Making the School an Effective Community: Belief, Practice and Theory in School Administration

Education Policy Perspectives

General Editor: **Professor Ivor Goodson**, Faculty of Education,
University of Western Ontario, London,
Canada N6G 1G7

Education and policy analysis has long been a neglected area in the United
Kingdom and to an extent in the USA and Australia. The result has been a
profound gap between the study of education and the formulation of educational policy. For practitioners such a lack of analysis of the new policy ini-
tiatives has worrying implications particularly at such a time of policy flux
and change. Education policy has, in recent years, been a matter for intense
political debate — the political and public interest in the working of the
system has come at the same time as the consensus on education policy has
been broken by the advent of the 'New Right'. As never before the political
parties and pressure groups differ in their articulated policies and prescriptions for the education sector. Critical thinking about these developments is
clearly necessary.

This series aims to fill the academic gap, to reflect the politicization of
education, and to provide the practitioners with the analysis for informed
implementation of policies that they need. It will offer studies in broad areas
of policy studies. Beside the general section it will offer a particular focus in
the following areas: School organization and improvement (David
Reynolds, *University College, Cardiff, UK*); Social analysis (Professor
Philip Wexler, *University of Rochester, USA*); and Policy studies and
evaluation (Professor Ernest House, *University of Colorado-Boulder, USA*).

School Organization and Improvement Series

Editor: David Reynolds, University College, Cardiff, UK

The Comprehensive Experiment
David Reynolds and Michael Sullivan with Stephen Murgatroyd

Improving the Quality of Schooling
Edited by David Hopkins

The Self-Managing School
Brian J. Caldwell and Jim M. Spinks

Successful Secondary Schools
Bruce L. Wilson and Thomas B. Corcoran

Whole School Approaches to Special Needs: A Practical Guide for Teachers
Edited by Arlene Ramasut

*Making School an Effective Community: Belief, Practice and Theory in
School Administration*
Mark Holmes and Edward A. Wynne

Education Policy Perspectives

Making the School an Effective Community:

Belief, Practice and Theory in School Administration

Mark Holmes
and
Edward A. Wynne

 The Falmer Press

(A member of the Taylor & Francis Group)
New York • Philadelphia • London

 A Publication of the Ontario Institute for Studies in Education

UK   The Falmer Press, Falmer House, Barcombe, Lewes, East Sussex, BN8 5DL

USA   The Falmer Press, Taylor & Francis Inc., 242 Cherry Street, Philadelphia, PA 19106-1906

The Ontario Institute for Studies in Education has three prime functions: to conduct programs of graduate study in education, to undertake research in education, and to assist in the implementation of the findings of educational studies. The Institute is a college chartered by an Act of the Ontario Legislature in 1965. It is affiliated with the University of Toronto for graduate studies purposes.

The publications program of the Institute has been established to make available information and materials arising from studies in education, to foster the spirit of critical inquiry, and to provide a forum for the exchange of ideas about education. The opinions expressed should be viewed as those of the contributors.

First published 1989.   Reprinted 1991.

Canadian Cataloguing in Publication Data

Holmes, Mark, 1935–   .
   Making the school an effective community
Bibliography: p.
Includes index.
ISBN 0-7744-0327-6
   1. School management and organization.   I. Wynne,
Edward A., 1928–   . II. Title.
LB2805.H64   1989   371.2   C89-093290-5

Library of Congress Cataloging-in-Publication Data

Holmes, Mark, 1935–   .
   Making the school an effective community: belief, practice, and theory in school administration/
Mark Holmes and Edward A. Wynne, p.   cm.
Bibliography: p.
Includes index.
ISBN 1-85000-486-2: $42.00 (U.S.).
ISBN 1-85000-487-0 (pbk.): $20.00 (U.S.)
   1. School management and organization. I. Wynne, Edward.
II. Title.
LB2805.H625   1989
371.2—dc19

Typeset in 10½/12pt California by
Chapterhouse, The Cloisters, Formby L37 3PX

Jacket design by Caroline Archer

Printed in Great Britain by Burgess Science Press, Basingstoke on paper which has a specified pH value on final paper manufacture of not less than 7.5 and is therefore 'acid free'.

Contents

Introduction

To the Reader

This book is intended for those who are already school administrators and who want to think more about their work and for those who are interested in school administration. It is neither an overview nor a manual, but something in between. It is intended to be both thought provoking and useful.

Theory and Practice

No choice is made between those two unrealistic alternatives. Theory in academic study usually refers to the discovery of true and verifiable insights and generalizations about the nature of a discipline of knowledge. In that sense of the word, there can be little or no genuine theory in educational administration. It is an applied field ultimately dependent on human will acting within a social context. Thus empirical truths tend to be low level and dependent upon the society and moment in time when they are discovered. However, I am not suggesting that there is no truth relevant to the school administrative task. Quite the contrary. There are important truths, for example, from history, from the sciences, from psychology and sociology. More important, the educational life of a school administrator should be imbued with truths drawn from philosophy, ethics and religion about the nature of education. This book is a study of the work of the school administrator in the context of beliefs and ideas about educational administration and interesting research.

Education itself is an applied field of study. It is about the upbringing, development, socialization and training of young people within formal organizations called schools. Necessarily, it is about what ought to be as well as about what is.

Educational theories are only a part of the social environment in which they were developed and must be considered within that framework. For example, the Getzels-Guba model (Hoy and Miskel, 1982, p. 58) was believed by some to be a theory of how organizations work. It purported to show how administrative behavior derives from a blend of decision making through the formal and informal networks. That idea, of parallel formal and informal networks, fits well with contemporary western society — but it does not necessarily fit some primitive societies where the formal organization is non-existent, and one could imagine organizations in a totalitarian society where the informal network is deliberately eliminated.

A difficulty with 'theories' in educational administration is that the more one tries to broaden them to make them generalizable, the more their usefulness decreases. For example, one could oversimplify Getzels-Guba to assert that administrators sometimes follow organizational rules and norms and sometimes do not. The value of such an insight is limited to directing us to the importance of the idea of administrative discretion. But in reality, the situation is often more complex than a simple blend of one organizational role and a straightforward contextual norm. Rules, norms, expectations, demands and personal desires form a complex web. And the individual cannot find the best decision by studying scientific principles, only by a thorough understanding of the situation and the application of a good set of beliefs, principles and values. No scientist is going to be able to sort out the various policies, beliefs and contingencies that come together to determine a particular decision at a particular moment.

Now it may well be that almost any theory involving human behavior, in psychology, history or sociology, is inevitably culture bound. A significant part of culture is concerned with ideas about the good, about what ought to be. The Getzels-Guba model is not very useful to the Marxist who objects that both the formal and the informal networks are structured to reproduce the capitalist system, and that massive structural change is required to produce a classless society. For the Marxist, studying how things work is a recipe for justifying the status quo. A theory is not really of much value if its operationalization requires that one suspends one's genuine disbelief and works within its particular frame of reference. It becomes then not theory but ideology.

So, it is unproductive to look for a set of theories of education, even less so for a set of theories by which educational administrators may guide administrative behavior. However, it is equally unhelpful to reproduce a list of rules for running a good school based on a series of war stories. The experience and interpretation of individual behavior in the past is not a useful guide for other individuals in different circumstances with different ideals. It is not that one cannot learn from the past (the past and what we create are all we have) but that one cannot helpfully set down a few rules, implicitly saying, 'These things will work for you because they worked for these individual people in some particular circumstance at some particlar time.'

So, if there is likely to be little useful theory in educational administration and if the recapitulation of old nostrums from individual narratives may not be very helpful, what can usefully be said about running a school?

The Purpose of the Book

The main purpose of the book is to give teachers and administrators a better understanding of how schools operate. There can be no guarantee that such understanding will make readers better administrators. Knowledge can be put to good or bad ends and it can be ignored. Educational administration, in this respect, is quite different from the practices of farming or medicine. Knowledge of those applied fields usually makes for better farmers and doctors; one would have to be perverse to use superior knowledge to produce poorer crops or prolong illness. But the goals of education itself and of educational administration by extension are not consensually agreed upon. That is a problem not found in most of the other major applied fields of knowledge.

Nevertheless, this book should make it possible for administrators to improve their practice and should also provide an incentive for them to try. The earlier point that there can be no universally true theory of educational administration should not be overinterpreted. Any opinion about what works or what is right is not the same as any other. The value of all educational research, irrespective of its methodological underpinning, should not be contemptuously dismissed.

If readers share some of my educational goals, if they share some of my assumptions about our society, then they will be able to apply some ideas that are likely to produce a set of desired, and I believe desirable, consequences. If they have somewhat different goals and assumptions, they will be able to attain a clearer understanding of the relationships among ideology, educational practice and educational outcomes. There is no comfort in this book for the person who wishes simply to make schools run 'better', regardless of its implicit goals. That person is asking a question to which there is and ought to be no answer.

The underlying approach used in this book is different from most writing on educational administration. I do not accept the assumption that an empirical science of educational administration can be built without a foundation of educational purpose. Equally, schools cannot be best administered simply by the application of practical, personal knowledge based on aphorisms passed on by others. The starting point in this book is that education is a moral exercise; it is a set of activities steeped in values. We educate children because we wish to change them from what they would otherwise become. The attempt to change human beings is the application of moral choice. We want to make children better, not worse. Once we have decided in which ways we want to change children, we can occasionally learn from empirical science which approaches are most conducive to bringing about certain selected changes. Running a school involves much day to day management, involving lower level decisions and a little discretion, as well as administration, involving the interpretation and sometimes the development of policy. True administration involves the application of moral choices; it involves the use of discretion. Even good moral choices and sensible techniques are not enough. Administration is also a moral task, and good choices must be pursued with honesty, courage and determination.

A Note on Intellectual Tradition

The approach used in this book is eclectic. It does not follow the recently popular empirical, positivist approach. At the same time, it does not rest on the post-Nietzschean assumption that each person individually constructs his or her own meaning, beyond which there is nothing.

Education should be seen primarily in its historical and cultural context. Individuals, parents, children, citizens are not free atoms making social contracts with the larger society. They are organic parts of that society, from which they have little real choice of physically or psychologically departing. Individual freedom and choice are important, but they are significantly constrained by physical conditions within and outside the individual, by ignorance, and by social and family rules, norms and expectations. The purpose of formal education in schools is to help both the individual and society reach an ideal, always within cultural restraints. The nature of that ideal is expressed in many different ways within western culture. Plato wrote of turning individuals away from the shadows on the wall of the cave to see the full light of day — the symbol for both truth and good. Christians think in terms of following Jesus' teachings and finding the kingdom of God. Jews use a more detailed set of guides from their cultural traditions to help them find the right way. Aristotle emphasized the specific virtues — of truth, courage, justice, friendship and moderation — that characterized the good life. What differentiates these interwoven traditions from, on the one hand, the logical positivist and utilitarian traditions and, on the other, the nihilist, existentialist and subjectivist traditions, is their assertion of central good, purpose and truth.

However, an assumption that there is some purpose behind education, beyond individualistic constructions from nothing, does not preclude the use of argument and evidence drawn from diverse traditions. For us, the purpose of education must be drawn from a study of our culture, our traditions and our sense of the ideal — not from mere individualism and not from, so-called 'objective', 'scientific' research. All manner of evidence should be used to discover and select the best ways to work towards the ideal, with the proviso that the methods should not be themselves inimical to the truth and good we seek.

Some readers may be impatient with this explanation of intellectual roots, believing they will decide for themselves whether the book is valuable to them, irrespective of its roots. For others, interested in the academic background, I recommend Bloom's discussion of the state of education and its philosophical background (Bloom, 1987), Shils' rare study of tradition (Shils, 1981) and, most of all, MacIntyre's fascinating reconstruction of Aristotelian philosophy for modern times, in which he makes interesting comments on social science and administration (MacIntyre, 1981).

Chapter 1

What Schools Do and Ought to Do

The Significance of Goals

This chapter examines the *is* and the *ought* of the contemporary school, from an administrative point of view. School administrators are, reasonably enough, expected by parents to hold a sense of direction, a philosophy of education. The expectation is that a sincerely held sense of direction will help direct the school and particularly its students toward the achievement of a set of common goals.

Discussions about goals and directions in educational administration are frequently confused, and not just because administrators, being concerned about schedules and toilets as well as philosophy, must necessarily oversimplify complex issues. They are further confused because there is usually a hidden premise that goals are roughly equivalent and interchangeable. Thus one principal may be more interested in attitudes, another in standardized test scores and yet another in physical fitness. For these and other reasons, administrative programs and textbooks typically neglect serious discussion of educational purpose.

It is sometimes suggested that we should not pass judgment on our fellow professionals' educational goals because they reflect individual values, ethics and religion. As well, administrators are sometimes expected at one and the same time to have an educational philosophy and also be flexible in the face of changing demands. Either way, most discussion is of methodology, practice and implementation. Values are not left aside as irrelevant. They are usually admitted to be important. But they are treated as though administration exists independently. The resulting situation is ironic. It is as if discussions of religious ministry and leadership were to be held in a training school for missionaries recruited from totally conflicting belief systems, including emissaries from Soviet communism, Islam and liberal humanism. Another reason is sometimes given by educators themselves as to why it is a waste of time to discuss values. Educational goals are motherhood statements, according to them. As everyone supports motherhood, there is nothing useful to discuss.

Making the School an Effective Community

Basic values are ignored because (i) there are believed to be many different sets of valid goals and administrators should not pass judgment on them; (ii) although goals are important, administrators have a job to do irrespective of the goals to which the school is working; and (iii) all goals are really the same anyway — it is only the means of achieving these statements of motherhood on which people differ.

The third argument is the least sophisticated and the most easily disposed of. Part of its problem is semantic, lying in the ambiguity of the word motherhood. Consider the following two goal statements: (i) all children should learn to read competently; and (ii) children should be given the opportunity to develop a moral framework related to the values of the larger society.

Both can be described as motherhood statements. But the first is an adequate goal statement. It is a motherhood statement in the sense that almost everyone will agree with it. However, consensus is no reason why a goal should be ignored. If there is consensus on a number of important goals, it is important for administrators to know.

The second statement is a motherhood statement in a very distinct sense. Most people agree with it because they interpret it in different ways. It could be translated as: (i) children should develop a moral framework that broadly reflects that of the larger society; (ii) children should develop a moral framework that takes into account but may reject that of the larger society; and (iii) children should be allowed to develop a moral framework but may reject or ignore that chance. Thus, any agreement on that goal statement is unhelpful, because it provides an illusion of consensus ultimately making the school principal's and the individual teacher's task difficult if not impossible. There is not in fact always agreement on fundamental goals. In the moral realm, some parents want specific virtues to be inculcated; others do not. Vague statements developed to conceal differences are neither useful nor honest.

The first two arguments, that administrators should be neutral about values and that administrators can work with any values, overlap. The first asserts that, as there are many competing educational goals and values, administrators should stay out of the argument. Their job is simply to implement policies. The second takes the matter further and suggests that the principal's job is the same irrespective of the school's values and goals.

The argument for the centrality of goals in a book on school administration is made at two levels. Firstly, schools are devoted to bringing about change in children. Administrators ought to be concerned about the selection and meaning of the goals towards which they and their organizations are working. Secondly, there is little evidence that administrative 'theory' actually works.

Those who advocate value-free approaches to educational administration may respond in this way. 'Certainly the administrator has to have goals — otherwise there can be no definition of success or improvement.

8

However, the administrator's own goals are only very indirectly if at all related to educational goals for children. The administrator's first goal is survival, i.e., success in the job. The second goal is the success of the organisation, in terms of continuity, growth and lack of upheaval. The advice given to administrators should therefore be directed to their own personal goals and not to goals they do not necessarily hold. And there are principles which, if generaly applied, can help administrators and their organization survive.'

One response to that argument is ethical and moral. Educational administrators are not normally employed mainly for their own and their organizations' survival. That is why this particular argument is not made publicly, even though it is often asserted privately. Schools are primarily for the benefit of children. Professional employees should put their clients' interests first. We would have little time for the doctor who said his work was directed more to his practice's survival than to clients' medical needs.

A subsidiary argument is often made suggesting that administrative skills are interchangeable among education, government agencies and corporations, buttressing the argument that educational goals are irrelevant to good administration. That argument raises a very different question that is not central to the theme of this book. Which jobs in education should be done by non-educators? Conceivably one could decide that the job of the superintendent, even that of the building principal could be carried out by a non-educator. If principals were not to make educational decisions, then our comments about knowledge of educational goals would be irrelevant. This book is written on the assumption that the principal is the symbolic educational leader of the school and is a professional educator. In that case, the school principal cannot be replaced by the manager of a soup factory.

Our second response to the main argument is that there is no empirical evidence of scientifically valid laws that promote individual or organizational survival. We do not deny that there may be some low level; common sense, usually tautological aphorisms that may be helpful, for example, don't antagonize the people who have the power to fire you; don't announce a policy change you can't implement; get to know the people you work with so that you understand their beliefs, values, habits, interests and other work related characteristics.

Some of these things may warrant a 'dos and dont's' check list or a training session; but they should not be confused with theory, with professionalism, or with graduate education. This book is intended to be practical but it is also intended to encourage administrators to think deeply about their work. The assumption is that the school administrator ought to be an educator as well, and therefore concerned with values and goals.

Educational goals are important because they should be the central focus of the professional educational administrator — just as the prolongation and the quality of life are central concerns for the physician. But, unlike the physician, the principal must face the perplexing reality of varied and conflicting goals.

The omission of discussion about education in most books and programs in educational administration is harmful for another reason. Not only do value-free approaches assume that all goals are essentially equivalent — that it is a matter of personal choice whether one prefers a goal of academic achievement or increased popularity with the opposite sex — they also implicitly assume that they are all equally attainable. Thus administrative principles are assumed to work in all contexts, for all goals and to the same extent. The idea that because we have a goal it can be achieved is equivalent to the equally prevalent falsehood that because there is a problem it can be solved. It should be obvious to any practising educator that schools are much more successful in achieving some things than others. For example, schools do a reasonably good job of teaching skills, for example, reading and computation, but it is much more difficult to establish that schools are effective in teaching higher level cognitive traits — such as synthesis and evaluation.

The failure of students of administration to consider the problem of what schools do and ought to do, and the tension between them, encourages bad practice in a number of ways. For example, some school districts decide that the development of 'self-concept' is a valuable goal. The 'expert', the administrator, knows as little about 'self-concept' as the elected official. Someone read some research somewhere that high self-concept is associated with good reading skills.

Soon, raising self-concept is a stated goal and is built into the curriculum. It becomes a 'necessary' prerequisite for the basic skills because 'achievement with low self-concept' cannot take place. All kinds of bad practice and foolish activities are developed because administrators have neither thought through the value of different goals and objectives and have failed to study the research on what schooling does and does not do.

The starting point for the professional school administrator should be knowledge of what schools do combined with serious thought about what they ought to do. One of the greatest disservices experts in educational administration can provide the profession is the idea that administrative practice can and should be divorced from ideas about school purpose. And ideas about purpose should bear some relation to what we know about schools' performance.

The Functions of Schooling

There appear to be four major distinguishable functions that are unlikely to be disputed. They are: (i) the distribution of young people among very different futures; (ii) introduction of some or most young people to the basic disciplines of knowledge; (iii) the provision of basic skills in reading, writing and number; and (iv) the provision of custody for young people, usually between the ages of five and sixteen, frequently up to the age of eighteen. There is broad agreement that schools do these things, not necessarily that they ought to do them or that they do them particularly well.

(i)   *The Distribution of Young People Among Futures*

In Canada, schools distribute young people among three broad and roughly equal bands — a group continuing to post-secondary education; a group going to work after high school graduation and a group dropping out before graduation. In other countries, the proportions may be different, but the principle is the same. In the USA, more go to some form of tertiary education and in Europe fewer. In West Germany and Switzerland, the combination of technical schooling and work is much more common within the school year so the untrained dropout is very rare.

Distribution takes place not only among those three broad bands but also within bands. Thus university bound students from the same school go in different directions. Some win scholarships, most do not. Some go to universities of high prestige, most not. Some gain entrance to a program of high prestige and limited entry. These programs include engineering and those leading to other major professions: law, pharmacy, medicine, dentistry, nursing, accounting. The competition may be held at the end of high school or during the undergraduate years but the principle is the same.

The results of this sorting process cannot be attributed solely to school experiences. Parental income, individual preference, luck, intelligence, and the influence of friends and family play an important part in the allocation of futures. But some combination of school marks and tests and examinations based more or less directly on what has supposedly been learned in school is a prerequisite factor.

An important question arising is whether the school has much independent effect on the allocation of futures or whether it merely acts as a societal surrogate, as a conduit, acting vicariously on behalf of parents. To those who have, it shall be given and from those who have not it shall be taken away.

It is sometimes argued that schools, individually and collectively, have little effect, independent of family background, on the futures of young people (Jencks, 1979, p. 306). According to this argument, schools give privileged youngsters privileged treatment and disadvantaged youngsters training for unemployment or, at best, casual labor. Empirical studies provide some support (Sewell and Hauser, 1975; Porter, Porter and Blishen, 1982). Against that, a British study (Rutter *et al.*, 1979) of twelve secondary schools in suburban London found that the best school achieved better external examination results with the lowest social group of youngsters than did the worst school with the highest group. That finding should not be overinterpreted — the schools in the survey enrolled a fairly homogeneous population. The schools did not make the daughters of laborers as successful as the sons of lords!

One way of determining the effects of schools, independent of parents, is to look at what happens to bright children. That is not easy as intelligence is related to social class. As advantaged homes produce bright children who do well in school, it is not easy to determine whether success results from intelligence, education or a favorable background. If we look at bright children from disadvantaged homes we find their success rate is much lower than that of bright children from advantaged homes (Porter, Porter and Blishen, 1982). Yet Sewell and Hauser (1975) found that measured intelligence does have some important effect independent of the family background.

So the evidence is far from conclusive. Certainly, much of the sorting effect of the school is of the processing variety, but there is strong evidence that the school also continues to provide an opportunity for upward social mobility. That channel may become even more important in the future, if, as we suspect, it becomes less used. After all, if schools and families combine to build a new super class of bright, rich, advantaged people and if their children tend to inherit their advantages, both intellectual and cultural, then it becomes all the more critical for the way to be kept open for an upwardly mobile minority to use the available opportunities.

Traditional class based societies were stable. People of lower status accepted their low status in life because there was no alternative; at least it was not their fault. For a much shorter period of time, modern democratic societies have also been stable — with a moderate degree of mobility — and the public believes in equal opportunity. However, the emergence of what is beginning to look like a permanent underclass in the USA, with lesser but similar problems in other western democracies, is a frightening phenomenon; frightening in the substance of the lives of the disadvantaged, and frightening in the implications for social stability. Administrators should not underestimate the importance of their role in keeping the channel of upward mobility open. The easiest way to 'help' the disadvantaged is to hold back the advantaged or to undermine their middle class values. That is not what we have in mind. We believe that all parents, and ultimately all children, should be given genuine understanding and the choice and responsibility that go with it.

The question of whether the school acts independently or merely as a surrogate for the family is an important one, but it does not affect the central issue here, which is the school's operational role in distributing young people among different futures. Even if the school's allocative role were largely symbolic, one of training young people in accordance with their social background (this idea is known as the correspondence theory) the function remains a socially necessary one. Some training for future schooling or work is necessary and there is strong competition for entry to many jobs and many programs. The future may be laid out for many in very general terms but it is not specifically predetermined.

Consider for example a town with five piano teachers, of greatly varying competence. The fact that only children with some combination of talent, parental interest and parental income are enrolled eliminates neither competition among the children nor the educational role of the piano teachers in the subsequent selection and sorting. One has to have certain advantages to succeed, but high social background is no guarantor of becoming a world famous concert pianist. Although home background is the best predictor of future success, it is a poor best.

Although the distributive function is one of the most obvious ones, it is rarely publicly mentioned as a purpose or goal for public high schools, virtually never in elementary schools. Yet imagine the consequences of stopping doing it. Suppose a high school were to, at one and the same time, cancel all vocational programs; abolish grading, graduation certificates and comparative home reports; refuse to conduct external tests; and refuse to write recommendations to colleges and universities. The school would very soon collapse. Most students would simply refuse to work if there were no grades and would drop out when they realized their academic progress would not affect their social and academic future.

As long as we have an economic system with a complex arrangement of differentiated labor and a differentiated reward system for the various jobs (and we should bear in mind that even socialist countries like Sweden and eastern bloc communist countries retain those two fundamental principles), there will have to be some means of allocating young people to different futures. The great advantage of having the school do it is that one can put some pill inside the sugar coating. A variety of requirements for high school graduation is developed to meet a variety of expressed purposes. The student who wants to become a lawyer will work hard for the required marks in school even if it means obtaining credits in such vocationally irrelevant subjects as outdoor education, human physiology, Shakespearean drama and instrumental music and may even find the subjects interesting.

There is a danger in either of two extremes. If schools concentrate solely on the narrow requirements of a post-secondary program or employment, they are apt to forsake education for training. If, on the other hand, their programs become extremely remote from the immediate material needs of their students, the schools are described as irrelevant and students see the collection of a variety of credits for graduation as just a part of a rather foolish credentialist paper chase. Educators sometimes try to persuade students that everything they do in school is somehow relevant to their later work, but it is not and ought not to be.

There are a number of possible reasons why administrators do not dwell on this most obvious of functions of schooling. Training and preparation for the future are not high status educational goals. They are also easily understood. Goals such as helping young people fulfil themselves, come to terms with their environment and learn complex decision making skills sound loftier, more important, more sophisticated — even though they often have little operational meaning. Publicity for the distributive role would highlight the significant failure of the contemporary school — with large numbers of graduates being unable to find a valuable niche in the labor market, even at times of low unemployment. A third reason for neglecting the vocational role of the school is that parents and students are well aware of the need for a 'good' education to obtain a 'good' job; over-emphasis of the material aspects of schooling only further undermines the school's other legitimate functions and purposes.

It is important that all those involved in school administration under-stand clearly that, even though some may wish it were not so, one of the central functions of the school is the allocation of socioeconomic futures. The school does not have total proprietorial ownership — many young people change their jobs frequently after leaving school and undertake new kinds of training; mature adults increasingly return to post-secondary programs for which they are not formally 'prepared'; the best and worst efforts of schools are frequently thwarted. Nevertheless, the central allo-cative role lies with the school in all developed countries.

It seems reasonable to assert that, as the job is to be done, it should be done well. Indeed, there are probably few things a school staff can do that will more promptly annoy students than to allocate marks arbitrarily, in-discriminately, or unfairly. The students know that their futures depend on the rewards provided in school. The significance of this function is illus-trated by the potency of grades and certificates in securing discipline in the secondary school.

(ii) *Introduction to the Disciplines of Knowledge*

This is the traditional respectable role of the secondary school and, to some extent, the later years of the elementary school. However, whereas everyone is affected, positively or by default, by the allocation of future economic status, not everyone learns the bases of all or any disciplines of knowledge. It would be foolhardy to estimate percentages because the problem is partly a matter of definition. Arguably, everyone learns some science, but clearly not everyone learns physics, chemistry or biology.

Before the days of mass secondary education, it would not be un-reasonable to assume that, generally speaking, academic high school gradu-ates had received a broad education in science, mathematics, literature, history and probably a foreign language. Such graduates would have learned a body of knowledge or a set of skills or some combination of both. One would be able to examine such graduates and differentiate them, on the basis of their knowledge and skills, from non-graduates.

Today, when nearly everyone in the developed world receives some secondary education, that sort of distinction is much more difficult, making it harder to determine the precise nature of the school's function in this area. The problem is illustrated by the first round of international studies. In the areas of literature and civic education, it proved quite difficult to discover any school factors related to achievement, including time in school and time in related courses. In other words, it has become very difficult to see what effect instruction in some subjects has on students as a whole.

As students are given more choice about the subjects they take, there is evidence that learning is difficult to adduce across all 'successful' students; the traditional academic function of schools is unclear. Of course, some students learn to write well and to understand French. There is evidence of learning from classes in 'hard' subjects like math and chemistry. The movement towards specifying levels of minimum competence and higher standards stems in part from the belief that schools do not demonstrate sufficiently clearly exactly what their graduates have learned.

(iii) *The Provision of Basic Skills in Reading, Writing and Number*

This traditional function of the elementary school remains powerful today. Despite sporadic speeches from prominent educators asserting that television and computers make reading, number and writing redundant, children still enter the primary grades generally unable to read, write and figure and learn those basic skills during two or three years. Now, it might be argued that they would learn the same skills without schools, but evidence from countries without compulsory elementary education suggests otherwise. If only half of the school-age population attends school, mass illiteracy appears to result. It seems reasonable to assume that a central and respected function of schooling is the teaching of basic skills.

A pattern emerges from this survey of functions. It is reasonable to assume that parents will be most upset if one of the central functions of schooling is interfered with, rather less if one of the peripheral functions is touched. Thus we stated that there would be acute parental and student unrest if a school abolished its grading system and all that goes with it. The unrest would be least acute in first grade, where the distance from the sorting is great, most acute in twelfth grade. In the disciplines, there is likely to be a problem if instruction in mathematics or physics is grossly interfered with, much less in the case of literature and history where the outcomes are diffuse and much more variable from one individual to another.

If it is correct to assert that instruction in the basic skills is one of the central functions of the elementary schools, it seems reasonable to assume that any attempt to tamper with them will cause considerable upset. This does not mean that the instruction cannot be weakened; merely that any weakening must be surreptitious, i.e., take place under the banner of some other form of improvement. We are not implying here that educators deliberately set out to sabotage the basic skills by introducing competing and less desirable programs, merely that new programs may under cover of well intended promises still lead to less effective instruction in the basic skills. Deliberate, stated, public de-emphasis of the basic skills is most unlikely. But we know that many schools perform very badly on standardized tests in these areas.

(iv)   *The Provision of Custody*

In most developed countries, formal schooling is compulsory for ten or more years. Although it is normally possible for parents to educate their children at home, the conditions, formal and informal, for so doing are stringent and few take the option. There are probably far more children of school age not attending school illegally than not attending legally. Even after adolescents reach the age of voluntary schooling, informal pressures against dropping out are formidable. For all intents and purposes, young people between the ages of six and sixteen are provided enforced custody. After that age, custody is provided for those adolescents whose parents choose it and who are prepared to enjoy or endure it.

Schools explicitly recognize the custodial function by punishing students for failing to attend school without a legitimate reason for absence, for skipping classes, for leaving early. Suspension from school is much more likely to result from unauthorized absence or unacceptable behavior — the two most obvious manifestations of resistance to custody — than from failure to complete assignments or do satisfactory work. As chief education officer of a small school district, Holmes once raised the possibility of concentrating the secondary schools' instructional hours in four days. He saw a number of advantages — a fifth day available for concentrated extra-curricular activities, reduced costs for energy and transportation. Apart from logistical problems, for example, transporting limited number of students for the fifth day, the only major disadvantage he could see was the lack of custody to be provided on the fifth day. The idea was considered worthy of serious investigation by teachers, elected school board members and students (roughly in that order of enthusiasm) but aroused fiery attack from parents at a public meeting, many of whom had not previously attended school related programs. The attacks were generally couched in educational terms, but the impression was that the problem of what people would do on the fifth day, beyond the supervision of working parents, was the major factor. In the same way, schools have been under increasing pressure to provide lunchtime supervision. Many schools are expected to provide early morning and late afternoon supervision; day care for pre-school children is becoming increasingly important. Schools are also experiencing problems with sick children who are sent to school because they cannot be cared for by working parents.

Major Functions of Schooling

Four major functions of schooling have been identified. Our argument is that virtually all contemporary school systems in the developed world fulfil fairly effectively these four functions. In priority, we would place them: (i) the distributive function; (ii) the provision of basic skills; (iii) the custodial function; and (iv) the disciplines of knowledge function. In other words, the greatest administrative danger is tampering with the distribution system. Even the most progressive private school helps the allocation of its graduates. It is inconceivable that any secondary principal would say or believe, 'We are totally uninterested in the future schooling and occupation of our graduates and will only participate in an advisory capacity in either their scholastic or their occupational placement.' Allocation affects virtually every young person, even though the allocation is neither final nor precise.

Almost as much can be said of the basic skills. Most sixteen-year-olds have some basis of literacy and numeracy. However, the place of the basic skills may be little less secure than that of distribution. Achievement testing undergoes periodic attacks, but public opinion polls suggests that the public is firmly determined to disallow, if it is able, the erosion of the basics.

Current employment trends do not suggest that in the near future employment will replace education as an occupation for young people in any significant way. Indeed, even if there is some movement in North America and Britain towards appenticeship programs on the Swiss and German models, that movement is at least partially offset by the tendency for young people to aim for higher educational qualifications, when, after all, the availability of jobs is related to years of schooling. Nevertheless, there are signs that some schools are trying to reduce the emphasis on custodial function. Whereas thirty years ago, schools tended to handle their own discipline problems, principals and teachers are today often advised to 'work with parents' to overcome difficulties. 'Working with parents' usually implies sharing responsibility for ensuring custody and sometimes greatly reduced responsibility for the school. Thus cases of truancy may be referred to parents as well as or instead of further action by the school or by district personnel. As responsibility for attendance is gradually shifted to parents, it becomes increasingly easy for students to be enrolled in name only, or even quietly disappear.

This change is not necessarily a deliberate attempt on the part of the school to shed responsibility for regular attendance. For a number of reasons regular attendance is normally and genuinely highly valued by school people. Funding and allocation of resources are usually related to some measure of enrolment. Frequent truancy probably leads to dropping out.

The regularity of progress through work is affected by irregular attendance and classroom disruption is associated with poor attendance patterns and incomplete work.

If school staffs have not notably relaxed their desire for regular attendance, what other reasons would there be for the apparent erosion of the custodial principle? One explanation is the increased awareness of individual rights, particularly evident in North America in the last twenty years or so. Jurisdictions at many levels have legislated a variety of codes. Schools are not exempt from the effects. Some administrators undoubtedly like to have an excuse not to have to worry too much about attendance; others are very concerned but throw up their hands in defeat.

A second reason for the apparent difficulty with custodial issues is change in the constitution of the secondary school population. In the first half of this century, elementary education was universal in the developed world, but access to secondary education was limited, somewhat so in the USA, much more so in Canada and Western Europe. Custody of young pre-adolescent children was assumed and fairly easily enforced. As secondary schooling was essentially voluntary (i.e., at the parents' volition) and competitive, fees frequently had to be paid, or exams passed or achievement levels reached — attendance at that level was not a major problem. Where there was a problem, parents were generally only too pleased that the school staff would take strong action, short of expulsion. Ultimately, attendance was a privilege rather than an obligation. At the elementary level, children are smaller, younger and more tractable. Although compulsory attendance is more challenged at the elementary level than it once was, it is at the secondary level where change is most noticeable.

Whereas 95 per cent attendance was normal in 1940, 90 per cent attendance would be considered good fifty years later and average attendance below 85 per cent is not unknown in large urban schools. The social and intellectual composition of the secondary school has changed so that today almost all young people experience some secondary education. If the distributive function is primary, clearly those who see themselves as being allocated to future unskilled work or even to unemployment are unlikely to accept custody very happily, particularly if aspects of the custodial care prove irrelevant, uninteresting, irksome, demanding, manipulative or paternalistic — and it is unlikely that compulsory schooling can completely avoid all those qualities.

The significance of instruction in the disciplines of knowledge as a major function is also in question. There is little doubt that many young people complete their schooling without being seriously apprenticed in any of the major disciplines of knowledge — literature, history, physics, chemistry, biology, mathematics, economics, psychology or sociology (and adding such fields as art, music, languages and geography would not affect the truth of the statement). Included in those not significantly apprenticed are some going to post-secondary education. That is not to say these people fail to pick up a smattering of general knowledge from school as well as from television, radio, magazines and friends. But knowledge and understanding and the ability to work within a field of study with specifiable skills and frames of reference are very far from being universal among high school graduates.

Goals and Functions

There is no reason to assume commonality between goals and functions. After all, custody and social distribution are unlikely to be listed in any official set of educational goals. Nevertheless, inculcation in the disciplines of knowledge forms the traditional core task and goal of the secondary school and it is noteworthy when it no longer forms part of an officially promulgated statement of goals. Similarly, the basic skills remain the core topic at the elementary level. Now these are not the only things that schools actually do. But they are the things that schools must do — the lowest common denominator. The remaining functions, which more clearly parallel officially stated goals, are more difficult to establish.

Other Functions of Schooling

The remaining functions of schooling are much more easily confused with goals. It is difficult to envisage a mass, public, compulsory school system that does not encompass the first four major functions, irrespective of whether they form part of a publicly stated list of goals. But goals are normally related to education rather than to schooling. Those four functions are rather obvious and almost undeniable because: (i) no agency other than the school evidently carries out the same function; (ii) major problems are caused when the school stops carrying out the function.

Neither of those conditions is absolute. We have suggested that some schools have surreptitiously or unintentionally down-graded the basic skills; some of the disciplines of knowledge have been partially abandoned and others, such as psychology and sociology, have never been clearly seen as being in the domain of the school. Parents undoubtedly influence their children's futures, directly and indirectly. Even so, no one denies that schools play a significant part in those four spheres.

The functioning of the school is more difficult to discern when the activities are shared with other agencies and when the effects are less obvious. For example, many secondary schools have effectively stopped teaching literary classics to some or all of their students even though the subject titles and time allocations remain unchanged. None of this means that the second set of functions, which are frequently shared and whose effects are less noticeable, is less important than the first. It does mean that the second set is less materially and evidently important to society. After all, if society felt that a particular function was of prime importance it would at least be evident that the school was trying to perform it. The remaining functions are not addressed by all schools, at least not with all students.

A Taxonomy of Educational Functions and Goals

It is possible to include both what schools do and what they might potentially do within a single set:

(a) intellectual
(b) moral/spiritual
(c) cultural and aesthetic
(d) social
(e) physical/biological/physiological
(f) vocational.

This taxonomy is one of many that could be used. Later in this chapter, we shall use it to develop a model set of educational goals for the elementary and secondary school. However, irrespective of the individual philosophy of the reader, any educational goal can be included under at least one of the above headings. That does not make the taxonomy ideal for all purposes. For example, some readers may believe that the school does not and should not perform any moral or spiritual functions, in which case that category is redundant.

A problem with classifying educational functions and goals is their tendency to overlap. Teachers do not separate intellectual instruction from social and vocational instruction. To that extent, any taxonomy is artificial. This taxonomy has an *ad hoc* purpose. It is useful because it permits the categorization of educational goals in a clear way. The taxonomy does imply that at least some schools do something under all of the headings. Some functions may barely be touched and schools and teachers vary. Further, none of the educational functions is carried out by schools alone. The average young person, aged 18, has spent approximately ten per cent of his or her waking hours in school. One good reason to consider carefully the tension between what schools do and what administrators and others think they do is that the school has limited time and shared responsibility.

The *intellectual* function is the most straightforward. Nearly everyone agrees schools should and do serve intellectual purposes. The basic skills are taught to and learned by most pupils; pupils learn a certain amount of general knowledge and they learn certain intellectual skills. Two of the basic functions already discussed — the basic skills and the disciplines of knowledge — fall under this heading.

The *moral/spiritual* function includes the aquisition of a number of much talked about qualities — character, self-respect, virtue, values, religious belief and attitudes. In the case of this function, there is a problem in identifying the instructional activity, and the effect. It is possible to see if a school is or is not teaching intellectual matters, irrespective of whether children are learning. In the case of character, it may actually be easier to establish that character has been changed than that it has been taught. There appears to be little doubt that 'total' institutions, such as boarding schools, where custody is provided twenty-four hours a day for the entire school year, have an effect on character. The British public (i.e., private) schools have a distinct and not always identical effect on their pupils (Wilkinson, 1964; Weinberg, 1967). In contrast to the traditional public schools, a progressive public school such as Dartington Hall has a quite different effect (Punch, 1977). However, the effect of the background of students in both traditional and progressive private schools cannot be separated entirely from the school effect. Nevertheless, there is convincing evidence that at both the school and the university level the effect on character is most pronounced and most enduring in institutions that make a direct, consistent and deliberate attempt to change their students (Holmes, 1986a). Peshkin's (1986) account of a fundamentalist school leaves the reader with little doubt that that school has at least some effect. But it serves a close, coherent community.

The influence of day schools on character is difficult to discern. Wynne (1980) argues that character education is the most important thing schools do and ought to do. His descriptions of various schools suggest that students' daily behavior is influenced greatly by the school. Their adherence to rules, their manners, their general deportment vary from school to school and are different from those of the unschooled. It does seem that manners are affected by school, although we do not know how long the effect lasts after students leave. Similarly, there is persuasive evidence that schools influence students' attitudes to work and scholastic success (McDill and Rigsby, 1973).

No distinction is made here between self-respect and self-esteem — and self-concept is frequently used as a synonym as well. It is popular to argue that one of the schools most important functions today is to build students' self-concept. It is not at all clear, however, exactly what function the school either has or ought to have in this area. There is some relationship between individual academic success and the individual's self-concept (but the relationship between the school is lower than that between measured intelligence and achievement). Because of that relationship, it is sometimes argued that schools should promote self-concept as a means of achieving academic success. However, even Purkey (1970), a strong advocate of the importance of self-concept, admits that there is no evidence that self-concept actually contributes to achievement. Simply, we do not know to what extent self-respect promotes achievement, successful achievement promotes self-respect and both achievement and self-respect are a result of supportive and cultured home backgrounds. From that it follows that we do not know to what degree the school functions to promote self-respect other than through being efficient in its intellectual function. Furthermore, many of the measures of self-concept have in fact been measures of what is called self-concept of ability. That is to say, students are asked how smart they think they are and that measure proves to be related to how well they do in school. But presumably, students' self-assessment of their ability is influenced by the grades they get from their teachers.

Comparatively little research has been carried out on school effects on attitudes and values. Some schools claim that attitudes and values are a major priority, but, once again the fact that someone has a purpose does not indicate that the institution fulfils the related function.

The situations with the intellectual and moral functions are not identical. The first problem in the intellectual area is whether intellectual teaching has very much effect. A secondary problem is to what extent students actually have the opportunity to learn, i.e., they are actually taught. In the moral domain, it cannot be generally assumed that students are even taught.

Consider the case of honesty. Most schools will assert that they do in fact promote honesty, if only indirectly. Suppose a ten-year-old child, who should well understand the meaning of honesty, tells the teacher that the assigned homework is not done because it was forgotten, left at home on the kitchen table. Typically in today's schools, according to teachers in our classes, that problem is dealt with as a homework problem; the homework must be supplied by some specified time. The possibility that this is an honesty problem — that the work has not been done and is not in fact on the kitchen table — is ignored, although most teachers will agree that that is frequently the case. In practice, dishonesty is thereby reinforced — it helps avoid confrontation.

Attitudes, which are unidimensional, only semi-permanent and more superficial, should be distinguished from values which form a more important and enduring part of our personality. Attitudes, by definition, may be changed. Values represent more fundamental choices and are changed much less easily. For example, it is not easy to convince an adolescent who believes firmly that dishonesty is the best policy, provided you can get away with it, of the virtue of truthfulness. Similarly, although honest adolescents may be easily led into dishonest ways, it is unlikely that they will quickly be unashamed of their new ways. In contrast, an adolescent with a negative attitude to serious literature may quite quickly come to enjoy a particular literary work given appropriate experiences over a few weeks. As an example, the Zeffirelli film of *Romeo and Juliet* has won many converts, temporary perhaps, to Shakespeare.

It seems probable, on the basis of this distinction, that day schools fulfil a greater function in the development of attitudes than in the formation of fundamental values or the development of virtue. In the first place, schools have simply much less time than the other influences of family, friends and media. In the second place, schools may sometimes work systematically to influence attitudes, towards other cultures; toward reading and literature; toward art and music; toward education. But they more rarely work systematically to inculcate virtue.

Indeed, it is not unusual to hear teachers and educational leaders specifically deny the school's responsibility for the inculcation of virtue. They argue that pupils must choose for themselves from an array of possible constellations. Typically, that argument does include a role for the school — a role in helping young people sort out the various possibilities. However, given the frequently powerful pressures of family, friends and media it seems improbable on the surface that a delicate helping hand toward free choice will very much influence the result. Indeed, if there is any effect at all, it is likely to be an undermining of any definite choice made by the student earlier under the influence of family or church. After all, the implication of permitting students to make a free choice from an array of possibilities is that it really does not make much difference which choice is made. Understandably, adolescents are more likely to make easier, less binding choices than strong ones which limit their freedom.

Even if one accepts the proposition that schooling can systematically present a range of values in an objective fashion, the proposition that this process will somehow result in better values being selected by students without formal instruction and prompting, appears to be, to put it mildly, implausible. If the choice is between having sex now and having sex five years from now, it would seem that some pretty strong arguments would have to be put forward if postponement of gratification is to be selected. Increasingly, schools abdicate authority in the area of values for fear of involvement in angry debates with parents and pressure groups of various kinds.

The actual function of the school in the area of attitudes and virtue is a matter of which we are relatively ignorant. It seems likely that the average school's effect is not of great magnitude and not very enduring. However, there are probably significant exceptions: exceptions in the form of individuals affected by individual teachers; exceptional schools (such as boarding schools and many fundamentalist Christian schools); exceptional teachers whose general influence transcends the confused message of the average school system; and exceptional students, who, for one reason or another, are particularly open to influence from both books and teachers.

The *cultural* function includes both the aesthetic realm and the habits and customs that distinguish one culture from another. Knowledge and understanding of one's country and ethnic background may easily be overlooked in a program designed to develop personal and social awareness. Civic awareness, and understanding of democracy and the Judaeo-Christian heritage are important parts of our western culture, to whose absorption and continuance schooling may contribute. It is difficult to determine the exact function of today's school in an area at once so diffuse and so closely linked with life outside the school. It is also probably the case that countries with considerable awareness of their cultural identity, for example, France, Denmark, Japan and the Soviet Union, carry out the most effective cultural programs in their schools, while countries with some doubts about their identity, for example, Canada, Belgium and modern West Germany, may have limited or rather ineffectual programs. Thus the separate effect of the school is particularly difficult to disentangle from the overall ethos of the society. It is arguable that those societies with the greatest problems of identity should be precisely those doing the most in their schools, just as those students who are least physically fit should be getting the most physical training — when the reverse is usually the case.

Aesthetic aspects of culture include awareness of beauty, color and tone in writing, art and drama as well as expression on a variety of ways. Once again, there is so much variation in the aesthetic exposure children receive outside school that it is highly likely that individual differences result more from the home than from the school. Even those achieving the most in the aesthetic domain are likely to have received intensive private tuition outside the home. Thus, while it seems very likely that some students are greatly affected by the aesthetic life of schools — in bands, drama and art — it seems probable that there are many more students, including both those who are totally uninterested in aesthetics and those who are most successful, who are little affected by the school. It is probably for this reason that poor performance in the arts is less likely to receive adverse reaction from parents than poor performance in the basics; some parents do not care and some of those who do pay for private instruction. This is not an argument for abandoning aesthetic work in school. It is an argument for giving an exceptional amount of thought to the deployment and direction of aesthetic programs.

The *social* function refers to the development of the individual's capacity to work in groups — cooperatively in work assignments, with friends, and within the larger society. This function is closely related to the moral/spiritual function. The individual who has a strong sense of independence, who has a firm set of values and attitudes (desirable or not) and who is competitive is quite likely not very good at group cooperation and may well not be a member of a group of close friends. Group cooperation involves some subordination of one's attitudes, values and interests to shared values and interests. A close network of friends requires a willingness to suspend one's own judgments, values and choices or, better, to merge them within a common and desirable set. In a very real way, the school cannot do everything, not because there is insufficient time, not because there is too much hindrance from the social environment, but because one reasonable objective frequently conflicts with another. Given this conflict of goals, between competitiveness and cooperation, between independence and friendship, between the selection of one's own values and attitudes and a willingness to suspend one's own judgments in the company of others, between having strong religious commitment and being non-judgmental and tolerant to others, it would be surprising if typical schools, which reflect this confusion of values, play a very strong social role, particularly as a consequence of any deliberate plan.

Nevertheless, even without direction or plan, the school organization may serve some social function. The change to block schedules in the secondary school has been widely perceived by educators as affecting the way young people behave in groups. When students mold together as a class, a solidarity of the group develops that is not the same when students are regrouped every sixty minutes. It is easier to belong to one group of thirty-five than five groups of thirty-five. The traditional schedule was difficult for the isolated who consciously wanted to be left alone — but good for those on the periphery who wanted to join but found it difficult. Traub, Weiss and Fisher (1976) found that children in an open classroom school (and hence large groups), in a school system in suburban Ontario, developed fewer friends than did children in traditional closed classrooms.

The function of the school in preparing young people for a competitive world is often commented upon, particularly by left-wing critics. The argument is that schools prepare a small conformist, competitive elite for managerial roles and processes and a sullen or rebellious mass for meaningless, docile lives in capitalist industry. There are numerous problems with this aspect of the so-called correspondence theory. Firstly, there is an inconsistency between critics such as Bowles and Gintis (1976), who believe that the malleable mass beneath the elite comprises something like two-thirds of the population and excludes an underclass comprising the minority of unemployed and non-unionized workers, and critics like Willis (1977) who argue that the mass proletariat, most of the population, is itself the underclass, trained to work in a world controlled by a dominating minority of capitalists. There is obviously a big difference between an underclass of perhaps one-fifth of the population and a proletariat of more than half. It is similarly not a trivial matter whether or not the mass of working people is victim or oppressor — particularly if the schools are supposed to have carried out the training. Secondly, if the schools are really teaching social subordination and docility, they appear to be singularly unsuccessful. The very presence of these numerous articulate critics, products of the formal system of schooling, speaks against any successful conspiracy, intended or not. Observers from other countries do not find students in English-speaking secondary schools in North America and Britain to be exceptionally docile. The strength of labor movements, the swings of electoral opinion and the high degree of social mobility found in contemporary democratic countries all tend to make improbable the idea that schools are effectively used to divide society into two or more fixed classes. It cannot of course be denied that schools inevitably to a significant extent reflect the society in which they are formed.

None of the above denies the reality of the role of the school in determining the economic and social futures of individual young people — the function of social distribution. It has already been pointed out that the school's social role in this respect is central and pre-eminent. A distinction is made here between the role of the school system in systematically creating and perpetuating social class divisions within society and the allocation of individuals to specific social and economic opportunities within society. The rapid changes in social structure in the western world in the last century suggest that mass schooling does not have a major function in preventing change; however, the second role seems inevitable and legitimate.

The *physiological* function operates in a way not entirely dissimilar from that of the cultural and aesthetic function. It is very difficult to distinguish the effects of the schools from those of the home. It may well be, for example, that if children spent less time sitting in school they would be fitter rather than less fit, except for those who substituted watching television for sitting in school. While some schools do ensure that pupils take part in regular physical exercise for the promotion of fitness, and test fitness regularly, many more do not. Thus the effect of the school on fitness is something like that of its effect on aesthetic development. Some students are greatly affected, many more not at all, some even negatively. One might hypothesize that in the case of fitness the variation from school to school is greater while in the case of aesthetic development the variation from individual to individual is greater. However, there are also individual differences in the case of physical fitness, particularly in the higher grades. While it is true that many of the most fit become fit as a result of out of school activities, others may be significantly affected by the regular school program and by extracurricular activities.

It is improbable that school instruction in areas such as sex, drugs and alcohol is very influential from a physiological point of view — although it provides some intellectual knowledge. There is no reason to believe that knowledge about sex, drugs and alcohol leads to less rather than more experimentation. It seems likely that more knowledge about contraception leads to greater sexual experimentation but fewer pregnancies. The effect of AIDS and AIDS education is still difficult to assess. There is conflict between those who advocate the teaching of safe sex and those who advocate abstention from sexual activity. If the teaching of safe sex has the same effect as teaching about contraception in the past, then its effect on the spread of AIDS depends very much on exactly how safe so-called safe sex really is. It is possible that the advocacy of abstention will be more effective when failure to comply with instruction will lead to possible death.

This domain cannot be intelligently addressed without simultaneously addressing the moral/spiritual and social domains, with which it is closely associated. Whereas one may assume a reasonable level of consensus with respect to the functions of schools in the intellectual domain and even perhaps in the cultural and sociological domains, consensus is obviously lacking in that area where the physiological and the moral/spiritual domains overlap. In general discussion, the actual effects of teaching about

AIDS, sexual intercourse, homosexuality, masturbation and abortion are overshadowed by the moral beliefs of those involved in the discussion — and rightly so. The ineffectiveness of a particular kind of instruction is relatively unimportant if one believes that the particular instruction is wrong in the first place.

The *vocational* function of schooling goes somewhat beyond the distributive function we have included within the social domain. The vocational function may be distinguished by the specific training provided for young people for a particular field of employment in which they will become, or are intended to become, directly employed. The distributive function is the process by which young people are sorted for materially and socially different futures. The vocational function is the actual training sometimes carried out within formal educational organizations for particular jobs. The vocational function within public secondary schools has been unfashionable in Canada and to a slightly lesser extent in the USA for at least two decades. Indeed, vocational education has never been strong in North America in the way it has been in West Germany and Switerland. In North America, the ideal has been that all young people should graduate from secondary education and that vocational training take place within the tertiary sector. This ideal conveniently ignores the fact that between one-fifth (the USA) and one-third (Canada) of the age cohort does not graduate from high school.

One exception to this general neglect of vocational education has been commercial or business education. Business education has flourished throughout North America training young people, mostly girls, for work as secretaries, clerks and bookkeepers. In addition, there has been more limited training in such areas as automobile mechanics, welding, electricity, carpentry and machine shop. The listing of those areas illustrates how the field of vocational education has ossified over the last thirty years — with the result that the vocational programs, where they exist, are likely to represent the employment picture of 1955 better than that of 1990. The newer and developing occupations in hotel work, restaurants, electronics, the use and repair of computers, dental hygiene, child care, care for the elderly, home and garden maintenance and specialty farming of vegetables and nursery stock are typically underrepresented in contemporary high schools. Even where vocational (often called technical) programs exist, schools often claim they are not primarily 'dead end' vocational programs but are aimed to prepare students for post-secondary institutions, a preparation which, incidentally, goes largely unappreciated by colleges who prefer students with a general academic background.

Educators typically give low priority to the vocational functions. There are several reasons for this. Philosophically, many educators see the school's purpose as being more to do with preparation for life than for making a living. It is difficult for vocational schools to keep up with changing technology. As the labor market becomes more diversified, it becomes more difficult to prepare workers for a precise niche, a niche that may not endure for more than a few years. The colleges have increasingly taken over the vocational role (but bear in mind the many who do not go on to post-secondary education). Parents and students alike, however utilitarian their attitude to education, see vocational programs as having low prestige. Finally, in many parts of the USA and Canada, the sparse population and diffuse labor market makes it difficult to concentrate specialized areas of training. However, it should be noted that while the prestige of secondary vocational programs has decreased, the prestige of college and university vocational programs (forestry, accounting, business, medicine, pharmacy, machine technology and law) has increased; there it is the general arts and social science programs that have lost favor in all but the most élite universities.

There has been some movement in some jurisdictions to what is called cooperative education — a plan whereby secondary students receive course credit for time spent working outside the school. Very often, these programs are not vocationally oriented. Such experiences may be useful but they are not strongly relevant to the vocational function addressed here. Recently, the success of West Germany in maintaining a low youth unemployment rate during times when many other western countries have had very high unemployment rates has encouraged Americans and Canadians to look more closely at their vocational training programs involving close cooperation, mandated by law, between the school and the employer. However, at the moment, the vocational function is weak in most school systems in the USA and Canada.

The Significance of the School's Functions

It is important to be neither controlled by nor contemptuous of the school's functions. It is easy to be so impressed by what schools actually do that one cannot imagine a system that is different. A standard criticism of the functional approach to educational analysis is just that: it defends the *status quo*. Some of the school's functions (notably in the aesthetic, physiological and moral/spiritual domains) are probably accomplished if at all, more outside school hours in extracurricular activities than inside. The school's moral/spiritual functions and increasingly its cultural functions are sources of heated debate. It is not clear just what schools do accomplish within those domains; still less is there agreement on what the role of the school should be.

If it is easy to be a slave to what the school does, it is equally easy to blithely ignore the functional analysis, on the grounds that it does defend the *status quo* and is therefore irrelevant to what schools ought to be about. This second position can be defended on a number of grounds. We cannot answer questions about functional effectiveness with complete authority; we just do not know the discrete contributions of school, home and community in the upbringing of our young, and there is no prospect that we shall soon discover them. It can also be argued that any description of functions depends on the eye of the beholder. And there is no question that left-wing and right-wing critics can disagree vehemently about what is wrong with the current school. The structural-functionalist describes both activities and outcomes — but the implication of a strong causal effect can easily be implied without careful argumentation. Despite such criticisms, there are good arguments for not ignoring reasonable evidence about what schools actually do.

Most studies of school administration adopt one of two approaches, or some combination of both. Some are based on organizational theory. Unfortunately, there is no empirically proven theory of school organization so such texts are reduced to describing scattered pieces of research held together with inconclusive argument. (Two very different criticisms of this approach can be found in Greenfield (1986) and Holmes (1986b).) Another approach is to describe what administrators do, with implicit or explicit suggestions about how they could do it better. The rationale underlying this book is different! The improvement of school administration must depend first on what it is that we want to accomplish. Education is a moral enterprise and therefore advice, implicit or explicit, only makes sense within some context of understanding about what it is we are trying to do. But education is above all a practical, applied field. It surely makes sense to take into account the possible when we discuss what it is we ought to be doing. This is not at all to discount the possibility of accomplishing things we do not currently accomplish, or of attempting some things more purposefully which we now attempt without success. But it would be foolhardy indeed to assume that because there is a problem, the school can solve it.

The Goals of the Elementary and Secondary School

With some idea of what schools do, it becomes a little easier to address the more complex question of what they ought to do. From the foregoing, it will be apparent that we are suggesting that one should be both realistic and idealistic. We do not intend to provide a potted history of educational philosophy. However, we consider it unwise to write about effective schools without some consideration of what it is one wants to effect. Our intent is to provide a short guide to the major choices facing the school administrator and to describe some of the assumptions lying behind the chapters of the book suggesting ways to make the school more effective.

However, it would be incorrect to assume that administrators typically choose in a reasonably focused way among a list of purposes to which they give some priority. It must first be asked whether or not the school should operate in terms of a set of given purposes, and if it should whether they should be explicit. Now it is true of course that if organizations continue they must be fulfilling some purposes for somebody. However, that does not mean necessarily that schools are directed primarily towards goals within the set of domains. Administrators do not necessarily confine themselves to goals concerning students. Security, income, personal happiness, continued organizational existence — all these goals may supplant what an outsider might consider to be a more legitimate goal.

The functional domains described, although all inclusive, are inclusive only in terms of students. It is not at all inconceivable that the day to day operational goal of some schools is survival. The staff wants the organization to continue as peacefully, as intact, as possible.

Thus the possibility of a school operating without a reasonably focused philosophy based on benefit to students cannot be put aside. It is possible to imagine a health service operated for the benefit of doctors and nurses, social services operated for the benefit of social workers. It is sometimes argued that large institutional bureaucracies have come to operate principally for the benefit of the staff employed by them rather than for the benefit of those for whom the service is intended. Illich made this part of his argument for 'deschooling' many years ago (1970).

An assumption behind this book is that the satisfaction of staff and administration is not an adequate substitute for success with learners — that the school's mission is to educate not to employ. A corollary of this assumption is that the adage, 'a contented staff makes a successful school' is not a reasonable philosophy for a school. Success does not necessarily follow from staff satisfaction, although skilful administration of staff may be one component of success with students. The conceptual point can be made in this way. It is possible to envisage a school where the teachers are well paid and provided good working conditions. They are given a great deal of professional freedom and genuinely believe in the illusion that students are progressing as a result of their teaching even though they have no real sense of what it is they are trying to accomplish. It is not at all illogical to assume that the staff is relatively content, and student progress very slight.

Even if it is agreed that school purposes should be grounded in educational terms rather than in the interests of the employees, it does not follow that the educational goals should be explicit.

An analogy can be made with the rule of law. As long as there is sufficient consensus about what ought to be done, law is unnecessary. Tradition, popular opinion and public pressure enforce compliance. It is when the consensus is challenged or disobeyed that a law or rule must be introduced. The British and American traditions are at odds here. The British tradition avoids codifying law unnecessarily, preferring to rely on reasoned judgment from past practice. The American tradition prefers the enunciation of grand principles, from which a broad range of judgments can then follow.

And so with education. Statements of explicit educational purpose are rare in England, the norm in the USA. In an ideal situation, we would prefer to manage without explicit statements of purpose, relying on consensual agreement among parents, teachers and students. However, that situation is rare today outside a few private and religious schools. Even in England, core curricula with clear goals and national testing of the achievement of those goals are being introduced. Generally in the Western world, as the central societal consensus erodes, as the centre weakens, the perceived need for the writing of educational goals has grown.

Most educational systems in North America have sets of goals; furthermore, many also have explicit objectives attached to them. There is a danger in this process. As lack of consensus becomes more and more manifest, even more detailed and explicit objectives become necessary. This leads to a vicious circle. As consensus disintegrates it is important for schools to codify their goals and responsibilities. As codification becomes more detailed, more frequent argument about the details erupts. This can lead to teachers' lives being industrialized as their room for professional discretion becomes more and more constrained.

Another problem with statements of educational goals is that they are often denigrated by educators as being statements of 'motherhood'. As we have said, that criticism is itself ambiguous. Sometimes it means that the goal statements are generalizations to which everyone will agree, at least until some very detailed specification is made. That kind of normative motherhood statement is useful. If one can agree on broad, general principles, disagreements can be kept in perspective. Much more troubling is the so-called 'motherhood' statement which actually says different things to different people. In this case, the goal is quite unhelpful.

Thus, it is increasingly necessary for one to have explicit goals and these goals should be clear and unambiguous; they form the backdrop, the context for most administrative behavior. Immediately, a philosophical difference emerges between those who want the goals to address the process of learning and those who want them to address changes to be brought about in the learner, learning outcomes.

Advocates of the first approach concern themselves with the way in which teaching and learning takes place, with learners' attitudes towards others and towards themselves. They are interested in learners' self-concept and their ability to learn how to learn.

Two different starting points bring educators to that conclusion. One is a belief that children grow in certain ways through certain stages — but at varying rates and by different paths. The other is the conviction that the adult world should leave the world of childhood alone to a great degree, so that children can make their own choices freely. Clearly the two propositions are of a very different order and to some extent are contradictory. The first set of ideas concerning growth seems to be an empirical hypothesis. However, closer investigation makes it difficult to determine to what extent the idea is really based on underlying theory and to what extent it is merely a means of attempting to classify observed phenomena into some framework of growth and change. For example, followers of Piaget and Kohlberg are not always in agreement on whether one should wait until a stage has been reached before giving instruction relative to that stage or whether one should help children reach and pass through the successive stages. In the case of Kohlberg's stages of moral development, it is not even clear to what extent it is preferable to be at a higher stage. If the ideas are theoretical, one should be clear as to whether one is discussing genetically determined, neurological changes or whether one is discussing changes that are primarily cultural in origin. Are the changes invariate? If not, what are the conditions under which they vary? Thus, although educational goals and instruction are frequently hooked to alleged changes, there are major educational problems. The fact that there are patterns of growth tells us little about what children ought to become and very little more about the educational processes one should use.

The second proposition, that one should prolong and enhance the freedom of childhood, is a moral injunction. It is based on ideas about the natural goodness of children. It is simply asserted that children ought to be left free to make more decisions about their lives, particularly about educational and moral choices without clear evidence or argument as to why this should be so. In practice, the argument is necessarily contradicted by the educational environment provided by progressive classrooms and schools, clearly limiting the range of choice that children can make. As an obvious example, children cannot choose firm rules and direct instruction in a classroom where those features are absent.

In our view, neither of those propositions provides persuasive argument for basing educational goals on process. The first proposition is empirical. If the ideas based on growth actually work, then it would seem sensible for teachers to adopt them. If they do not work, or if they do not work as well as competing methodologies, based perhaps on sequential, cognitive learning steps or on behavioral conditioning, then there seems to be no *a priori* reason for their adoption. The second proposition is impossible to refute in a final way. If one believes that process is more important than outcome as an article of faith, it is unlikely that argument or empirical evidence will convince one otherwise. However, progressive educators who hold this belief in process should be clear and straightforward about their faith, as of course should those who hold conflicting beliefs. Very often the argument is made that process goals are preferable because children learn more effectively that way. The argument becomes empirical at that stage and should be subject to large scale empirical testing. If in fact process goals are favored only because they allegedly produce better results, logically they should be abandoned as soon as it is established, as it has been, that they generally do not. But advocates of process goals are generally unwilling to forgo their goals even if they can be shown that their methodology is less effective than others in some important respects. Typically they respond that there are other things that are more important than the stated learning outcomes.

Responses to the second proposition fall into one of two categories. It is pointed out that large scale research into the teaching of basic skills does not generally favor progressive methodologies. More fundamentally, the proposition is attacked because many people believe that education is intended to bring about clear changes in students, not least that it should make them better human beings.

A major practical problem for those who support the second proposition is that, translated into practice, it becomes inconsistent with many assumptions underlying contemporary school organizations. This is recognized by Sarason (1983) who argues that the contemporary school cannot possibly achieve progressive goals. He effectively abandons the school and argues that education should take place mainly outside the school context. There is some logic in that position as the very notion of compulsory schooling, required homework, scheduled periods, subject centred instruction, specialist teachers, and motivation by grades and certification run counter to progressive philosophy.

Our own view, which is shared, according to recent polls of public opinion on education, by the majority of members of the public but probably not by as many educators, is that school goals should be outcome oriented. The outcomes may include non-traditional goals in, for example, the social and physiological domains, but the goals are changes to be brought out in children, not processes to be used on them.

If the assumption is made that education in schools is intended to bring about changes in young people that would not come about to the same degree or so efficiently if schools did not exist, then administrators must know which changes they want to bring about. What is distinctive about the professional educational administrator is the discretionary power to make moral choices. Obviously, the range of choice in choosing and emphasizing educational purposes is always and necessarily limited. Governments and elected school officials and other adminisatrators in the hierarchy all have much to say about legitimate educational goals. The school administrator cannot substitute important personal goals for those of the legitimate authority. Nevertheless, there is frequently considerable room for the exercise of professional autonomy. High level goals are often very vague or ambiguous. Priorities among them are usually left very much to the individual school. But even at the school level, the school administrator frequently is appropriately constrained by the wishes of parent groups, teachers and others. Even so, none of this makes the codification and clarification of goals unimportant.

The set of goals that follows (table 1) is intended for use in a typical public school, where we believe it will receive consensual public support. The set should be read and used with the following assumptions in mind:

(i) *A set of written goals is necessary.* Today, we come across very few public schools where one is not necessary. Disagreement about significant purposes is common among staff members as well as between staff and parents. Goal setting may sometimes be difficult and divisive, but a legitimate set of goals is generally necessary for an effective school.

(ii) *Goal statements can either be more or less general than this particular set.* Some schools are likely to find parts of the goal statement redundant, i.e., some parts they will see as being self-evident from other parts. However, deletion should not result from fear of divisiveness. It is precisely the areas of lack of consensus that require definition. To include only those things on which agreement is complete is to carry out a redundant exercise.

(iii) *As this set is intended for elementary and secondary grades, some goals will be unnecessary for either an elementary or a secondary school.*

(iv) *Some goals will be specifically prescribed or proscribed by the legitimate authority.* Where a goal is mandated, there is generally little point in further discussion, although it should of course be included and be clear. Where a goal is not permitted (for example, the development of particular religious beliefs), it should be left out. There is generally no point in raising for discussion areas for change where no change is legally possible. However, administrators should avoid using their own distaste as a criterion for impossibility of application.

(v) *The goals do not apply equally to all students.* Some goals cannot be achieved by some students. Other goals can be achieved by virtually everyone. The subject areas and levels where goals will be addressed should be included in a more detailed set of objectives. Nevertheless, goal statements should be as universal as possible. There is an important distinction between not making every child honest, because of human frailty, and not making every child musical, because music is an option.

(vi) *Minimum levels of competence and levels of excellence should generally be covered in sets of objectives or in program statements, rather than in goal statements.*

(vii) *As goals are matters of major interest to the legitimate authority and to parents as well as to staff and students, there should be widespread, genuine consultation.*

(viii) *Principals should be open about their own position on goals. They must also be flexible in areas not fundamental to their own educational philosophy.*

(ix) *Administrators should be prepared to leave the school, without recrimination, if the goals derived consensually by others (the general public, the school district, senior administrators, parents) fundamentally differ from their own.* They do no one a service if they either work towards or try to subvert goals with which they personally disagree. On the other hand, they should not feel too concerned about or constrained by vague goals developed for some short term single interest purpose with few if any intelligible implications for school program. Resignation on principle should stem from a major difference of views, not from a non-event, however irritating or demeaning.

(x) *The decision making process for the development of goals, possibly beginning with a working set developed by the principal or principal and staff, should be clear, fair and open.*

Table 1:   A Model Set of Educational Goals for Elementary and Secondary Schools

---

(i) *Intellectual goals*
Students should learn:
   (1) to read with comprehension and interest;
   (2) to write and speak and listen effectively and accurately;
   (3) basic computational skills and the everyday use of number and measurement;
   (4) to think, analyze, synthesize and evaluate using reason, imagination, curiosity, logic and moral integrity;
   (5) to approach problems using appropriate skills and criteria, in the context, where applicable, of overriding moral judgment;
   (6) to communicate competently in the second official language (Canada);
   (7) fundamental ideas in the disciplines of knowledge;
   (8) the general geography and history of their country, its neighbors and the world;
   (9) basic knowledge in the physical and biological sciences and the ability to apply the basic scientific skills of observation, sorting, classification and inquiry:
   (10) how to use and operate a computer for purposes of word processing, learning and other everyday applications.

(ii) *Moral/spiritual goals*
Students should:
   (1) appreciate, value and practise the virtues of truth, courage, justice, compassion, friendship and integrity;
   (2) pursue and value virtue and the overall good;
   (3) develop their latent capacities to improve morally, intellectually and socially;

Table 1: (cont'd)

---

      (4) develop a confident awareness of self, including a judicious blend of self-respect, humility and a sense of control of their own destiny;

      (5) understand the importance of their own moral behavior within the contexts of family and society;

      (6) be encouraged and given the opportunity to develop an appropriate religious or spiritual framework in accordance with their family tradition and wishes, at the same time learning respect for other frameworks that also reflect fundamental virtue.

(iii) *Cultural/aesthetic goals*
Students should:

      (1) discover and appreciate the culture (for example, language, history, literature, the arts, social development) of their own civilization, including the characteristic culture of major social groups found within their own country, together with a tolerant understanding of other cultures;

      (2) learn to form grounded opinions in artistic fields (literature and the arts), become aware of prevailing standards, and develop artistic preferences based on knowledgeable choice;

      (3) develop the capacity to create and express a blend of emotional, intellectual and aesthetic ideas with the aid of the required skills in artistic, musical, literary, dramatic and sculpted forms.

(iv) *Social goals*
Students should:

      (1) understand and appreciate important principles and ideas underlying our social system: political democracy; freedom of expression; respect for law; individual spiritual equality without discrimination by sex, race, language, ethnic background or age; respect for the discipline of work and such attendant traits as punctuality, reliability, and industry;

      (2) make rational plans for their future based on an understanding of their own characteristics and of the society in which they are going to live;

      (3) understand the economic organization of their country, including parts played by organized labor and public and private corporations;

---

    (4) understand and appreciate the role of the family as a social institution and their own role within the family;

    (5) understand the political organization of the country, the province (or state) and the local municipality together with the citizen's rights and obligations;

    (6) learn to work and play cooperatively and productively with others, in a variety of structured situations — as leaders, as team members, as subordinates, depending on the nature of the task;

    (7) consider others when making both simple and complex decisions.

(v) *Physiological*

Students should:

    (1) achieve and maintain a high level of physical fitness;

    (2) acquire an understanding of their own behavior and how and when to control or change it;

    (3) know and apply good health habits;

    (4) know and apply standards of safety in leisure pursuits, in work, on the highway and in daily life;

    (5) acquire a general understanding of the anatomy and physiology of the human being;

    (6) learn, always within the context of the moral/spiritual and social goals, about sexual reproduction and the effects of common licit and illicit drugs, including alcohol;

    (7) develop psychomotor skills, in particular those associated with readily available healthy, recreational opportunities within the community.

(vi) *Vocational Goals*

Students should:

    (1) know the characteristics (entry standards, type of work, pay, employment prospects) of a broad variety of employment opportunities, including those areas in which they are interested and those for which they may be potentially qualified;

    (2) know the school's assessment of their own level of functioning in academic and other relevant terms, including work habits and attitudes;

    (3) be prepared either for post-secondary education or training or for employment;

Table 1:   A Model Set of Educational Goals for Elementary and Secondary Schools
(cont'd)

---

       (4) learn about adult work experience, in the form of
           apprenticeship training or in volunteer work or in
           part-time employment;
       (5) learn the skills, general behavior and personal res-
           ponsibility that will be required when they move from
           school to adult life.

Relationship between Functions and Goals

Earlier in this chapter we argued that there are four functions that the
school undeniably fulfils. Social distribution, the basic disciplines of knowledge and the basic skills are all clearly included in the set of goals. Custody
is not. We went on to argue that schools should be concerned with what can
be done as well as with what ought to be done. Custody is a means to the end
of education rather than an end in itself. If the ambitious goals included in
the model set are to be appreciably achieved, a long period of compulsory
attendance is necessary. It is true that custody is frequently demanded
outside the usual educational framework. Schools are expected to provide
custody over the lunch-time break, after school and before school. Increasingly they are being expected to provide day care for younger children.
    While we see nothing illegitimate in the extension of custody in these
ways, it is important that a distinction be made between custody required
for educational purposes and custody required for other purposes. It is not of
course that one suspends all educational effort during the non-instructional
part of the day. But it is administratively important to determine reasonably
precisely which hours of the day are intended for formal education, with the
necessary personnel, planning, and program thereby entailed, and which
are not. In terms of cost accounting, it is important that day care not be
included in the cost of education. For example, it is extravagant to employ
highly paid people to oversee essentially custodial activities (which should
not necessarily be non-educational).

Why These Goals?

We have listed a specific and carefully developed set of goals for two reasons.
Firstly, as one theme of this book is that school effectiveness is only as
valuable as the goals being effected, it is important for the assumptions
behind the book to be made explicit. The goals set out here are in general the
ones we believe today's school should be working towards. Secondly, it is

useful for administrators to have a set of goals as a starting point for their own or as a basis for comparison.

Several kinds of reaction to these goals are likely. Some administrators will sigh at the sight of another set of goals, thinking that the problem is not with goals but with their realization. We sympathize with that reaction and most of this book is about exactly that topic — how to realize goals effectively. Others may say that all sets of educational goals are 'motherhood' statements, a statement which is not very helpful. Others may argue that unimportant or wrong goals are included, and important areas excluded. Some of the aspects of that last reaction will be addressed on the basis of comments received from teachers and administrators who have used a similar, preliminary set in graduate classes. The three most controversial domains are the moral, academic and vocational.

A crucial choice in the moral domain must be made between the teaching of virtue and teaching about virtue. The point is not whether instruction is formal or informal but whether specific values are assumed and inculcated or not. Our goal set makes it clear that virtue (of fundamental values) ought to be taught. We are not addressing here the question of how they might be taught, merely the fact that they should be.

The philosophy underlying this chapter's position may be found in MacIntyre (1981). Holmes (1986c) has applied those ideas to educational administration. It is no coincidence that the virtues broadly represent the Judaeo-Christian moral tradition. Further, it is clear that most parents expect schools to uphold the basic values quite explicitly. Finally, the only alternative to what is often called rather derisively 'a basket of virtues' approach is a relativist world where all moral choices are fundamentally equivalent, where teachers may help students to reason but where they must make no judgmental comments as to right and wrong. The consequence of accepting a set of moral goals is important. Principals and teachers must conscientiously reinforce the basic virtues and must not condone attacks on them. In practice, many teachers tacitly condone lying, particularly if it seems irrelevant to the job at hand; they do not expect courage — in fact they help children avoid situations that may require the exercise of courage. To avoid a decision on this vital issue is to choose the relativist position; if clear values are not enunciated, relativist values replace them. There is no middle way.

The academic goals, like the rest of the set, are oriented towards outcomes, towards what students should be able to do when they have completed satisfactorily their school program. We have already indicated that progressives will argue that the whole approach is wrong, that education should not be subject or discipline centred, that what is important is the learning process, that young people should learn how to learn rather than pieces of knowledge or sets of skills. We do not deny the importance of children learning how to learn, but we do believe the goals one wants should be clear. Once again, the consequence of choosing a set of clear, desired academic outcomes is significant. Universities, colleges and employers look for specific qualities and a failure to acquire such qualities will put the young people in question at risk. If we put functions and goals together, it becomes clear why academic matters related to intellectual goals form the major content of school life. Although it is undoubtedly better to be good than to have a great deal of knowledge, the average day school's effect on virtue is likely to be much more limited, in the best possible circumstances, than is its effect on learning. This does not mean that moral goals are of secondary importance but it does mean that most of the time will be spent working towards intellectual goals which can be achieved rather than by repetitious moral instruction which (like repetitious academic instruction) will be ineffective. This is not to say direct moral instruction is unimportant — but modelling and expectations are also good modes of instruction.

Some critics will object to the entire category of vocational goals. We refer here not to the objection that they should be subsumed under some other domain but to the more fundamental objection that schools should not be concerned with vocational choice and material ends but with personal fulfilment. Part of the answer is the functional reality — that schools everywhere in the developed world must distribute students among their futures. Beyond that, it should be realized that young people, like adults, have a mixture of motives. Remove the vocational relevance of secondary schooling and some students will leave. In the same way most teachers will not stay in school if their pay cheques cease. One must remember that the most academically inclined students are strongly motivated in vocational terms. They are typically thinking of the superior jobs that will result from their success in school, university and perhaps even professional school. We have no wish to dwell on the vocational aspect of schooling and the material ends, but educators are irresponsible if they fail to recognize the legitimate demands by society for trained workers and the legitimate request from secondary students that there be some sense of connection between their school work and their future.

Much of the remainder of the book consists of the application of ideas (drawn from belief, logic, practice and research) for the better achievement of that set of goals. Thus rejection of these goals *in toto* is likely to make most of the rest of the book uninteresting.

Are All Goals Equivalent?

From the administrative point of view, there are two dimensions in which goals vary. They vary in importance and they vary in their ease of attainment. Consider the goal of physical fitness. It is quite low on most people's priority list. But it is one of the most easily attained (twenty minutes of hard exercise a day will increase the level of fitness of most young people and bring virtually all to an acceptable level). Take the goal of virtuous character. It is a vitally important goal, but one very difficult to achieve.

Thus the customary administrative approach of giving administrative emphasis to those categories of intellectual goals considered most important is not necessarily a sensible one. If, for example, achieving second language goals is easy, first language goals very difficult, it may not help very much to give high priority to the latter. Indeed, a half-hearted attempt at the former may be much more successful than a whole-hearted attempt at the latter. We are not arguing that we should abandon the difficult goals and replace them with more easily achieved ones. We are arguing that one should take difficulty of achievement into account.

If character development is very difficult, then minor changes in program are unlikely to have much effect. Great efforts will have to be expended and their success closely monitored. Similarly, if first language fluency is important but difficult to achieve, then doing more of the same — simply extra classes or extra writing or more reading time — is unlikely to be effective. Different approaches will have to be tried and evaluated. On the other hand, if direct instruction in basic mathematics proves to be very effective in raising mathematics achievement levels, perhaps all that is required for overall improvement is formal allocation of time to focused, sequential mathematics instruction.

Furthermore, the school does not have equal responsibility for all goals. We happen to believe that character is the single most important aspect of education. But the family has greater opportunity and responsibility in that domain. On the other hand, the school has the greatest responsibility in the academic domain.

Conclusion

The theme of this chapter has been a dual one — what schools do and what they ought to do. There are four important tasks that schools everywhere in the Western world carry out: they provide a mechanism for social distribution; they provide custody for youth during much of the working day; they provide instruction in the basic skills, generally successfully; and they provide, at least for some, introduction to the basic disciplines of knowledge, which themselves lead for an important minority of young people, to further education at the post-secondary level.

Within the six domains of education — intellectual, cultural/aesthetic, moral/spiritual, physiological, social and vocational — other functions are fulfilled, perhaps at a low level for many, at a higher level for a few. In contrast, a reasonable set of educational goals is ambitious. Few educators would feel happy to be confined to the four major functions. Are the goals then really the icing on a rather dull cake? Are they merely the public legitimation of a rather pedestrian, but very expensive, undertaking? We think not. We believe that, although the school does not have equal responsibility for all domains, they should be taken seriously.

If administrators act as though all that is required is to determine the relative importance of the goals and then encourage the school to make efforts commensurate with their ranking, the result is likely to be unsatisfactory. The goals are not interchangeable; they are not all equally sensitive to educational effort. Furthermore, there is in fact no simple logical link between the importance of goals and the efforts expended on them. Many administrators and teachers have their own priorities, conflicting with those of the public. If schools are to be made more effective, one must know what they are now doing, one must know what one wants them to do and above all one must know how best to achieve an extremely varied set of goals.

Further Reading

The philosophy behind this chapter, and the book, stems from Alasdair MacIntyre, developed most fully in *After Virtue* (1981). The ideas of Edward Shils in *Tradition* (1981) are also important. In terms of educational philosophy, our position most closely reflects that of Jacques Maritain (1943).

Mark Holmes has developed the ideas of schools' functions more fully in articles in *Curriculum Inquiry* (1980, 1985a). Seymour Sarason has appealed for a more liberated education and radical change in *Schooling in America* (1983). He and Holmes debate that approach in Holmes (1985b, c) and Sarason (1985).

Hoy and Miskel (1982) is probably still the best general text on educational administration written from a positivist, scientific perspective. In contrast to the perspective developed in this book, most other modern texts adopt the same fundamental assumptions, although they are frequently more practical in their approach, for example, McPherson, Crowson and Pitner (1986).

A thoughtful attempt to place values within administration is found in Hodgkinson (1978). Although we are sympathetic to many of Hodgkinson's ideas, our view is that educational administration is fundamentally different from, for example, business administration. Hence our stress on the idea that the school principal should determine what the school is about before trying to 'improve' it or make it more 'effective.'

Chapter 2

The Influence, Power, Authority and Role of the School Principal

Power, Authority and Influence

Power, authority and influence are distinguishable. Power is the capacity to have others do what they do not want to do. If a boy suggests to his girlfriend that it would be good to go to a rock concert, there is no evidence of a power relationship just because she chooses to go. She may want to go to the concert herself. It is probably not even a power relationship if she happily agrees because she loves the boy and wants to be with him, but actually hates rock. The relationship becomes a power relationship when she does things she does not want to because she feels she must. Power does not have to be exercised in the form of a command, but evidence for its existence requires that another's will be broken. Principals have limited power. They only on rare occasions, for example, have power to make all teachers do something they do not want to do.

Authority has a number of meanings. One talks of a scientific text as having authority. One means that its influence has legitimacy. Authority may also derive from a role or position. Principals and teachers have certain privileges and rights stemming from their legal appointments — these privileges and rights form the core of their authority. Yet one often adds an overlay to that *legitimate authority*, when one talks of some people, doing the same job, as having more authority than others. If the first is bureaucratic, *legitimate authority*, the second is *moral* or *informal authority*. This second form of authority is also found in relationships where there is no hierarchy; sometimes, a younger child in the neighborhood will have considerable authority over other older children not enforced by power or by legitimacy but by charisma, intelligence or a proven track record. Authority and power frequently co-exist and overlap when someone has both the power and the authority to carry out certain actions. Power is usually used in a bureaucratic setting over people. Authority is a more broadly applied term. It is possible to have legitimate authority without power. Bureaucracies pass all kinds of rules and regulations, but they may prove impossible to enforce. A principal may have the authority to suspend the entire teaching staff, but it would be a rare principal who had the effective power to sustain such a suspension. One can certainly have moral/informal authority without power — indeed such authority is most obvious precisely in the situation where there is no possible power. When a friend recommends a particular film, her authority rests on her reputation for good or agreeable judgment. School staffs sometimes have authoritative, informal leaders.

It is possible to have power without authority. Any strong adult can make a child act against his or her will. In the absence of physical domination, it is more doubtful that such power can last. Power at least requires either the illusion of authority or the illusion of strength.

Power and authority are both categories of *influence*. Influence is the broadest and most general external cause of behavior. Influence is frequently seen in the absence of power and authority, but it is highly unusual to see power or authority without influence. Power without influence is latent or unknown. Authority without influence may also be latent or unrecognized; in a school situation authority may have been disarmed — where the principal of a school is openly ridiculed and barely tolerated by teachers and students. It is possible to have influence without intent, and to be influential or influenced without awareness. Authority and power are usually recognizable when they are used. Influence is often covert — unrecognized, denied or forgotten.

School jurisdictions legislate authority for the principals and teachers in their schools. The legislation is often so general that rights in specific situations are not at all or very crudely spelled out.

A teacher may have authority to give homework, but the ability to exercise the power to ensure that it be done is dependent on other sources outside the classroom — the principal and parents. One of the principles behind corporal punishment is that it gives a potent form of power; however, in extreme conditions a child may still refuse to submit. Exclusion in the form of suspension and expulsion is the ultimate power of school administrators but the power is also not readily exercised. Most teachers and parents want the good things that schools have the authority to provide; but there is much reluctance to exercise the power sometimes required to ensure they be provided.

Why should administrators concern themselves with the nature of power, authority and influence? Many successful principals have run schools without the benefit of such inquiry. Moreover, the very act of inquiry may be counterproductive, filling administrators with the self-doubt and insecurity which will serve only to reduce their power, authority and influence. Most principals in elementary schools, like elementary teachers, rarely give much thought to the painful possibility their instructions may be disobeyed. Their very assurance helps make disobedience unlikely.

There are two reasons why the nature of authority is of interest. Firstly, the pursuit of knowledge and understanding is an end in itself and cannot be guaranteed to provide immediately helpful results. That may sound smug, but once one refuses to confront truth, particularly in education, one is surely in trouble. Secondly, schools are becoming more complex places where the traditional exercise of power and authority is no longer accepted easily by teachers, students and parents. Just as written goals become necessary in the absence of consensus, so written definitions and agreements on authority are required when it is frequently challenged. If it is to be pinned down on paper, it should be understood.

The Nature and Use of Power, Authority and Influence in the Schools

Teachers have the unusual professional responsibility of being responsible for ensuring that others do what they are 'supposed' to do. Principals, even more unusually, have authority over fellow professionals. Yet, as Chapter 1 showed, what learners are 'supposed' to do is frequently complex, ambiguous, debatable and ill-defined. Professional educators differ then from doctors, dentists and lawyers, who are essentially responsible for their own professional actions and not for the actions of their patients and colleagues. Doctors may have some limited responsibility for the behavior of nurses. But doctors have bureaucratic authority over nurses in situations where they have responsibility. Principals sometimes have very little hierarchical authority over teachers but are still held responsible for the teachers' behavior. Later in this chapter, we shall deal generally with the ethical use of authority and shall turn later to problems of professionalism.

The concepts of power and authority override the concept of influence as matters of importance in the school. A dentist may decide to emphasize preventative dentistry in her practice, relying on influence and the authority of her status. The school principal can rarely decide any change of direction independently and is constantly concerned with the exercise of legitimate authority to ensure custody for all enrolled students. Even in the case of private school students whose enrolment is in a sense voluntary, once enrolled the voluntary aspect recedes, for it is usually the parents rather than the students who operationalize the choice. Even in the private school, custody is of central importance. In this respect, the private school is more like the public school than it is like the dentist's office. Authority is an ever-present concern.

Some principals try to adopt the position that schools provide an array of offerings, and that it is up to pupils' parents to take advantage of what is offered. But they cannot normally invite pupils to leave if they don't like the offerings. There is a world of difference between an optional evening class for adults, and a fifth grade class for children. The evening teacher has a responsibility to provide an offering; she is more like the dentist. The fifth grade teacher has a responsibility to see that the children learn, to make them learn even if they do not wish to. The teacher's strategy may be to let the children learn 'at their own rate', 'in their own way' but the strategy, however well meaning and however effective in a particular circumstance, is dishonest if it purports to give the child genuine control. The teacher knows he is accountable for the learning of children; the most permissive of parents still holds the teacher accountable for the child's failure to learn. Thus even though an educator may seek to work through influence rather than through authority and the power lying behind it, the functional realities of school life dictate otherwise.

Some Propositions about the Nature of Power and Authority

1 Power is necessary for the continuing execution of authority, but power sometimes creates resentment in the ruled.
2 Legitimate authority requires either power or informal authority to make it operational.
3 Informal authority is less dependable than legitimate authority, less comprehensive and more easily rejected.
4 Informal authority is a greater potential force for major change than power or legitimate authority in institutions that are not highly bureaucratized.
5 Legitimate authority is never expended.
6 Power is expended, when the subordinates cease to care about the consequences of disobedience, when its use creates counterforces, and when it is required for the normal operation of legitimate authority.

The Zero Sum Nature of Power

Is power in an organization additive or zero-sum? In other words, is power gained by one person or group automatically lost by others, or can the total amount of power within an organization be augmented? The question is important because there are increasing pressures for principlals to share power with teachers. There has been a trend for teachers, singly or collectively, students, parents and school district offices to gain power in the school over the last ten or twenty years. But has the principal lost power? And does it matter?

One way to conceptualize the problem of the zero-sum is to examine the circumstances in which decisions are made. Let us imagine that for ten years a high school principal has alone decided which teachers will teach which subjects at which levels to which grades. Then suppose that a new collective agreement between the teachers' union and the school district determines such matters as: minimum class size; maximum class size; maximum number of course preparations; maximum number of sequential classes; and maximum number of pupils taught. At the same time, the elected council of teachers from the staff demand that it be consulted before any major scheduling decisions are made. Clearly the principal has lost a significant amount of power, authority and influence. Nevertheless the loss may be less than it at first appears. Those with enormous amounts of legitimate authority rarely have the time and interest to exercise power in all areas. Frequently, traditional principals with considerable legitimate authority officially delegated authority to vice-principals and to others. Just as frequently, informal power devolved to influential members of staff. If Mrs. Fisher has become accustomed to making staff allocations in 'her' English department, it is difficult for the principal to reclaim the exercise of that legitimate authority. Even a new principal would find it difficult. That said, the zero-sum principle still stands in this case. No new power is created. And in some circumstances there may be a major transfer from principal to teachers. The effect on the principal's informal authority, as well as legitimate authority, is likely to be very considerable if that one example of change is just one among many.

In other circumstances, in contrast, it is possible for new power to be created. Consider the example of a school purchasing a computer. Control of access to the computer is a new form of power and authority, provided that teachers and others want access to it. New funds may be made available to the school for additional spending. Extracurricular activities may be expanded. Teacher aides may be hired. Volunteers may be introduced. New methods of evaluation may be brought in. All these additions create new responsibilities — and hence additional authority. The principal may then delegate some authority without a necessary net loss. In turn, however, the net gain in total authority may be less than it at first seems. As activities increase, other activities may well decrease.

If authority within a school is reduced by transfer of some of it to central decision makers, the problem facing the principal is a difficult one. The few remaining areas of discretion become more obvious, not only to the principal but also to the staff and students. Such awareness may lead to increasing scrutiny and challenge. The principal may become increasingly determined to exercise discretion in the small remaining area. That may result in increasing objection to the principal's 'arbitrary' and 'capricious' use of power. The principal may then become despondent, and be increasingly disinclined to make discretionary decisions that only appear to cause trouble. The vicious circle continues. Superordinates decide that principals cannot be trusted to use their authority effectively so make central policy decisions and sign collective agreements with the unions whereby power is effectively shared centrally between senior administrators and union leaders. Teachers, pupils and parents soon sense weakness and grab what remains of the principal's power or quickly appeal to higher authority. As an administrator once remarked, 'Once the lion is wounded, every hyena comes creeping out of his den to take a bite.'

Power needs to be used occasionally, or at least be visible, if it is to remain in force. Yet, the more power is exercised, the less effect it usually has. The child who is never chastised does not respect parental power; the child who is constantly chastised loses respect for parental power because the blows (physical or psychological) appear to come indiscriminately.

If power within a school is increasing as a result of decentralization, it becomes possible to share power without loss of informal authority. But generating power is difficult if enrolment is declining, or budgets are being cut, or options reduced. The most obvious way to increase power and authority is to increase the work to be accomplished, by developing new curricula, by having more extracurricular activities. However, increasing the amount of work to be done is not easy at a time when administrators' authority is under general scrutiny and when make-work projects are particularly suspect. In fact, one of the easiest ways out, in the short run, when there is a grab for a diminishing supply of power, is to compensate groups for their relative powerlessness by reducing workload. In that way, peace, for a time, can be achieved by reducing the working day, reducing homework, lengthening periods, allowing more spares and reducing maximum class size. Most of this can be aided by the simple expedient of increasing both average class size and minimum class size. A way to simulate increased areas of authority is to cut administrative decisions into smaller parts so that more can share. For example there may be an increase in departments or committees. But that expedient makes more work, and increased workload is less popular than increased power.

Thus while power is not necessarily an unchanging constant within the school situation, it certainly cannot be easily expanded. In practice, trends to centralization combined with tight budgets make it likely that power is contracting in most schools. It becomes important in that circumstance for the principal to understand the power and authority remaining and use them intelligently. Carelessly delegated authority or its prolonged disuse may disempower the principal entirely. Principals should realize that, without power and authority, they are no longer administrators.

Bureaucratic, Traditional and Charismatic Authority

Max Weber (Gerth and Mills, 1958, pp. 295–301) described three kinds of authority: bureaucratic (legal), traditional and charismatic. Within the organization, people do what they are supposed to do either because of established rules, because things have always been done that way or because the force of personal character, of a superordinate or co-worker, compels them to do it. Charisma cannot be relied on regularly within any organization as most people do not have enough of it. Schools are very rarely set up, let alone continued, on the basis of charisma, exceptions being the occasional private school. Even charismatic individuals cannot guarantee their charm will work in every circumstance with every individual. This does not matter so much in voluntary organizations such as churches. But control in the public school depends on mass compliance on the part of both teachers and pupils. Even parents have to comply to some degree. Traditional authority has served the school, particularly the elementary school, well. When a colleague was told about this book, his comment was that the school principal was the last bastion of authority in our society. Many principals would doubt that, comparing their diminished authority with that of their predecessors. However, in many elementary schools, notably in rural areas, the principal is still very much in command, and the teacher has comparable delegated command in the classroom. Much of that authority comes from the tradition that the principal is in charge, that, 'if you're going to do well, you have to do what the principal says', and that, 'if you don't learn to behave, heaven help you when you go to school when the principal gets hold of you.' Those traditions may be dying as school districts and parents both move to constrain the application of the principal's power, but they are far from dead.

Traditional authority is less evident in the modern secondary school which, being often new, has fewer and less firm traditions. It is possible to inherit or adopt traditions — as new elementary schools frequently do. But there is no strong body of tradition governing the large contemporary, comprehensive secondary school, with a clientele most of whose counterparts fifty years ago were not in school at all. Individual teachers and principals may sometimes depend on charisma, but bureaucratic authority is the least unstable underpinning of the secondary school.

Bureaucratic authority is the all-pervasive, reliable form of school control — certainly in the secondary school, increasingly in the urban elementary school. Chapter 5 deals with the question of the discipline of students. Here, we note that the secondary school principal has considerable legitimate authority over students (as well as over teachers) but that the principal's authority is increasingly challenged and threatened. Sanctions, such as transfer or expulsion, are possible if there is an individual problem. But large scale non-compliance with bureaucratic rules by either students or teachers is difficult or impossible to deal with. Such non-compliance has not been unthinkable since the 1960s. Membership in bureaucratic organizations, for example, banks, factories, colleges, governments, even the armed forces in most countries, is voluntary. Only prisons, psychiatric hospitals, conscripted armies and schools are based on involuntary membership. Yet observers frequently expect schools to be particularly benign examples of service organizations where extreme voluntarism is normal.

There is a contractual relationship between an employer and an employee. There is a contractual or quasi-contractual element in the citizen's involvement with a bank or a government department, such as taxation or water supply. In contrast, the citizen's involvement with a library, play park, entertainment centre or sports club has minimal contractual implications. The citizen can choose to participate or not, almost on a daily basis. Such organizations have minimal authority; but they normally do have the authority to exclude difficult clients. In turn, individuals simply choose to participate in a particular set of activities or not. The custodial aspect of the contemporary school, frequently ignored by parents and school people alike, has major implications for its authority structure. One great advantage of the private school is that involvement is voluntary on the part of parents. There is even a slight spillover to some private school students who share the spirit of voluntarism, aware that their school is being chosen and paid for, sometimes at considerable sacrifice by their parents.

Ultimately, if schools are to work as bureaucratic organizations there must be reasons for members (teachers and students) to want to remain as members; and the principal (or other legitimate authority) must have the power and the authority to exclude members who flout the rules. But bear in mind the maxim that power much used is power abused, power restrained is power maintained.

Some readers, particularly those who have not worked in large bureaucratic schools, will demur — surely this account is too cynical, too calculating. Most students enjoy school and do not have to be controlled by authoritarian powers. That response arises from a confusion of happiness with freedom, a frequent mistake in modern times. It is perfectly possible, indeed it is normal, to be happy in a state of less than complete freedom. Relationships, such as friendship and marriage, inhibit freedom in very significant ways, but they also may promote the greatest of happiness. The complete absence of freedom does simply imply unhappiness, particularly in a society like ours where we have been brought up to believe we have a 'right' to be free. However, complete freedom, the absence of all constraints, is no guarantee of happiness. It is not at all inconceivable that a class of 6-year-olds, sitting in traditional rows learning the phonic code, may be extremely happy. Whether they would be happier learning in centres or individually is an empirical question — and one that probably depends very much on the context, i.e., the personality of the teacher, the children's expectations, and their feeling of success.

The fact that the organization requires some authority, charismatic, bureaucratic or traditional, to continue operation does not mean that its members must be kept in miserable thrall to an authoritarian boss. The refutation of that alleged need for authority requires a demonstration of one of the following: that formal organizations survive without authority, which is untrue by definition; that there are other forms of authority; that members are so happy with the organization that authority is irrelevant; that individuals receive such great intrinsic, psychic rewards that authority becomes irrelevant. That last point is the most relevant to the point under discussion. However, before turning to the examination of indiviual incentive systems and the glue they provide social organizations, we do point out that the most zealous progressive educator in the public school is unlikely to argue that all school activity can always be maintained for all pupils on the basis of intrinsic rewards. And that is what would be required if schools were to divest themselves of authority and turn themselves into voluntary sports clubs. Furthermore, it is worth foreshadowing ideas developed in later chapters concerned with the importance of genuine, spontaneous relationships — relationships much more easily developed under traditional than under bureaucratic authority.

Incentive Systems

The sociologist Peter Blau (1964) has analyzed the ways in which members of organizations are persuaded to behave in the desired way. He suggested a classification of three types of incentive. The *unilateral* incentive is the use of power: members have to do certain things because there is no alternative. In the case of the school, staff usually have to do certain things, for example, arrive regularly and punctually, use acceptable language, and keep pupils orderly, or face reprimand and ultimate dismissal. Similarly, pupils who habitually use physical violence against teachers or extreme violence against other pupils are excluded. There are certain things that have to be done if the organization is to continue. The way in which that list is first determined and then communicated, overtly or covertly, is an important task of the school administrator. It is important to establish that even the most progressive, private school has some unilateral incentives, however few they may be. The question for the administration is not whether there are rules — but their nature, communication, enforcement and consequences.

The *intrinsic* incentive is focused on the nature of the task. Teachers are willing to do many things for students because they consider them an integral part of their professional lives and, not incidentally, a source of psychic returns. A notable example is the extracurricular activity, in which participation is usually voluntary. The return for both parties is largely intrinsic. Note in this context that teachers are generally not willing to take two or three pupils to the cinema on a Saturday afternoon even if the film might be valuable and enjoyable — it would not be seen as part of their job. Indeed, many parents would suspect the motive of the teacher who suggested an outing to the movies with a young or adolescent child. But the same teachers are often quite willing to referee a basketball match on the same Saturday afternoon. Even the cinema might not be objectionable if the film were *Julius Caesar* and the target audience and curricular relevance were clearly established. Teachers probably tend to overestimate the intrinsic returns to students from regular school work. For their part, adolescents underestimate the return. It has become fashionable for young people

to denigrate academic work, even academic success, a phenomenon identified in the American high school by Coleman (1961) over twenty years ago.

The *extrinsic* incentive consists of the promise of rewards not
emanating directly from the task itself. Teachers receive rewards in the form
of pay cheques, performance reviews and comments of commendation.
Students receive their rewards in the form of reports, marks (most important
in the secondary school) and approval (from teachers and parents).

The usefulness of this taxonomy lies in its illustration of the ways in
which school administrators can use their authority, both legitimate and
informal. By definition, tasks will not be completed if there is no incentive
— this is a classification system not a theory. Administrators with a strong
managerial bent are apt to believe that rules, even suggestions, are self-
sustaining. The more frequently such exhortations are ignored, the more the
administrators' authority is eroded.

There are dangers in becoming too mindful of incentive systems. Some
teachers foolishly try to rely entirely on intrinsic incentives — subverting
difficult goals because reaching them may be hard or unpleasant. Others
cynically assume children will only respond to material rewards. Good
schools use all three types harmoniously. Another danger is that administrators may be seen as being and may in fact be Machiavellian manipulators
— always on the lookout for insincere, hidden persuaders. Too much
material return for the teacher is as insulting as too little, because it implies
there is no professionalism in the teacher. Different incentives often blend.
Praise is an extrinsic incentive, but it frequently legitimates the intrinsic
satisfaction received from a job well done. Blau's taxonomy, taken as a
whole, does imply that there must be something 'in it' for the participants,
but lack of complete understanding of Blau's ideas may easily lead to interpretation of incentives in a narrow instrumental way. The usefulness of
Blau's taxonomy is that it helps the administrator recognize both the
potential and the limits of influence. Teachers will not maintain professional concern if administrators act on the assumption that they respond
only to material rewards. It is important for the administrator to see how a
variety of incentives may work in conjunction, not to choose one in isolation
as the 'good' one.

Clark and Wilson (1961) developed a taxonomy that also has some
usefulness in the school setting. They classified incentives as material,
solidary or purposive. The *material* incentive is similar to but a little
broader than Blau's unilateral incentive. Blau's incentive is essentially
negative — one does something because of the power of the sanction that
will, one believes, be invoked if one does not. The material incentive also
includes many of the incentives Blau would classify as extrinsic — marks,
promotion, privileges, exemption from unpleasant duties.

The *solidary* incentive combines some of Blau's extrinsic and intrinsic
incentives, for example, both the external praise and the inner satisfaction
that derive from working more closely with one's reference groups. In the

case of teachers, these may either be their collegial associates, or groups of pupils, or groups of parents.

The *purposive* incentive also combines some of Blau's extrinsic and intrinsic incentives — the credit received for good work well done and the sense of satisfaction received from the execution and completion of the work.

Cameron's (1984) recent work in New Brunswick suggests that teachers are much more interested in purposive and material than in solidary incentives. Lortie (1975) and Jackson (1968) have painted convincing pictures of the isolated life led by teachers. Psychic returns tend to be related more to pupils and their perceived progress than to cooperation with other teachers or parents. This provides an explanation as to why attempts to persuade teachers to work cooperatively in groups and teams are so often unsuccessful. Perhaps some teachers choose teaching precisely because they enjoy the individual responsibility and the direct relationship with young people. As for pupils, the purposive and material incentives are probably also most powerful for them — particularly in the middle and later grades, and in academic classes, where individual competition is most apparent and most helpful.

Clark and Wilson's taxonomy is an attractive one for school application. The principal may be able to conceive of material, solidary and purposive terms more readily than unilateral, extrinsic and intrinsic incentives. However, both sets are conceptually blurred at the edges. Teachers often think young children are getting intrinsic satisfaction from their work when they are in fact heavily dependent on the teacher's extrinsic approval, illustrated by smiles and praise. Marks, grades and test results are probably best classified as material incentives in the Clark and Wilson typology, but they cannot be finally distinguished from purposive achievements. Often, grades certainly indicate material success and material prospects; but sometimes they provide satisfying recognition of educational progress. Indications of students' successful academic achievement are in turn purposive incentives for teachers and vitally important ones. Teachers as a group frequently oppose external testing on the grounds that the test results may be used to compare and evaluate them. However, as soon as the tests are completed, teachers usually ask for their own results in terms of other peoples' results so that they may evaluate themselves.

Incentive systems illustrate the ways in which principals and teachers use power, authority and influence. It is remarkable how wide and variable is the range of activities in which principals and teachers participate. Doctors typically have no superordinates and live much or all of their working lives outside of bureaucracy, for example, as independent practitioners; within a very small bureaucracy, for example, working in a group practice with a few colleagues and a small support staff, or as external, independent consultants to a bureaucracy, for example, as a surgeon with right of access to a hospital. In all cases, their purposes and organized behavior are quite closely prescribed by some combination of tradition and professional ethics. Their goals are primarily about healing, secondarily about maintenance of health and prevention of disease. Even more striking, the daily behavior of one doctor is much like that of another. Their professionalism lies in their independence, in their lengthy training and above all in their discretion in determining special modes of treatment for the individual patient. Doctors may specialize in ears and noses or in pediatrics just as teachers may specialize in physics or kindergarten. But principals and teachers vary much more in their range of choice of activities. Some secondary teachers of English, for example, spend large amounts of time teaching grammar, others none at all. Some spend most of their time analyzing literature, others spend most of that time encouraging student reading and writing — and all these with equivalent clients. This is an equally valid observation of educational administrators who spend varying amounts of time on discipline, parental involvement, staff involvement, evaluation and curricula. Their goals are often unclear.

Thus principals and teachers face similar problems. They both live in an unusual bureaucratic arrangement where the clients' participation is typically not entirely voluntary; they have some power but ready application is discouraged, considerable legitimate authority but few sanctions to support it, and a wide array of potential tasks and associated areas of influence. They are professionals, in that they have lengthy, specialized education or training and have considerable discretion both in choice and treatment of tasks, but are subject to many of the norms and regulations of life in a hierarchical bureaucracy. The application of the idea of incentive systems to the school situation suggests there will be great difficulties in accomplishing tasks, no matter in which domain principals choose to concentrate. None of the incentives described by Blau or Clark and Wilson is nearly sufficient in itself to run a good, effective, public school in a heterogeneous social setting.

School Principals — A Typology

Table 2 presents a typology of school principals based on their use of power, authority and influence; incentive systems; and decision making styles. It is not set up to distinguish 'straw men' from one ideal choice. We could describe our ideal principal, but that single ideal would certainly not suit all personalities or all circumstances.

There are innumerable ways in which principals can be classified. A typology developed by Leithwood and Montgomery (1986) classifies principals on the basis of their major sphere of activity — managerial tasks, personnel development, program development and implementation, and problem solving. Leithwood argues that these four categories form an ascending scale, with the problem solver being at the pinnacle. Insofar as the ascending scale increasingly includes those characteristics most desired by contemporary professionals, his typology is valid and appropriate — but only providing that one's criterion of success is assessment by contemporary peers. Most educators and laypersons will readily agree with Leithwood that administrators should be more concerned with major decisions than with day-to-day trivia. However, there is a danger in Leithwood's approach that the ideal type will become cast in concrete, the form merely reflecting what happens to be currently fashionable. There will be a danger too that principals will quickly learn to classify most of their own work as problem solving. It is unhelpful to assume that all personalities, all preferences, all philosophies may be subsumed in a single role description suitable for everyone.

The position taken in this book is that two general criteria should be used in choosing and evaluating the role played by an educational administrator. In Chapter 1, we discussed the selection of educational goals, the first criterion. We suggested that schools should give particular emphasis to character because it is centrally important and to intellectual development because it is the central domain of the school. In this chapter and succeeding chapters, we address the second criterion — the effectiveness and efficiency with which those goals are achieved.

The typology in table 2 is based on Weber, Blau, and Clark and Wilson. The decision making types are drawn from Holmes's observations and from readings in educational administration. The decision making processes all involve some deployment of power, authority and influence. Judgments as to the potential influence and the most suitable environments are based on observations and on discussions with graduate students. Students (mainly teachers and school administrators) can often fit principals they have known within one of the types, but not infrequently they cannot. They point out that some principals truly blend two or three types; others vary their approach with the circumstances. The utility of the typology lies in the light that it sheds on the administrative use of influence. We do not believe that there is one right type, although the following discussion of the various types and references to them later in the book will illustrate that we do not believe they are all equally valid. Most important, we do not suggest that the most important quality of the second administrator is the administrative style. The most important qualities are the educational goals, including the priority among them, and the degree to which they are addressed, always taking into account the difficulties of the context. The practical value of this typology should be the aid it gives practising and potential administrators in understanding, choosing and recognizing the consequences of adopting a given style.

The *Despot* is obsolescent. The category is included principally for conceptual completeness as it demonstrates extreme reliance on the use of power and unilateral incentives. In the past, there was probably considerable overlap between the charismatic and despotic types. Principals were

Table 2: A Typology of School Principals (By Use of Influence)

	Type(s) of Influence Most Used	Types of Authority Most Used	Types of Incentive (Blau)	Types of Incentive (Clark & Wilson)	Potential Level of Influence	Conditions Where Influence is Greatest
DESPOT	Power Legitimate authority	Traditional Charismatic	Unilateral	Solidary Purposive	Very high	Voluntary membership by students and teachers; external problems
BENEVOLENT DESPOT	Power Legitimate authority Informal authority	Traditional	Unilateral Extrinsic Intrinsic	Material Purposive Solidary	High	Forceful/Expert leader and disorganized interest groups
DEMOCRAT	Informal authority	Bureaucratic	Intrinsic	Solidary	Very low	High level of professional excellence and commitment; commitment to democratic ideology

Table 2: (cont'd)

	Type(s) of Influence Most Used	Types of Authority Most Used	Types of Incentive (Blau)	Types of Incentive (Clark & Wilson)	Potential Level of Influence	Conditions Where Influence is Greatest
POWER BROKER	Informal authority Legitimate authority	Bureaucratic Charismatic	Extrinsic Intrinsic	Material	Very low	Competing, powerful interest groups
BUREAUCRAT	Legitimate authority	Bureaucratic	Unilateral Extrinsic	Material Purposive	Low	Strongly unionized, highly bureaucratized; Centralized
CONSULTATIVE BUREAUCRAT	Legitimate authority Informal authority	Bureaucratic Traditional	Unilateral Extrinsic Intrinsic	Purposive Material	Medium	Competing interest groups; lack of consensus
CHARISMATIC	Informal authority Power	Charismatic	Intrinsic	Solidary	Very high	Combination of charismatic personality and fragmented interest groups

expected to show strong 'leadership' and charisma is a characteristic that is used to produce major effect, as dictators such as Hitler and Mussolini have demonstrated.

Some thoughts about the *Despot*:

1 The type is obsolescent because (a) power relationships are much less socially acceptable than they once were; (b) the development of unions and the growth of special interest groups provide checks to unbridled power; (c) the traditional and legitimate authority of the principal has been significantly curtailed by changes in laws and in their interpretation; (d) a growing lack of respect for authority in society generally erodes power even further.

2 The solidary incentive can be very powerful when despots pull an organization together to compete with or fight external forces; however, for those members who do not surrender to the organization, whether they are students or teachers, life can be extremely hard in the absence of tolerance. In more stable countries, maintenance of despotism is extremely difficult.

3 The despot is *likely* to be effective in the following circumstances: (a) there is traditional acceptance of the exercise of power; (b) there is general consensus about goals and objectives; (c) there are alternative, available placements for teachers and pupils who do not share the despot's aspirations; (d) there is a perception of an external threat; (e) there is an existing power vacuum — or no recognized legitimate authority.

The only condition under which despotic school administration is defensible today in Western society is where there is genuine choice of membership for both teachers and students. Otherwise, the restrictions on both students and teachers are likely to offset the advantages of firmness of purpose and unified sense of direction a despot is able to provide. The advantage of excluding dissenters from a school trying to establish some sense of direction should not be trivialized.

The demise of the despotic leader leads to a significant conclusion about the exercise of power. Even in the case of an extreme despot, there must be some acceptance of power for it to exist. School principals have little recourse against massive non-compliance with their wishes. The person who issues frequent executive orders in the absence of such compliance is courting rebellion. The traditional acceptance of the superintendent's and principal's authority is waning. Thus the so-called 'democratic' behavior of many urban, secondary principals, however sincere, is also a pragmatic accommodation of comtemporary social relationships. It also frequently represents a simple lack of moral courage.

The *Benevolent Despot* is probably the most frequently found type — at least in the perception of teachers and ourselves, if not in that of principals. This is particularly true at the elementary school level where traditional authority is still often strong, and in rural areas. Elementary principals can often act independently in matters such as attendance, punctuality, and work habits.

The reason for the popularity of this type despite the disdain in which its operating principles are held by experts, probably lies in its efficiency. Pure despotism is efficient too in the unlikely event that the despot's orders are accepted and respected — but it becomes inefficient if enormous energy has to be devoted to non-compliance or covert subversion. In contrast, the Benevolent Despot generally avoids giving orders that will be unhappily received or disobeyed. The Benevolent Despot listens carefully and works within the traditional framework of the appropriate role for the principal.

There is a paradox here. Most contemporary texts and academic discussions about the role of the principal focus on the principal's role as curriculum leader. Yet, empirical evidence suggests that, even in the case of elementary principals, program leadership is not common; at the secondary level, it is extremely rare. One explanation for this paradox is that most principals are Benevolent Despots working within an accepted, traditional framework. Their authority over the discipline of students, the allocation of duties to teachers, the allocation of resources, the organization of classes and the supervision of teachers is tacitly accepted by teachers and parents. But their role in curriculum is narrowly circumscribed. Teachers reign almost supreme within most classrooms, providing that they adhere to some generally accepted norms: order is maintained; there is reasonable emphasis of the basic skills; there is nominal compliance with the official curriculum; they do not interfere with one another; they do not transgress on the traditional parental role. Thus to ask the Benevolent Despot to adopt a central role in curriculum is to ask that there be a major change in the moral order and social structure of the school. Whether or not such a change is desirable, it will not be easily accomplished. The problem of program change is addressed in Chapter 6. Other types will not necessarily have an easier time dealing with curriculum, but the traditional sphere of influence of the Benevolent Despot does not include curriculum, particularly at the secondary level.

Some thoughts about the *Benevolent Despot*:

1 The type can best be adopted in conservative times, in traditional communities, in the context of a traditional, probably unwritten consensus about the purposes and functions of schools. It is dependent upon a high level of traditional authority.

2 The long-term prognosis for the type is difficult to predict because it is attacked on numerous sides:

(a) The traditional consensus on education is gradually being eroded;

(b) Elementary teachers are increasingly reluctant to accept benevolent despotic rule because (i) they are increasingly well educated; (ii) they are increasingly men, or feminist women who will no longer readily accept the traditional, submissive, female role; (iii) there are increasing numbers of well qualified applicants for promotion to the principalship, with a resultant increased level of awareness of administrative matters at the school level; (iv) they are increasingly likely to resort to collective action to challenge the power and authority of the principal; and (v) they are increasingly likely to learn in graduate school that Benevolent Despotism is bad;

(c) The Benevolent Despot is generally not respectable in expert circles.

3 The Benevolent Despot is likely to survive in the school where there is greatest consensus about goals and directions, for example, private schools, elementary schools.

4 As a Benevolent Despot is dependent on the goodwill of his or her subjects, the role requires very careful deployment of a wide array of incentives.

5 The Benevolent Despot makes most sense in the traditional school, whose social structure is more like that of the traditional family than that of the modern, bureaucratic factory.

The *Democrat* has developed as a type as a result of two very different developments: (a) progressive ideology in education and 'people oriented' ideas in industrial management and (b) to a lesser extent, increasing bureaucratization. Progressive ideas, which have flourished in North American schools intermittently since the 1930s, hold among other things that children should participate fully in choices about their own education. 'People oriented' management ideas require a relaxation of the traditional line hierarchy from management to worker. On the other hand, in systems also affected by trends towards bureaucratization, written rules and the precise delineation of authority become increasingly necessary. Both those trends make despotism, however benevolent, more difficult. The Benevolent Despot must be in charge and must be seen to be in charge. In important curricular areas, despots tend to delegate much of their legitimate authority. Progressivism increases the authority of children vis à vis teachers and, teachers vis à vis administrators. Bureaucratization reduces the discretionary power of administrators and teachers.

In keeping with the idea that the school should provide an environment in which children find learning rewarding and fruitful, the Democrat aims to provide an administrative environment where teachers will feel free to develop their own creative ideas and provide a creative environment for pupils. This does not imply that all progressives are Democrats, or that all Democrats are progressives — merely that, originally, Democrats were likely to profess a progressive ideology.

Obviously, progressive ideologies can be, and frequently are, imposed in an authoritarian manner. Equally, the principal may be influenced by the Democratic ideology without believing in learning by doing. The Democratic type is an accommodation of the assertiveness of better trained teachers and of the breakdown of consensus. Its inefficiency lies in its reliance on consensus. In contrast, we shall show that the Broker builds co-alitions to achieve a majority. Both types accept the breakdown of consensus and are likely to lead to schools with little sense of community and even less sense of direction. Even so, the development of the democratic type is a logical response to trends that reduce both the legitimate authority and the power of the principal. If it is accepted as legitimate both within the school district and within the community (an unlikely event), the democratic type permits responsibility to be reduced commensurate with authority.

The term Democrat, it should be clear by now, is not being used in the usual educational sense — denoting a mid-position between being 'authoritarian' and being 'laissez-faire.' And it is not, of course used in its strict meaning of the practice of representative government. It is used to denote the development of greater equality of educational roles, and an attempt to level the organizational hierarchy. The Democrat consults all those with expertise or with a stake in the decision and may use influence to attempt to reach consensus. A major aim for the Democrat is to bring people together to work consensually towards an agreed objective.

Some thoughts about the *Democrat* are:

1 Teachers become irritated by the time taken to reach decisions and gradually extend the areas of decision making to be excluded from the democratic framework.

2 Areas excluded from the democratic framework are often not handed back to the principal for decision making. They may be handed to committees, individuals or to the union apparatus.

3 The type is most effective where (a) there is consonance of administrative method and educational philosophy, and a consensus among the staff on both; (b) teachers are highly competent professionals not requiring supervision.

4 Where there is not consensus among the staff, the principal's traditional authority is assumed by aggressive teachers, consultants and parents.

5 There is little concerted emphasis on evaluation, of either teachers or students, and little on academic progress, as consensus on either the purpose or the process is most unlikely to be forthcoming.

6 The type is mainly found in small elementary schools where its limitations can sometimes be overcome.

7 The type is unstable and short-lived.

The democratic type, somewhat popular in the 1960s and 1970s, is not common today and is likely to remain rare. It is unlikely to be popular with administrators themselves because the potential influence in the role is so limited. Although some principals may be happy to retreat to a powerless, symbolic status, they are likely to be fearful of being held responsible for something over which they have delegated control. Current trends do not favor the type. The thrust towards unionization and bureaucratization favors the more formal bureaucratic type rather than the democratic type. The thrust towards accountability and excellence favors the Benevolent Despot and the Consultative Bureaucrat.

The *Power Broker* is a relatively new type, promulgated as appropriate, particularly for senior administrators, in the difficult years of the 1960s and 1970s. The Power Broker can be seen as a reaction to the upset and rebellion that took place in schools and colleges during that period. The Power Broker uses influence to effect decisions but very little authority, unless there is some latent charismatic authority. The Power Broker acts as a mediator among conflicting factions and uses influence, persuasion and occasional authority to bring about an agreed decision, always in conformity with an apprehension of the power equation.

The Power Broker is significantly different from the Democrat, whose philosophical origins go back much further and whose thrust is itself more philosophical than practical. While the Democrat is concerned, as a point of principle, to ensure that those affected by a decision have the option to influence it, the Power Broker is interested primarily in finding the fulcrum of power — it being assumed that the administrator has little. The Power Broker in educational administration has most often been a school superintendent and the type is less clearly applicable at the school level. Nevertheless, in situations where elected and senior administrative officials are active, parent groups make frequent demands, and teachers are unionized, this type is an option at the school level as well.

Ironically, the causes that gave an impetus to the mediator's role in educational administration also imply that the occupant of the role will have a short life on the job and that the type itself may not last very long. The irony is the more marked because it was assumed that brokers would have long lives percisely because they had no commitment to any particular philosophy or platform. But American school superintendents have found it does not work out that way; mobility in senior administrative ranks has been greater since the growth of the Broker than it has ever been.

There is no easy answer to being a principal where there is widespread lack of consensus. Becoming a Broker means that the principal loses the committed support of most or all groups. If there is one group (teachers, elected officials, left-wing, right-wing) more powerful than others, the Broker is likely to become aligned with it — and will lose support when that power group loses support. If there are many groups jostling for power, the Broker is easily sacrificed when things go wrong; after all the Broker is not a genuine, card carrying member of the group in question.

Above all, the Broker is likely to be seen by all parties as being 'unprofessional' precisely because there is no ideological or philosophical commitment. This is most obvious when it becomes clear that the best interests of children are being sacrificed as teachers' unions, elected officials and public pressure groups jostle for power. The Broker ignores the powerless, and strikes the best bargain among those possessing clout. It is ironic that administrators are often urged to become more flexible, only to be disdained as lacking vision and professionalism when they do.

Some thoughts about the *Power Broker*:

1 The type is likely to become less common because: (a) conflicts among power groups are unlikely to be satisfactorily resolved if the central purposes and functions of schooling are not agreed upon; (b) continuing disagreements about fundamental purposes are likely to result in schools differentiated by purpose and clientele within which commitment rather than mediation will be required; (c) the role is professionally unsatisfying; (d) the role does not give the job security which was its original main attraction.

2 The type is likely to be inefficient and ineffective over the long term as peace among special interest groups is likely to be paid for by educational losses.

3 Professional principals will come to dislike the image among colleagues of being vacillating 'politicians' devoid of both educational substance and real power.

4 Contentious urban secondary schools are the most likely sites in which Brokers may survive.

The *Bureaucrat* is one of the most common types. Charisma is rare. Tradition is being eroded. Bureaucratic authority remains. It is important to recognize that there is no pejorative connotation in the use in this book of the word 'bureaucracy', although we do deplore the excessive bureaucracy often implicit in the uage 'bureaucratization.' All schools are bureaucracies. There are rules governing the behavior of the members. There is a hierarchy and there are formal and informal norms of behavior associated with the various roles.

Bureaucratic is frequently a word of opprobrium in the school context. It is taken to refer to school administrators who appear to concern themselves too much with pettifogging rules and regulations and insufficiently with education and children's lives. To some extent this perception reflects the increasing complexity of modern life evidenced by: the large size of many schools; the size and complexity of school districts and their associated hierarchies; and the proliferation of schools' responsibilities for: food services, driver education, exchange visits, medical, dental and social care, sex education, cooperative education, special education services and parental involvement. The Bureaucrat develops systems, rules, policies and regulations to reduce to a minimum any possibility of crime, mistakes, upset, surprise, ambiguity and, unfortunately but inevitably, discretion. This type is essentially a reaction to the difficulties of wielding authority when every action is likely to be challenged and when authority beyond the legislated, legitimate authority is minimal. If the Despot and Benevolent Despot are the traditional types, the Bureaucrat and the Power Broker are the archetypical modern types. The Bureaucrat is not necessarily as purely reactive as the Power Broker. Creative Bureaucrats are likely to follow the traditional administrative adage 'make it easy for them to do the right thing.' The implication is that the bureaucrat has some idea about what the right thing is. The bureaucrat does not necessarily have a philosophical thrust, but it is not excluded by definition. Of necessity, it becomes obscured.

Some thoughts about the *Bureaucrat* are:

1 With this type, rules and policies become increasingly lengthy and detailed as new rules are developed to deal with proliferating ambiguities in the old ones.

2 Administrators' and teachers' discretionary authority is gradually reduced.

3 Informal systems develop to by-pass the complex regular channels.

4 The organizational arrangement is generally and minimally effective but not highly efficient.

5 Significant change is increasingly difficult to introduce as the bureaucratic framework becomes more elaborate, more entrenched and more accommodating of different interests.

The *Bureaucrat* is, we believe, a permanent response to the complexities of modern life, while the Democrat and the Power Broker are more likely to be short lived and occasional aberrations, the one pursuing a philosophy not easily accommodated by the institution of the school, the other reacting in a fundamentally non-educational manner to very real problems. One difficulty with a bureaucratic school system is that the bureaucracy and its survival become ends in themselves, and the goals of schooling become subsidiary. There are a few ways to force bureaucracies to change. One is to remove the demand for their services. Although a bureaucracy may be totally bereft of ideas about how to fulfil its legitimate purposes, it can often move quickly to perpetuate its own life. Another way is to provide strong competition. Educational bureaucracies have not yet had to meet either challenge in a serious way, but they will. The first signs of this are already apparent in England and Wales, where local schools are to be permitted to choose independence from the local authority and receive funding directly from the central government.

The *Consultative Bureaucrat*, as the name suggests, is closely related to the Bureaucrat. Just as the Benevolent Despot replaces the Despot, so the Consultative Bureaucrat develops to allow for more thrust than is possible with the pure Bureaucrat. The Bureaucrat needs rules and policies to ensure the smooth running of the organization in circumstances where charisma is non-existent or insufficient and the force of tradition is spent. But the power behind bureaucratic rules is disarmed, as is all power, by massive non-compliance. The Bureaucrat ultimately requires not only legitimate authority but some moral authority. In a typical industrial hierarchy a superordinate has five to seven subordinates. A typical secondary school may have sixty teachers, several support staff and three administrators. Department heads are quasi-administrators but they usually ally themselves with teachers at times of collective action. In traditional schools, where complex bureaucratic rules are less necessary, department heads may be seen as an arm of the administration — selecting teachers, allocating workload, even carrying out evaluation and recommending dismissal. When the centre fails, when the hierarchical, administrative authority is seriously challenged, the battle lines can quickly be drawn between the principals and vice-principals, the bosses, and the teaching staff, the workers. When the school is turned into an industrial shop floor, the ratio of 'managers' to 'workers' of 1:20 or even 1:30 becomes unmanageable. The reason for the disparity is that teachers are not 'workers', they are independent professionals.

Thus bureaucracy, in its pure form, does not work precisely when it is most needed. A bureaucratic administration serves the day to day requirements of the school engulfed in competing interests moderately well. The management may be smooth. It is ill-fitted to stresses, particularly to massive challenge from within or from without. When the chips are down, 'managers' simply cannot run the school by sticking to the rules; the school is not that kind of organization.

The Consultative Bureaucrat, who recognizes the need for bureaucratic rules and procedures during times of declining consensus, takes the initiative to advance the goals of the organization, i.e., the goals of education reflecting the school's purposes. This pro-active behavior serves two functions. It give administrators professional legitimacy; they are able to advance their own educational ideas rather than just react to requests, proposals and complaints from other parties. It also makes the implementation of the agreements legitimate, precisely because they result from recognized and approved methods of consultation.

Brokers involve only those with clout, and only to the extent of their clout. Any effect they have is as the instrument of others. Democrats consult to achieve consensus on significant decisions. Unlike Power Brokers, they are concerned if those without clout are ignored, and so promote their participation. They may also be concerned about educational issues (although it is not unusual for the Democrat to be consumed by process), but their efforts are frequently ineffectual unless there is strong consensus among a powerful staff, because Democrats deliberately divest themselves of legitimate authority. Bureaucrats manage to legislate mainly by reaction to others. Unlike Brokers, they ensure that the required, formal consultative procedures are duly followed. In contrast, Consultative Bureaucrats persist through their own agenda of problems and decisions to nail down policy, to tidy the hierarchy, to provide legitimacy for administrators' and teachers' behavior, and to permit incremental improvements in education. They utilize a formal consultative structure to legislate and legitimate their own ideas.

Some thoughts about the *Consultative Bureaucrat*:

1 The type becomes more common as benevolent despotism becomes less acceptable. It is a compromise between the Bureaucrat and the Benevolent Despot.

2 The type thrives in or leads to a situation of clear division between management (administration) and workers (teachers), particularly when the administration plans reform and change.

3 While it is an effective management style in a given context, it is less efficient than benevolent despotism because the procedures for decision making are more formal, less flexible and more complex.

4 There is a temptation for Consultative Bureaucrats to become Power Brokers in difficult times, when failure to heed those with the greatest clout will lead to a breakdown in the organization, e.g., grievance, work to rule, demonstrations.

5 The proliferation of agenda items, from administration and from teachers, leads to a reduction of discretion for individual members of the organization, who are bureaucratized from both sides.

6 The style, like that of the Bureaucrat, will not survive difficult times.

The *Charismatic Leader* is the administrator who influences others by dint of force of personality and character. It is doubtful that charisma is a dichotomous characteristic, even if some individuals appear to have none and others powers that are frighteningly mysterious. If charisma is distributed along a continuum, as seems likely, administrators of all types will all benefit from a modicum of it.

It is natural to think of religious and political leaders as examples of charisma — Adolf Hitler, John Kennedy, Winston Churchill, Billy Graham, Pope John Paul, Pierre Trudeau. What they share is an unusual willingness in their supporters to suspend any disbelief, cynicism and scepticism with which they normally greet public pronouncements, a suspension that is at least temporarily replaced by enthusiasm, in the traditional sense of the word.

Charismatic principals (and teachers) have a personal advantage. For a time at least, they may well be effective, and will almost certainly appear to be effective. But the famous examples used above are useful as cautions as well as illustrations. No reader will be glad of Hitler's effectiveness in pursuing aggressive foreign policies against neighbors and genocide against his own and others' citizens. Readers will have varying reactions to some of the other leaders, but none is without severe critics, particularly after the fact. Charisma certainly produces ardent followers — but that is not advantageous if the path chosen is undesirable and if the character of the leader is tainted. Many of the checks and balances faced by most administrators are reduced or eliminated by the enthusiasm of the charismatic leaders' following.

Some thoughts about *Charismatic Leaders*:

1 If the enthusiasm of the mass of followers is not solidly based, for example, on a sound philosophy and consensual directions, the opposition, based on those who do not share the initial enthusiasm will grow as the magical powers wane.

2 Charisma is not necessarily equally influential on all groups, on males and females, teachers and students, parents and students, and this adds to the danger of divisiveness.

3 Charisma is often allied to thrust because charisma makes the persuasion of others easier, but thrust itself may bring divisiveness and disaffection.

4 Charisma is most usefully effective when it is combined with another type of leadership style or if the Charismatic leader is allied with other administrators in an effective team. For example, one might imagine a charismatic principal with tendencies towards despotism being most effective in a highly unionized situation when the vice-principals are Consultative Bureaucrats.

The Charismatic Leader is the victim as well as the beneficiary of charisma. Natural leadership does not imply any superior moral sense. Indeed, the ease with which one gets one's way often encourages a lack of moral sensitivity to others. In general, Charismatic Leaders may be expected to work through one of the other styles — benevolent despotism being perhaps the most likely because charisma makes its practice easier. However, it is conceptually possible that charisma may permit its own idiosyncratic style.

None of the styles is, of course, discrete. Not only do many administrators change their style over time and in different situations but they may create combinations of the styles. However, in general, a certain stability of style is required in administrators as they are expected to be predictable, fair and universalistic. The Charismatic Leader is able to get away with more inconsistency but this is not advantageous in the long run.

Choosing the Best Type

There is no hero among these types. The aspiring principal may be confused and disillusioned — where is the correct role model? It would be possible to find examples of apparently effective principals and describe what they do. However, it would not be easy, outside an extremely large and extremely difficult study, to separate what they do from the multitude of other variables that affect excellence in schools such as: the principal's intelligence, education, personality and genuineness; qualities of the teaching staff; characteristics of the student body; and the ecological environment of the school community. Even when we identify good schools, taking their student population into account, does the leader make a good school, or does the good school make the leader look good? To put it another way, we cannot be sure that what principals are doing is in fact the important cause of whatever it is that constitutes excellence in a school. Of one thing we can be sure, there is a great deal of variation among principals in good schools.

The typology presented has a number of limitations. It does not accommodate all of the variables that have been developed by leadership studies. Later chapters will consider problems involved in the administration of teachers and students and other aspects of school life. The concern here is with the use of power and authority. It provides neither final answers nor even highly reliable guides. But it does provide a picture of the conceptual choices and some likely consequences.

The Principal as Leader

The term 'leadership' is one of the most difficult in educational administration. To some, a leader is simply one who is followed. Presumably by that definition, a good leader is one who is followed consistently and reliably by large numbers of people. But that leads to the difficulty of Hitler being a 'good leader.' So, some will argue either that leadership itself involves both followers and a good sense of direction or that, at least, *good* leadership involves an approved direction. The latter distinction leaves one with the ambiguity of the 'bad leader' being either one who is not followed or, very different, one who is followed but in a disapproved direction. In addition to those definitional problems, some people believe they know what 'good leadership style' is. It may be 'democratic or 'decisive' but whatever it is its supporters know it is 'good.' Such people are likely to substitute the criterion of style for the criteria of having followers and having an appropriate direction. Some people go even further. They assume that good leadership style is an important end in itself. They give their favored style an attractive name like 'democratic leadership.' In that way, principals who have a 'democratic' style are automatically deemed good, even though they may be ineffective and unpopular. The ineffectiveness and unpopularity are explained away; the principal is not 'really a democratic leader, because, if she were, she would be effective and popular!'

As the concept of leadership is so obscure, leadership is a term that should be used with great care and only in circumstances where it is carefully defined. Our typology of types of style may be seen as a typology of leadership only if one limits the term leadership to the exercise of power, authority and influence.

We distinguish an effective leader, who gets results, from a good leader, who achieves good things. But does a good leader *always* get plentiful, good results? Some principls appear to be effective in some circumstances but not in others. Do they then suddenly change from being effective and, perhaps, good leaders one year to being ineffective leaders the next? The answer is probably yes. Thus leadeship can be seen to be as much an outcome of the internal and external working environment as it is a quality of the leader. Thus Winston Churchill was a good and effective war time leader but not a very effective leader in peace time. The reverse might be said of Franklin Roosevelt.

There are dangers in dwelling heavily on desired leadership character-istics. It is easy to assume that there must be a set of leadership character-istics that will somehow work whatever it is one wants to do. If that were true, the implication must be that the effective leader is inauthentic, in-sincere, being able to act out a number of different roles — yet authenticity is frequently identified as being one of the key characteristics of good leader-ship! At times, a particular teacher or group of teachers may make good, effective leadership in a school impossible, just as some students may make good teaching in a particular class impossible. Different administrative styles or types probably make sense depending on the school, the system, the personal characteristics of the principal and number of years in the position.

On balance, given our high level of ignorance, it is unwise to become highly concerned with the concept of leadership. It is more important to consider how we can best get the job done of running an effective school. And among other things, the principal must decide how to deal with power, legitimate authority, moral authority and influence.

Choosing a Type

The choice facing the principal is less overwhelming and confusing than it may at first appear. Charisma is more a gift than an option. Being a despot is usually not a choice. Table 3 is a semi-serious decision making tool. No one, we hope, will actually make a major decision on the basis of such a flimsy framework. But many administrators and future administrators are con-fused and uncertain. One principal is criticized as being too 'authoritarian', but another as too 'indecisive.' One is 'afraid to move without the permission of the union', another 'consults us about things we cannot possibly change.' In running through the checklist, it should be borne in mind that one cannot be simultaneously two inconsistent things — both a democrat and a bene-volent despot, yet one can often combine elements of two different types. For example, one can be benevolently despotic over some trivial things, consultative over others.

It should be evident that we do not see all types as being equally valid, although circumstances may make all of them understandable. If one

Table 3:   Choosing from the Principal Typology

---

1 Is there a high level of consensus about educational directions within the school community of teachers, pupils and parents? If yes, go to 2. If no, go to 6.

2 Do you believe that the school is best handled by a firm, friendly hand acting through careful informal consultation with those affected by decisions, with decisions being made in the best interests of the entire community? If yes, BENEVOLENT DESPOT. If no, go to 3.

3 Do you believe that there should be regular consultation varying with the importance of the decision with all significant groups in the community and that decisions should be made in the light of such consultation? Do you also believe that the administrator should try to influence decisions in a significant way? If yes to both questions, CONSULTATIVE BUREAUCRAT. If no to either question, go to 4.

4 Do you believe that important decisions, and any decision considered by members of an organization to be important is important, should be made collectively with the principal acting as chair, advisor and guide? If yes, DEMOCRAT. If no, go to 5.

5 Do you believe that administration can best be carried out by the careful elaboration of appropriate procedures, by the clarification of role responsibilities and by the resolution of differences in written policies? If yes, BUREAUCRAT. If no, go to 6.

6 Do you believe that the principal's responsibility is to wield, manipulate and orchestrate power in such a way that there is the greatest chance of a secure, settled solution being reached? If yes, POWER BROKER. If no, go to 7.

7 You are probably in trouble. Perhaps you think you have charisma. Do others recognize this characteristic? If not, go back to the typology. Is there some type that is left out? How will it use power and authority? Is it a combination of two or more types? If so, how will any inconsistencies be worked out? Is the preferred type one that relies more heavily on influence than on power and authority? If so, how will policies be implemented when some staff members reject influence? Can you help create some consensus, thereby making the bureaucratic and consultative bureaucratic options more practicable? If these questions are unhelpful, go to 8.

8 RESIGN. If there is no consensus, no chance of developing consensus and the amorality of power brokering does not appeal, the professional administrator should not remain. There is no substitute for some agreement on professional purpose.

---

believes, as we do, that the principal should aim to be an educational leader, i.e., the person who tries to focus the school's energies on achieving desirable educational goals, then it follows that types with little possibility of thrust are less valid. Two types do stand out as being reasonably popular, broadly applicable and as having a reasonable chance of leading to desired results. They are the Benevolent Despot and the Consultative Bureaucrat. The individual's choice of ways of deploying power and authority to make and influence decisions will depend on a number of factors besides those analyzed here — certainly including personality, personal preferences and the people in the organizational setting.

Much of the remainder of the book looks at the flexibility available to school administration — in the management of time, staff, pupils and programs. But a premise, which most principals like to accept, is that administrators have sufficient potential influence to make efforts in some of those areas worthwhile. Yet the general perception by teachers is that principals, particularly secondary principals, are, in practice, little involved in program or staff training. Principals are generally unaware of the importance of instructional time as a variable. Their involvement with pupils is often mainly in the area of discipline. At the same time, it is generally conceded that they are industrious, zealous people. What do they do? They apply themselves to day-to-day management. They sometimes complain of being buried under the 'paper blizzard' and 'administrivia.' This leads to a significant question: If the power of the principal is decreasing as a response to environmental changes, if principals find little time for substantive educational activity, would it be sensible either to increase the legitimate authority so that it is more nearly commensurate with the apparent responsibility, or to reduce the responsibility so that it is more commensurate with the available power? In our view, the principal should generally possess some clear, accepted legitimate authority — and the accompanying responsibility.

The alleged gap between power and responsibility appears inconsistent with our previous discussion of the typology of principals. There it was suggested that the Benevolent Despot probably remains the commonest type. Continued prevalence of this type suggests that the principal retains a fair amount of power, in many people's minds too much. However, one qualification of that argument should be borne in mind: Benevolent Despots often have tacit moral authority in some domains — but those domains may exclude, for example, program.

The continued prevalence of the Benevolent Despot underlines the enormous variation in the situation and role of the contemporary principal. In many school districts, the style would be unthinkable. Even where benevolent despotism reigns, it is often a retreat from the more extreme despotism of the past. Benevolent Despots not only present a kindly image, they genuinely try hard to avoid unpleasantness. The best way to avoid unpleasantness is to avoid confrontation, to avoid giving an instruction that may be challenged, to couch instructions in the form of suggestions (following which there is not too much loss of face if they are not accepted). While it is not denied that many principals remain genuine rulers, the retreat first to, and now from, benevolent despotism reflects some loss of power. The classroom teacher under many benevolent despots may be rather like the proverbial housewife: 'My husband makes all the major policy decisions — about world affairs, politics and economics; I make the local decisions about budget, the home and family, and vacation and retirement plans.' As long as teachers are left in charge of those matters they consider most important, then they may be willing to concede tacit tolerance of the principal's strong role in the dominion of 'administration.' Frequently one finds a joking relationship between the usually male elementary principal and the predominantly female teaching staff. (And the elementary school is the main redoubt of the Benevolent Despot.) A joking relationship, according to social anthropologists, reflects an asymmetric, rather difficult liaison, for example, between young men and older women; between son-in-law and mother-in-law. The joking relationship may cover a situation where the assumption of power is a mask. No one challenges it as long as the Benevolent Despot does not play the game for real. This also explains why the Benevolent Despot may sometimes be just as reluctant as the Democrat to enter a classroom to evaluate a teacher, unless the evaluation be confined to soporific, 'helpful' clichés. The unwritten contract between elementary principal and teacher is often that the principal reigns supreme outside the classroom, the teacher within. That contract makes supervision a tricky matter. The principal typically avoids the problem by giving nearly every teacher a glowing evaluation, the exception being the teacher who has already been consensually rejected by the staff.

If these observations are valid, the continued existence of the Benevolent Despot is not necessarily evidence that the principal retains considerable power and authority. The authority of the Benevolent Despot is limited and carefully used.

One solution for the perceived discrepancy between the principal's power and responsibility is to increase the power. The most obvious way is to make the principal once more fully in charge of the building — with strongly entrenched rights to transfer or dismiss teachers and to suspend or expel pupils. An additional aid would be to increase the administrative staff to provide a more normal hierarchical span of control, for example, by excluding principals, vice-principals and department heads from the teachers' union.

Such a solution may be impractical or undesirable. Clearly, it would tilt the role of the principal away from that of Power Broker or Democrat towards one of Benevolent Despot, or at least Consultative Bureaucrat. The principal might become more accountable to the school district just as staff and students would become more accountable to the principal. Thus the bureaucratic hierarchy would be strengthened and bureaucratic authority would be shored up to compensate for the decline in traditional authority.

The opposite solution is to reduce the responsibility of the principal — to bring the role more in line with that of a university president, who is normally considered responsible for the grand line of university policy, for example, overall standards of admission; the development and closure of programs; the university's public image, but not for day-to-day staffing and teaching. Even university department heads are not normally held responsible for the quality of their colleagues' teaching and research. It is easy to envisage a school principal doffing responsibility for program and quality and even, perhaps, for teachers' competence. It is more difficult to imagine who would take on the custodial supervision of pupils.

Current trends in the public and the private sectors are different.

Private schools, both of the religious and the élite type, leave considerable power and authority in the hands of principals. Parents choose a philosophy to their liking and delegate authority to the principal and staff. In public schools, in contrast, teachers and individual parents both assume increasing powers. Whereas in 1960, it was normal for the principal to tell parents what were and were not legitimate reasons for lateness and absence, today it is normal for principals to accept parental authority except in the most extraordinary cases.

Both solutions, of increasing power and reducing responsibility, may be equally unpalatable as deliberately chosen policies. But the absence of decision makes many principals *de facto* school managers — without the power of the traditional principal and without the distinct status of the university president. But if the central thesis is correct, some corrective action will be necessary in schools in the militarized zones of the big cities of Western society.

Solutions to the Problem of the Mismatch between Power and Responsibility

The problem of power in the modern school is a real one. The institution, in its contemporary form, is not much over a hundred years old. It has not adapted well to changing conditions and is not in a shape where it can be expected to address realistically many of the probably optimistic expectations held for it. In many bureaucratized schools, there is a gap between the principal's power to develop and implement policies and decisions and the paper responsibility for those same policies and decisions. Senior administrators implicitly understand the problem and therefore try to avoid holding principals accountable for what they cannot be expected to accomplish. But turning a blind eye only permits schools to slip further into chaos.

In difficult urban schools, any increase in the power of the principal is likely to be compensated for by new checks and balances. Thus the price for increased power may be sometimes the disappearance of the role of Benevolent Despot.

For example, the power to dismiss teachers and expel pupils requires safeguards to ensure there is no arbitrary or unfairly discriminatory bahavior. Thus safeguards frequently exist today but they often serve to deter principals from taking any action at all. Some school boards do have effective structures to permit or encourage the dismissal of non-performing teachers but many do not. And very few school districts have effective means for expelling students. Principals often go to inordinate length to transfer students or let students go by informal methods — to avoid the opprobrium they believe they will receive from senior administrators and from school board members.

In practice, it is extremely difficult to reinvest the principal's power and authority in urban and suburban settings where there is lack of agreement on educational purpose. The very conditions that have produced the problems prevent the exercise of authority. Decentralization of authority to individual teachers or to groups of teachers holds little promise in such situations. After all if the principal cannot represent an absent consensus, it is unlikely or impossible that groups or many individuals could agree to represent the non-existent.

This is not to assert that all effective schools are characterized by strong and effective principals, although many are. Leadership is frequently delegated or assumed by default; generally, however, we assume that the good principal will want to have some direct effect, some clear influence, will want to represent an educational consensus. It will become clear in later chapters that this statement does not imply for one moment a single ideal role description; it does imply a sense of direction, determination and moral courage. The fact that some effective schools do not have effective principals is not an argument for the development of ineffective principals.

We do not believe there is one simple solution to an enormously complex problem, but we do suggest that the aim of authority wielded firmly and fairly on behalf of a clear set of educational purposes should be fully appreciated by all. In some instances, energetic, courageous, moral leaders manage to transcend the constraints and complex policies and collective agreements; they cement the school and its community of parents behind a common vision. In other cases, schools, both public and independent, come to represent a coherent vision of one sub-community within a larger geographical area. Either way, common purpose is achieved.

Power and Morality

The first chapter emphasized the moral aspects of educational administration. As professionals, school administrators must make choices with consequences for right and wrong. That chapter stressed the principal's moral responsibility to work towards consensually derived goals with which they themselves must fundamentally although not necessarily entirely agree.

The authority of the principal, particularly as used by a Benevolent Despot, is often seen as being bad in itself, a holdover from older, more traditional times when it was acceptable for some people to rule categorically the lives of others. Thus, although few would go as far as to assert that no one should have power over someone else, many see the ideal society is that in which power of the few over the many is reduced to a minimum.

This book does not share that perspective. We assume that complex, modern societies will remain democratic, bureaucratic and significantly free market. Those fundamental, political characteristics imply: the subordination of some roles, but not the spiritual inequality of human beings; the legitimacy of authority within its context; and the morality of personal choice and personal responsibility. That certainly does not mean that professional ethics are irrelevant to administrators as they manipulate power and authority. It does mean that there is nothing intrinsically shameful in possessing and exercising authority. It means also that there is no principle that less authority is better.

What follows is a statement of ethical principles derived from the first two chapters. If a school has a comprehensive set of educational goals and if school administrators must have legitimate authority, careful consideration should be given to the ethics of its use. Each principle is followed by a short explanation. These principles will become clearer in their implication in later chapters dealing with teachers, pupils and the moral tone of the school.

The Ethics of Educational Authority

1 *Authority is to be used to further the legitimate, public goals of the school and the school's continued operation.* Two common errors are to disavow authority in an attempt to be more collegial and, sometimes at the same time, to use administrative authority for private rather than educational advancement.

2 *Members of the school community are to be treated with the dignity and forbearance consistent with fundamental morality.* There is a natural tendency, particularly in unionized situations or times of dispute, for administrators to stick together and treat teachers, pupils or parents as the enemy. The authority granted administrators does not make them superior in any sense other than that derived from tradition or law although they may well earn some additional moral authority. The truly good administrator never forgets the fundamental equality of all, including and particularly the most powerless.

3 *The long-term collective and individual interests of pupils should always be uppermost.* Teachers have considerable power over school administrators. Administrators sometimes try to ingratiate themselves with teachers to disarm this power, sometimes to join with them against pupils. The views and statements of teachers and pupils should not be given equal weight. Quite the contrary, teachers have legitimate authority over pupils. But the convenience of teachers should not be allowed to override the educational interests of students.

4 *Professional staff should be consulted about all educational matters which affect them professionally.* This point will be developed more fully in later chapters. Suffice it to say here that it is

a matter of ethics, not effective management, to show care and deference when interfering in areas of professional activity.

5 *The different authority of the principal and parent must be carefully agreed upon and, when necessary, put in writing.* In traditional schools, this problem was slight. Today, as they become less common, there must be more discussion and clarification. Administrators should not condone let alone support immoral development of children by parents, for example, the encouragement of dishonesty or illicit sex. However, they should not set their own ideology against that of parents. For example, Western society supports equal opportunity for both sexes and all ethnic and religious groups. It does not follow that administrators should use their authority to compel girls to choose professional training rather than a more traditional route leading to emphasis on marriage and family. They should not *compel* members of religious sects to choose educational goals which alienate them from their religion and their family. On the other hand, if young adults (not children) exercise a legitimate and morally acceptable *choice* of equal opportunity, the school administration should support them even against the wishes of the family.

6 *Honesty must be the guide for all communication within the school.* If the twin, central tasks of the school are intellectual and moral, it is essential that in all matters, administrators model, inculcate, expect and work towards truth, the centrepiece of both domains. We shall examine later the trend towards administrative manipulation of fellow professionals.

7 *The good of the school should come before the narrow interests of individuals.* This principle should be used in conjunction with the recognition of the fundamental equality of all members of the school community. Thus individuals should not be used as objects for some selfish, non-educational purpose. On the other hand, a stable community requires rules (or norms), respect and hierarchy. When members break those rules, the continuance of the community and the good for which it stands must be placed before any calculation of short-term advantage or disadvantage for the individual. Moreover, to hold members of a community responsible for their behavior and to persuade them to lead better lives is to respect their human individuality and value. To assume people are not responsible for their acts (except in very special cases of young children, the insane and those who have temporarily lost their senses) is to devalue them, to see them as not being fully human.

8 *Teachers as professionals should not have a final say over educational purposes or over the evaluation of their own success, although they may participate actively in both processes. They should have major discretion over their teaching.* The implications

of these distinctions will become clearer in later chapters devoted to teachers, program and evaluation.

Further Reading

Peter Blau's book, *Exchange and Control in Social Life* (1964), is a classic study of the sociology of the organization. Willard Waller's fifty-year-old study of the social relations in the school is still worth reading (1965). However, the reader must be careful to put aside the specific cases Waller presents, which may seem strange and outdated to the modern reader, and consider instead the underlying themes, which we believe to be still important today. Metz (1978) provides a thoughtful, incisive look at the problem of authority in the modern school. Sara Lightfoot (1983) provides interesting descriptions of principals in action, but readers should be careful to consider what evidence there is that all of these schools are in fact effective. It seems possible that some of the schools she describes are more noteworthy for attracting potentially effective students. Mintzberg's classic study (1973) provides an interesting view of the administrator at work. It differs sharply from the mainstream 'theory' driven studies. Halpin (1966; pp.131–249) carried out an impressive study of the principal's characteristics, demonstrating a clear understanding of principal/teacher relationships but follow-up work has failed to yield any relationship between Halpin's findings and student achievement (Holmes, 1985d).

Chapter 3

The Administration and Management of Space and Time

Schools are about people — pupils, teachers, parents, administrators and support staff. Most of their budgets go to salaries. Most of administrators' time and energy are spent dealing with people. So space and instructional time are often overlooked as administrators react to the exigencies of the day — all related to people.

Space and time are the two non-human commodities over which administrators have influence. Of the two, time is much the more important, because material support is generally taken for granted in the affluent, developed world to which this book is addressed.

Planning Schools

This book is intended for those interested in the administration of schools, within buildings that are for the most part already constructed. It would be out of place to devote a major section to architectural considerations. However, as principals and teachers ought to be and frequently are consulted about new school buildings, it is worthwhile mentioning some aspects of school buildings that are sometimes given insufficient attention by architects unfamiliar with the social workings of schools. Some of these points are relevant when additions or renovations are planned.

Appearance

Everyone prefers a nice looking building, other things being equal. However, other things are rarely equal. In Britain, after World War II, hundreds of schools were built with walls of glass. Large glass windows, particularly those facing south and west (in the northern hemisphere) are today among the most irritating architectural problems in many schools — cold in winter, unbearably hot in spring and fall. Blinds and drapes are unsatisfactory palliatives. They are frequently ugly, spoiling any effect of fine windows. They wear and are expensive to replace. Inflammable materials are often inflexible and smelly. Fashion has taken us from one extreme to the other from walls of windows to windowless schools. Few people enjoy working in situations where there is no natural light. Indeed, most people would choose to live with access to fresh air. Note that there are few air conditioned homes that do not have opening windows.

Educators should be wary of any striking architectural innovation that may prove to be dysfunctional or expensive to maintain. Holmes was founding principal of a secondary school built over a large area in seven square buildings to serve a population of 1200 students. Needless to say, supervision was a problem. Setting a school well back from the highway may give it a more imposing appearance. But is ground being wasted? Will there be enough money to maintain the pretty gardens sketched on the architect's drawings? Will the entrance road become a speedway?

Heating

Holmes was principal of an elementary school where there were neither opening windows nor air conditioning. The air circulation pump was quite incapable of coping with the heat caused by the sun in fall and spring (there were large windows on all sides). The secondary school to which we referred earlier was built with very expensive air conditioning equipment on Canada's Atlantic coast where high summer temperatures are extremely unusual. The assumption at the time, that all schools would soon operate year-round, was ill-founded.

Supervision

Architects cannot be unaware of the problem of supervision given the publicity it has had in recent years. Nevertheless, school people remain at a disadvantage when confronted with an implicit question, 'What are you running, a prison?' Long halls may be unsightly, but they are efficient. Toilets, in particular, need to be kept away from remote corners and as close to heavily travelled, closely supervised areas as possible.

Building Materials

Materials must be hard wearing, easily maintained, easily replaced in whole or in part, difficult to mark (with spirit markers, etc.) and easy to clean when marked. Walls, floors, ceilings, lights, doors and fire alarms are important things to watch.

Facilities

Facilities are often determined by the application of a formula devised at some central jurisdictional level. Only rarely are cost-benefit analyses conducted for an individual school. For example, in most suburban areas where schools are now being constructed, level well-drained land is very expensive, yet new secondary and elementary schools typically have a large area of playing fields and playground. Additional gymnasia, exercise space and swimming pools may sometimes be lower cost alternatives, although of course the cost of ongoing maintenance must be included in the cost-benefit analysis. The cost-benefit analysis should include estimates of usage, number of students and hours, and the value of the usage in terms of educational objectives.

School facilities are, reasonably enough, expected to serve community as well as school purposes. The problems of joint use and joint management are often not addressed until after the architectural plans have been drawn. Administrators are often put at a psychological disadvantage by architects who imply that they are interested in aesthetics and education while the principal seems only interested in management and custody.

Building, Equipment and Maintenance Budgets: Shared Use

Careful consideration should be given to the relationship between the building and the equipment budget. It is not unknown for schools to have magnificent libraries and music rooms — but few books and fewer instruments. Maintenance budgets should also be considered carefully. How much janitorial service will be available? How much will it cost to maintain the swimming pool? Will the municipality pay for some of the costs in a shared use program? If facilities are to be shared what will the real cost be to the school, including maintenance, heating, repair, supervision? Increasingly schools are being asked to provide day care for young children and supervision for school aged children before school, at lunch time and after school. The extended use of school buildings for numerous purposes is surely to be applauded provided that no one thinks that the additional uses come free. The cost sharing arrangements should be made before building begins. Similarly, parts of the building used when most of the school is not in use should be physically separable. Careful consideration should be given to the ways in which students may contribute to the maintenance of the school — and hence to their safety.

Cafeterias and In-School Supervision

Administrators must plan for accommodating significant portions of their populations at times when they are not undergoing formal instruction. In the secondary school, it probably means an informal area where supervision can easily be provided and a more formal quiet room, which may be the library itself, or a work room adjacent to it. In the elementary school, some kind of common facility is increasingly necessary even if a full cafeteria cannot be supported.

The practice of providing secondary schools with cafeterias designed to serve full meals on the assumption that the catchment areas are large and adolescents need a hot midday meal, and providing elementary schools nothing at all, on the assumption that young children go home to mother, requires revision. Most secondary students do not purchase proper lunches at school; fries and gravy hardly justify the capital expenditure on big kitchens. It is possible that school cafeterias could be somewhat reduced in size and greatly reduced in facilities if alternative areas for quiet and informal gathering could be provided. Elementary facilities, in contrast, need some augmentation.

Classroom Space

Traditionally, classrooms have been cubicles with sufficient capacity for between thirty and forty pupils. The assumption has been that average maximum class sizes would be in that range. Before 1950, classes of forty-five or fifty were quite common in the elementary grades, as they still are in the developing world. If a school was built to accommodate 600 pupils, it would typically have had, in 1955, twenty classrooms built to house thirty-five pupils comfortably, forty at a squeeze. Since the late 1960s, important exceptions from what has been rather scornfully called the egg crate model were made.

The Open Space School

The idea of the open space school, implemented mainly at the elementary level, is that the traditional one-class, one-teacher configuration is desirable neither for best learning conditions not for the appropriate social development of children. The question of varying approaches to instruction is discussed in Chapter 6. At this point, the following points are worth noting:

1. 'Open' classrooms can exist without open architecture. For example, some classrooms are organized around learning centres. 'Open' schools have often operated with symbolic walls, sometimes substantiated with plants or filing cabinets.

2. Open architecture only makes sense when all those involved are working systematically according to informal methodologies virtually all the time; and will be doing so for the life of the school.
3. Open, informal classrooms may well lead to lower levels of achievement in some conditions (Traub, Weiss and Fisher, 1976).
4. Larger and informal groupings of pupils may sometimes make the atmosphere more pleasant for pupils, but they also reduce their circle of immediate friends (Traub, Weiss and Fisher, 1976).
5. Open architecture is administratively helpful for: activity centred instruction; individualized instruction; team teaching supported by aides and parent volunteers; project based instruction; tutoring by older and more advanced pupils.
6. Open architecture is not administratively helpful for most forms of direct instruction; oral second language instruction; music; drama and formal testing.

When a new school is being built, educational philosophy should determine the architecture, not the reverse. That statement seems stupidly obvious, but, school architects sometimes have very strong opinions about what is the appropriate educational setting for the future, and school administrators may be reluctant to appear conservative or old-fashioned. Certainly there have been many schools with open classrooms that have been changed to traditional classrooms in one way or another.

Variable Class Size

As the notion of the traditional one-teacher, one-class model of instruction has been challenged, architects have responded by designing schools with large and small areas. Most of these arrangements tend to be extremely inefficient, making traditional calculations of required floor space per pupil obsolete. A few moments thought should explain why this should be.

It is virtually impossible to schedule a large lecture hall for continuous usage in a normal school. Even on the rare occasions when team teaching is used, it is difficult to regulate the length of the lecture — in practice one needs both small rooms and a lecture area available simultaneously, so that students can move from one to the other at the most propitious time.

Classrooms of variable size create problems. A small class of twelve can be scheduled into a room for fourteen — but three or four new pupils create problems. Yet, transfers into small classes are likely precisely because classes that have reached their maximum size cannot be increased. The exigencies of scheduling and reasonable workload allocations make for classes of similar size.

Art specialists may recommend that art rooms be built to accommodate sixteen or twenty pupils; for similar reasons, electrical laboratories are built for sixteen; physics laboratories for twenty; clothing rooms for fifteen — all on the advice of subject experts, sometimes supported by state or provincial recommendation or regulation. But the administrator has to wrestle with the realities of the schedule, pupils' choices and teachers' rights according to the collective agreement. Everyone may agree that the physics class should not be larger than twenty, the number for which the laboratory is built, but what happens when the twenty-first applicant for twelfth grade physics arrives on 5 September? Wherever possible facilities should be equipped for a greater number than the ideal maximum.

Many of the space problems are compounded by collective agreements which specify maximum, minimum and average class sizes for different subjects. These agreements do not always take into account the physical arrangements with which the school administration must work. Thus a maximum class size of thirty-five may appear to work well — until one takes into account that the laboratories were built for twenty, the shops for eighteen and so on. Those small classes push up the sizes of the remaining classes.

Obviously architects and educational administrators sincerely plan for schools for what they think will be good instruction. Equally clearly, many new schools built at considerable expense have proved to be inadequate in many ways. One cannot forecast the future. Schools in 1960 were not built for computers. But one thing does stand out. The standard class, somewhat reduced in size, with one teacher, has survived innumerable innovations. It would generally be unwise to build a school based on the assumption that the standard class is about to disappear.

Research suggests that academic gains could be made by teaching very small classes, twelve to fifteen children, in the primary grades. But it would be still unwise to begin to build schools with small primary classrooms. Perhaps there will be increased enrolments and a shortage of teachers. Consider also the lesson learned recently from Japan. It is possible that some of their success results from their very intensive teaching of larger classes, and fewer teaching periods per teacher.

Space Limitations

Administrators sometimes let their facilities direct instruction rather than have instructional needs determine the use of facilities. For example, a middle school may have fourteen classes and one gymnasium. The school operates on a thirty-five period week. The principal therefore solves the physical education problem by giving each class two periods a week and keeping the remainder as spares. Alternatively, seventh grade classes may be given three periods. If a policy of providing 150 minutes physical education instruction a week is either in place or proposed this principal may argue that the policy cannot be implemented unless a second gymnasium is built.

Yet some schools provide a physical education program without any gymnasium at all.

An analysis of the physical education curriculum would probably show that a large proportion of the objectives could be addressed in any room. A classroom could be converted to an exercise room. A portion of the cafeteria might be used. Two classes could then alternate in the gymnasium and the make-shift exercise room. For much of the year, many activities can take place outside in many climates. And within the gymnasium, an exercise program could easily accommodate three classes at the same time. In the same way, the absence of sufficient science laboratories, music and art rooms, does not prevent the delivery of high quality programs in some schools. Yet schools with 'insufficient' facilities often design programs simply to fit the available time in the rooms available.

The Elementary School Library

Small elementary schools often do not have libraries. Sometimes there is no room for one. In other cases, room is available but books are decentralized to classrooms. The rationale provided is two-fold. First, pupils will read more if the books are close at hand. Second, there is no supervision of the central space. The arguments in favour of a central resource appear more potent, which is why most new schools have central libraries. A central resource provides a much more varied offering to the children. Supervision can be more easily provided in one place, by parent volunteers and aides, for example, than in nine places — it is unlikely that all nine teachers will supervise the book collections carefully. Classroom resources tend to restrict children to 'their' grade level and to topics related to school subjects. Many children are excited precisely by the things that they choose to do rather than the things assigned to them.

Space Ownership

The territorial imperative is strong among teachers. Teachers, particularly in the elementary school, become very possessive about 'their' classroom. They take pride in the social climate, and an equivalent pride in the physical appearance. Indeed, the easiest way to distinguish between empty secondary and elementary classrooms is to look at their walls. In the secondary room, the rooms most 'owned' by a particular teacher are the ones most likely to be similar to the elementary classroom, for example science laboratories, art rooms, geography rooms.

Effective schools are usually the more attractive, better kept ones (not the best buildings but the most cared for) (Rutter *et al.* 1979). The explanation may be that the kind of teacher who worries about the classroom's appearance is the kind of teacher who cares about student's work. In any case, it is preferable for the teacher and for the students to have a more pleasant rather than a less pleasant environment. The reasons why secondary teachers are less identified with a particular space are two. Firstly, the scheduling system in the secondary school is more complex. Secondly, secondary teachers tend to have more time for planning and preparation, often teaching five periods when their students take seven. This means that teachers are often allocated fairly randomly to rooms. At best, the room in which they teach is likely to be shared with other teachers. At worst, they teach in five different spaces.

Administrators should respect and take into account the territorial interests and ambitions of teachers as much as they can. Possession of territory gives teachers some security, a sense of belonging. They know where everything is. They can find the chalk. They have access to the materials they want — learning materials, overhead projectors, micro-computers. They are less likely to bump into swinging doors, opening cupboards and suspended lights. They have an incentive to make the space attractive. The reward of space should not be dismissed lightly. It is so easy to scorn the bureaucrat's concern about office size and not recognize that this concern appears to be one of almost all human beings. At home or at work, most of us are concerned about the quality and the quantity of our space. It is worth considerable effort to give as many teachers as possible a place that they can consider their own — as secure and private as possible. These ideas should be applied to the school's common areas — entrance, reception and halls. Posters, exhortations, art, honor rolls, trophies, photographs of the life of the school, bulletin boards all give life and meaning to the school.

The Importance of Space

There are some good reasons why space is only rarely considered by administrators. Overall, its effect on students appears to be slight compared with that of time or teachers. More importantly, there is not much that administrators can do about what is already there. And they have other more important things to think about.

Even so, space can be very important in the lives of teachers and students. Most administrators and architects value their own offices. They should not decide that the territorial imperative in teachers is inappropriate. Some secondary schools have homeroom and floating teachers. The homeroom teachers often have possession of their room — whereas the floaters move from room to room to teach. Despite the additional work involved in being a homeroom teacher, in a good school there will be competition for the status of having one's own room and one's own class.

It is important that space be used with two significant criteria in mind:

How can it best serve the educational interests of students? How can it make life easiest and most pleasant for teachers, who have to live with the conditions for many years, perhaps a working life? In this area, the interests of teachers conflict directly with those of custodians who do not like clutter, models, plants — the very things that give the room identity. Here, teachers should come first. In return, teachers should be held responsible for the condition of the room at the end of the day.

Time

The Principal's Time

Before addressing the important question of pupils' time, a few comments about the allocation of the school administrator's own time are in order. In a sense this entire book is about the school administrator's time. It addresses issues such as developing goals, working with teachers and improving instruction all of which involve the principal's time.

As in the case of instructional time and educational purposes, it is incorrect to assume that there should necessarily be a close relationship between the principal's priorities for the school and the distribution of the administrator's own time. For example, high priority for the secondary principal may be excellence in English. But perhaps the school is blessed with a first-rate English department headed by an exceptional person. The department delivers excellent results, taking into account the composition of the student body, year after year. It would be unwise to spend much time trying to change the instructional program, although the good principal will still spend some time praising, reinforcing and evaluating that program. More generally, the principal should consider not only what is most important but how much effect administrative effort is likely to have. The principal should be both efficient and effective.

Imagine a doctor and a priest arriving on a battleground littered with dead and dying. The doctor may decide to ignore those with mortal wounds and concentrate on those whose lives or limbs can be saved by immediate attention. The priest may temporarily ignore the dead and lightly wounded and concentrate on the dying. Both are thinking of the effects of their use of time, not only their major goals. So principals should consider the likelihood of their intervention having some effect before determining a precise allocation of their time.

Principals are sometimes exhorted not only to become 'democratic' or 'consultative' leaders, ideas discussed in Chapter 2, but to concentrate on, for example, instructional leadership (for example, Leithwood and Montgomery, 1986). Usually, the central argument advanced is that curriculum is a crucial component of the school. That may be true, depending on how the various terms are defined. However, even if the cliché does have some general validity, it is not a self-evident truth that a particular principal in a given set of circumstances will have or should have much influence on the instructional program.

Circumstances vary. Some schools are forced to work within very narrowly prescribed curricula. That situation is very different from one where there is only some vague and frequently ignored guideline. That too is different from the situation where there is no guideline at all, perhaps nothing but a distant examination, or perhaps not even that. Some schools are tightly unionized, with such tight rules that the principal will require very unusual qualities to work with teachers effectively in areas of curriculum where teachers' committees have developed the program of studies. The entire question of working with teachers to improve instruction is extremely complex and is discussed in the next chapter. It is not unreasonable to suggest at this point that big efforts are not necessarily rewarded by big results.

Principals themselves vary. Some principals are knowledgeable about and interested in curriculum and student evaluation. Others are not. If a school district really wants principals to become involved in those areas it may decide to provide in-service training. But even that raises the question of how effective it will be to train professional educators to do things they would rather not do — that is, whether or not the in-service work should be compulsory.

The administrative enterprise is so complex and varied that it is dangerous to advocate that the principal should do specifics X and Y, rather than A and B. So much depends on the circumstances and on the individual. This book describes some administrative possibilities. It does not directly advocate a particular role, style and focus, although some foci will certainly appear to be more productive than others in most conditions. Our position is that principals should be evaluated in terms of their overall effectiveness, and not in terms of the role they adopt and the way they allocate their time. Good evaluation of their effectiveness must take into account the limitations set by the learners themselves and by the setting.

None of this should be taken to mean that principals should be treated by senior administrators in a hands-off, *laissez-faire* manner. Once again, senior educational administrators differ, and their effectiveness will vary with their individuality and competence. Some of them are likely to be very interested and competent in curriculum, some not at all. In one case, it may be entirely appropriate for a principal to be by-passed, by mutual agreement, as district staff implement a curriculum in the school with the benign but distant support of the principal. In another case, that may be totally infeasible. The central principle, however, is that the school administration is responsible for the overall results. It matters comparatively little whether the results are achieved by reliance on heavy involvement with parents, by direct action working with small groups of teachers or by delegation and support to a team of teachers.

Studies of school administrators show that they spend much of their time on activities that may not help the school achieve its goals. Much time is spent reacting to squeaky wheels and memoranda, many of which problems would be resolved in the absence of the principal. Administrators tend to spend a great deal of time dealing with managerial and disciplinary issues. Large numbers of pupils only see the principal when they lose a bicycle or require punishment — and in large schools not even then. Studies of business organizations, whose findings may not be transferable to schools, suggest that the best managed firms are those where the managers are visible, are interested in both the employees and the product and spend comparatively little time in their offices. Our experience suggests that a determined effort must be made if time is to be spent around the school, in classrooms, in the staff room, and chatting to students in the halls. An open door policy, whereby anyone — student, teacher, parent, or cleaner — may see the principal if available or may make an appointment without explaining the purpose to a defensive secretary — is a minimum, certainly not a sufficient requirement of accessibility.

Our own preference is to become directly and integrally involved in a variety of activities. Examples are: take on supervision duties (either regularly or as a relief); coach or help coach sports teams; act as a helper in athletic events; help supervise school dances; teach regularly, or at least occasional classes for absent teachers; help with school plays and music festivals. There is a danger to be guarded against. The behavior may appear 'out of role', an inauthentic and condescending pretence to be 'just a teacher' or even 'one of the kids' — an act that is foolish and demeaning, even though it may bring short-term applause. For such involvement to be effective, it must be genuine — 'I am doing this because the activity is important, I want to help, and I want to find out more about what is going on.' But the principal is always the principal. That means that some activities are constrained by the principal's involvement — there can be no 'unofficial' smoking after the play rehearsal, no covert stop at a tavern on the bus ride home from a football game. If the principal really wants to turn a blind eye to some activities — and that is usually dangerous, particularly in modern litigious times — then there can be no direct participation; a blind eye cannot be seen to see.

This book is about effective administration. So, in allocating time, the principal should be looking for effects. Working with teachers in cooperative decision making should result in both higher morale in teachers, and better decisions. Working on curriculum, discipline, or improved tests of achievement should result in better learning for students. Working on day-to-day managerial tasks should produce a smooth running school, a tight ship. The collaborative involvement just described has several purposes. Most importantly, it should bind administrators, teachers and students in a common endeavor — it should symbolically announce, 'These things are worth doing well; administrators care about them.' It should help strengthen the mutual bonds of trust, respect, obligation and affection. It announces that the school is more than an organization that carries out a set of prescribed curricular tasks with pre-ordained outcomes. Clearly, the statement implies something about the philosophy of the school and of the principal. But that should be no surprise — all activity should stem from a clear philosophical underpinning.

Research is badly lacking in this area. Even if it were available, it would likely not show that nearly all principals who follow the pattern we suggest are more effective than nearly all others. There has been research to test hypotheses about the relationships between principals and teachers (for example, Gross and Herriott, 1965) and research that has included some activities of principals and a host of other variables (for example, Rutter *et al.*, 1979). None has been very conclusive about what principals should do.

Leithwood and Montgomery (1986) argue that practitioners recognize the effective principal and are able to develop a schema of growth, from concern with school appearance and day-to-day operations, to inter-personal factors, to program and, finally, attention to all factors within a larger decision making framework. This idea raises a number of questions. Is there such a thing as the profile of the good principal? Are good principals recognizable by other administrators? Is the growth pattern unidirectional? Will empirical evidence confirm that principals perceived as good decision makers are more effective in terms of pupil outcomes? We remain sceptical that research will ever establish clear types of behavior for the principal which will in most cases be conducive to better outcomes among students. However, dysfunctional behavior is more obvious.

One problem, as Brookover and Lezotte (1979) show, is that teachers and principals do not always know whether or not their school is effective. The principal and staff of one of the deteriorating schools, in terms of academic achievement, were blissfully unaware of their deteriorating status. The school had a middle class clientele and above average achievement norms. There is no reason to expect a high level of recognition of effective principals by external or internal observers. There are many reasons for confusion. Different circumstances require different treatment. There is no one right way. And being effective is easily confused with being nice. There is probably a stronger relationship between the identification of a 'good' principal by observers and the social class of the school, simply because it is easier to look good in a more congenial setting. There may also be a positive relationship between identification as a 'good' principal by observers and qualities currently seen as being desirable, such as those described in Leithwood's framework. The more we discover about principals and their effects, the more complex the problem will become. The final problem, to be taken up again in Chapter 9, is the extent to which the principal makes the school effective and the extent to which an effective school makes the principal look good. Observers sometimes argue backwards — that an effective school must have an effective principal. But that is not always so (Holmes, 1988a).

There seems to be no particular reason why the growth pattern of the principal should be unidirectional, although it does seem likely that the problems around program are among the more complex and therefore require a high degree of self-confidence in the administrator. Very likely, some principals become less effective over time.

Over the last thirty years, there has been a major thrust in educational administration towards interpersonal factors. Some studies of educational administration focus almost entirely on the interpersonal concerns. Many beginning principals have been trained to believe that interpersonal relationships are the key to administrative success. They may therefore begin with explorations and efforts in that area only to be turned by force of circumstance and by lack of success to the day-to-day regularities of school life. Thus they might be seen as regressing on Leithwood's scale, without necessarily regressing in terms of effectiveness.

Kelsey (1983) has looked at recent supervisory reports on a group of Canadian school principals. He supports Leithwood's position that programmatic concerns are high in the perceived hierarchy — actions in that sphere are reported more often than actions in any other sphere. Equally interesting is the finding that the group of low rated principals received one-third the number of mentions relating to steady state activities, but more than twice as many mentions of innovative and developmental activities. One could interpret the finding as suggesting that successful principals have arrived and do not have to innovate. Less charitably, one could suggest that innovations often get the principal into trouble. It is very easy for onlookers, particularly supervisors, to confuse high morale with success, and peace with progress — yet there is no particular reason to believe that either denotes effectiveness among students. Many innovations are unhelpful; but desirable change may also cause confrontation, as we shall show later in the book.

So what does all this tell one about the allocation of the principal's time? One conclusion is that time should be carefully allocated with an eye on reasonably anticipated effects. We are sceptical that a formula will ever be developed that will work well in nearly all circumstances for nearly all people. Chapter 9 looks further at the role of the principal in the effective school.

We have already looked at some of the problems with the idea of leadership — does it merely require followers? Or successful achievement of goals? Or successful achievement of the right goals? The good principal, for us, is the person who is most effective and efficient in the achievement of desirable goals. There is no one formula for appropriate time allocation — or at least if there is we certainly do not know it. As principals themselves and the settings in which they work are so different it seems impossible that any one formula could apply. The abilities, interests and competence of the various professional staff with whom the principal must work are themselves enormously variable.

Nevertheless, there seem to be some patterns of time allocation that are least likely to be associated with effective administration. Some will emerge again as specific aspects of the principal's work are examined.

Some approaches likely to be ineffective are:

1 *The Reactive Approach — Management.* Many principals stay away from such difficult issue as goals, program and evaluation by retreating to day-to-day events. It appears unlikely that such a definition of the role will lead to school improvement; indeed it is difficult to see why such principals should be educators with high salaries. It would be better in such circumstances to have a school manager will trained in management techniques who would carry out policies developed collectively by teachers and parents together with those delivered when necessary, by the school district.

2 *The Morale Building Approach — People Person.* Some principals believe that by building a good team good results will necessarily follow for students. This may work if the team rather than the principal has authority and responsibility, making it easy for teachers to live comfortable lives without tension. Comfortable lives without accountability are unlikely to produce good results for students. We are not here questioning delegation to vice-principals, department heads and others. Hire good people and let them get on with the job remains a sound maxim. But their authority must be bounded, just as the principal's is.

3 *The Committee Member — Absentee Landlord.* Some principals become very active on district and other committees away from their school. Perhaps, they believe thay can influence external policy. Perhaps they seek to escape the day-to-day school regularities. Perhaps they seek personal visibility and promotion. There is every evidence that good principals are there — in the building as a manifest presence, giving force to their priorities.

4 *The Individual Student Specialist — The Amateur Psychologist.* Some principals spend large amounts of time with individual students — particularly those with psychological problems. Even if the principal is able to deal with some problems — and that is doubtful in the extreme — the overall goals of the school are neglected.

The above should not be seen as an attempt to develop high level theory. Quite the reverse — the above four statements are essentially truths by definition. There is no conceptual reason to believe that day-to-day attention to problems that happen to be brought to the attention of the principal will in any way improve educational policy and practice in the school. There is no conceptual reason to associate high morale among staff with high outcomes among students. Common sense tells us that good morale may be a necessary condition for enduring effectiveness, certainly not a sufficient condition. A principal who is absent from the building for much of the time is simply not influencing what goes on in the building. A person who spends most of the time closeted with individual students is obviously not affecting the vast majority of students with whom time is not spent.

Once the simplicity of those four statements is understood, the enormous range of activities that may (or may not) be helpful will be readily apparent. What is left? What are the most promising sets of activities? Once again, speaking in conceptual rather than research terms the following would seem to be strong candidates: working with teachers and parents developing and invigorating school goals and policy; working with and talking to teachers — encouraging, questioning, suggesting, judging; working with groups of students; planning and carrying out symbolic events; collecting ideas and information; and developing and implementing plans to evaluate students and programs.

The Learner's Time

The instructional time of the student is one of the most important forms of wealth the school possess, and certainly one most manipulable by administrators. Yet it is also one about which most texts on school administration are silent. Teachers, buildings, materials, curricula, policies, philosophies — all these go to make up a school, but rarely are most of them easily manipulable. Throughout this book there is a dual theme. The principal should be concerned both with what is of greatest worth and with what will have greatest effect. This is what characterizes the true professional — a combination of knowledge, expertise and wisdom with practical knowledge about their application.

Some years ago, Karweit (1978) wrote that, although the average high school graduate has spent 12,000 hours in school, 'we have little knowledge, apparently, about how time is spent in school and what the learning consequences are of spending different amounts of time or spending the same amount of time in different ways' (p. 1).

Wiley (1976) provided a starting point, 'It is clear that if a child does not go to school, he will not directly benefit from schooling. If a child goes to school every day for a full year, he will achieve maximum benefit from that schooling, other circumstances being equal. If he attends school less that the full year but more than not at all, the benefits he derives from schooling should be intermediate. That is, the quantity of schooling should be a major determinant of school outcomes' (p. 227). In general, more time is likely to be more effective than less. At the very least, time is an important commodity whose distribution requires careful thought.

School administrators usually have little influence on the total instructional time available. To the principal, two aspects of time allocation are of interest. First, there is the question of allocating available time in the context of competing school goals and subjects. Second, there is the mechanical means of allocating time, i.e., the school timetable or schedule. The first issue is of great educational significance. Most school administrators would probably claim that, while the matter of time allocation may be important to researchers, the schedule is of more immediate, practical importance. The implication is that administration is about means not ends, about management rather than about real choice. To be fair, it must be admitted that educational goals and objectives are frequently determined with little or no reference to school administrators. Nevertheless, the school unit, particularly at the elementary level, often has major descretion in the area of time allocation and therefore has a corresponding responsibility to ensure some consonance between time allocation and the agreed goals. Although we remain somewhat ignorant about the relationship between time and learning, there is little excuse for one to ignore what is known.

Allocated time. Although Wiley's famous pronouncement on time is essentially undeniable, it is misleading. It can be used to support the assumption that the more important a subject (or goal) is, the more time that should be allocated to it. The implicit assumption has long been that there is a simple linear relationship between time and learning — in all subjects, towards all objectives. Thus, if some students are found to be leaving school unable to write well, the usual solution is to increase the time allocated to English. If adolescents are taking too many illicit drugs, then the schools plan to expand the unit on drugs within the health program.

What evidence there is does not support such simplistic logic. In the late 1960s and early 1970s, one of the largest and most expensive investigations in the history of educational research was carried out, known generally as the first round of international studies. (See, for example, Purves and Levine, 1975; Wolfe, 1977). Beginning school earlier, at age five instead of six or seven, was found not to be associated with high levels of achievement in subsequent years. Neither was continuing school later, to age nineteen instead of eighteen. Instructional time in a particular subject was found to be related to achievement in the case of some subjects — English and French as second languages, senior science and mathematics — but not in others — civics, reading and literature. There was also a general, but far from universal, finding that 'opportunity to learn' is related to achievement. Thus, in some subjects at some levels the amount of learning appears to be quite sensitive to the time allocated to instruction. In some subjects at some levels, usually the same ones, a second important variable is the exposure children have to instruction in the tasks to be accomplished.

In the late 1970s, Holmes (1979) examined the relationship between officially allocated time and achievement in a large but non-random sample of Ontario intermediate schools at the eighth grade level. The sample was biased towards rural schools. Two findings were noteworthy. Firstly, there was enormous variability in time allocation among schools — from five to forty minutes a day in written expression, from twenty to eighty in mathematics, from twenty to ninety in social studies, from ten to fifty in science and from five to fifty in French. This finding was substantiated by investigation in two large urban systems, where comparable variability was found, except in one case in French. Thus the discretion in terms of the importance given to provincial goals and objectives at the school level is, in practice, enormous. In other school districts, we would expect, in the elementary grades, comparable variability although there are doubtless exceptions. Certainly we would expect to find considerable variation among school districts throughout North America.

The second noteworthy finding was essentially consistent with the international studies. The coefficients of correlation between mean school achievement and allocated time in various subjects are shown in table 4. Additionally, in the case of English numerous correlation coefficients were calculated between a variety of time measures (including numbers of writing assignments) and a number of measures of outcome (written expression, reading, language). None of the relationships proved significant — the coefficients ranging between -0.17 and 0.15.

One must be wary of overinterpreting a single small scale research study, particularly where it differs from the findings of the international studies. Nevertheless, the differences between subjects with a strong positive relationship between time and achievement and those without are:

   (i) The subjects with strong relationships involve instruction with relatively 'new' subject matter, i.e., learning is developed in sequential steps;

   (ii) The former objectives are more clear and straightforward;

   (iii) Instruction in the former subjects tends to be teacher-centred and directive;

   (iv) Learning in these subjects (with high relationships) is more concentrated in school, as distinct from the home or other external sources, for example, the media.

Other explanations for the data should be considered, but none seems particularly probable. For example, do schools with more intelligent students give more time to French? Perhaps; but the relationship between time and achievement in the second language has been so widely researched that this explanation cannot be tenable. Do schools with perceived weaknesses in language give more time to language on that account? There seems to be no particular reason why more time would be given to language and not to, say, mathematics. There is evidence from other studies of the compa-

Table 4   *Relationship between Achievement and Time Allocation in Ontario (Grade 8)*

Subject	R	N	Level of Significance
French as a second language	0.60	27	0.01
Mathematics	0.35	39	0.05
Geography	0.49	22	0.05
Canadian studies	0.19	22	—
History	0.11	22	—
Science	− 0.40	21	0.05

Note: The school is the unit of analysis.

rative insensitivity of language skills, in the middle and senior grades, to changes in instructional time.

The implication for school administrators is important. Schools have, officially or unofficially, considerable discretion in the allocation of time and the utilization of that discretion has greatly varying consequences. Consider two hypothetical extremes. Intermediate School A provides twenty minutes a day for mathematics, five minutes for French, 125 minutes for language and fifty minutes for science. School B provides eighty minutes for mathematics, forty-five minutes for French, sixty minutes for language and fifteen minutes for science. If the research conclusions are valid, then there will probably be no difference in achievement between the two schools in language and science but School B will perform significantly better than School A in mathematics and French.

There are a number of possible rejoinders. It may be argued that teaching in language and science could be made more effective, and so more sensitive to varying time allocations. Perhaps, but that should be demonstrated. It may be argued that it is easier to measure change in French and maths because the learnings are more immediate, more tangible. Probably so, but the other less immediate, less tangible learnings in English and science should at least be described qualitatively and researched. The point we are making is that either the research sould be refuted, or account should be taken of the findings in time allocation, or instructional changes should be introduced which may demonstrably invalidate the research findings.

When thought is given to time allocation, three criteria are either explicitly or implicitly considered. How important is the goal or subject matter? How much time will it take to cover the content? Will the time allocations fit the circumstances — staffing, specialist rooms, etc., (i.e., is it convenient)? The appropriateness of the first question is unchallengeable. If the goal is sufficiently important, then time is usually justified. The third criterion, of convenience or expediency, must also be acknowledged. If there is only one teacher able to teach French, and the instructional load is 1,200 minutes, then that time must be shared by the classes requiring instruction in French in some sensible way. However, the rigidities of staffing, like those of physical accommodation, are sometimes allowed to direct time allocation in an unreasonable way. It is often possible to hire a second French teacher (instead of a third grade teacher perhaps), even if that action means major rescheduling. Available time in a gymnasium, we have noted, is often used to justify limited minutes for physical education, without consideration of the actual capacity of the gymnasium or the usefulness of alternative space for some fitness activities. So while there are logistical limitations to time allocation, they are rarely as pressing and important as they are made to appear. Often, concern for managerial convenience overrides instructional requirements.

It is the second criterion that is most open to abuse. There is rarely a simple answer to a question concerning how long it will take to 'cover' some content largely because the meanings of 'coverage' and 'content' are rarely very clear. It may reasonably take one teacher three hours and another 140 hours to 'cover' *Macbeth*. The notion of coverage should be replaced by criteria that take into account the varied relationships between time and achievement. Instead of asking vaguely how long it takes to cover curriculum, administrators should be asking what can be achieved in ten minutes a day, twenty or sixty. The answer should be set against what one wants to achieve. Time is the school's wealth, and it should be spent carefully. Thus there may be a goal that everyone agrees is very important, but, if that goal cannot be significantly achieved even with five hours a day, it is worth spending one's limited wealth? On the other hand, there is no point in doing something just because it can easily be done.

Consider the case of drug abuse and a proposed change in the health course. If education about the properties and effects of illicit drugs is being considered, then the probable effect of such education should also be taken into account. There is little point in vaguely hoping it will serve to reduce drug involvement if the research suggests that such education is more likely to lead to increased experimentation. The link between information and desired behavior is seldom direct and sometimes different from that intended. Information about differences among ethnic groups, intended to increase understanding and tolerance, is sometimes used merely to promote further evidence for negative prejudice. Good intentions are insufficient.

Let us suppose there is some time in the schedule available and the school staff wonders what to do with it. One could teach more maths and French, because it seems likely that there may be a good return from the investment of additional time in those two areas. One could teach more English, because the public is very concerned about the state of language competence. But there is little point in teaching more French if the additional French is not wanted at the next level or school. There is little point in teaching more English if there will be no more learning as a result. If custody is a basic requirement (and it usually is), there may be something more pleasant and more useful that could be done with the time than either of those alternatives. For example, more time for physical fitness classes would certainly improve physical fitness and might even help academic achievement.

Many principals will smile at the thought that a school may have time available to spread around. There is a popular idea that as schools are being asked by parents and others to do more and more, the demands on instructional time are too great to be met. While it is true that many demands are made of the school, it is not true there is too little time available.

Suppose it is claimed that a number of similar, neighboring households have insufficient income on which to survive. Suppose, on investigation, it is found that one spends $50 a week on food, another $140. One spends $70 a week on shelter, another $210. One spends $20 a week on clothing, another $55. It would be reasonable to conclude, given that the needs are similar, it is possible to get by with the lowest expenditure in each category. And so with instructional time. If some schools and some classrooms can spend so much less time than others on a given subject, how can there be an overall shortage of time? When pupils reach seventh grade or ninth grade, they are all put together whether they have been spending twenty minutes a day on mathematics or fifty. Of course, if one asks subject consultants how much time is 'needed' for their various curricula, and if one adds on time for the various things demanded by parents and other community groups, for example, sex education, drug education, street-proofing, etc., then there is not enough time to go around. But, as we have said, that appears to be the least reasonable way of assessing time needed — unless one is also going to accept that one should find out from the grocer how much money we should spend on food, the tailor how much on clothes and the travel agent how much on vacations.

In summary, time is one of the most important forms of the school's wealth, and its distribution should be made with careful thought about goals and likely instructional effects. The greatest variability in time allocation within a jurisdiction is found in elementary schools. In secondary schools, a number of factors combine to reduce the variability — increased specificity of the curricula, the impact of computerized schedules in block schedules, the prevalence of the credit system which equates learning in all subjects to formal instructional time and the existence in many jurisdictions of external examinations.

Observations of school curricula, in combination with the available but limited research, lead to the following tentative suggestions:

(i) Children should be taught regular routines, discipline and required work habits early in the year.

(ii) Material should be arranged in a sensible sequence and taught thoroughly the first time.

(iii) More time should be spent on intensive, sequential instruction in mathematics, reading and language so that nearly every student learns nearly every skill the first time around. This should begin in first grade.

(iv) More time should be spent on direct instruction in writing, for different purposes, for different audiences, in a sequential, structured program. This is important in the middle grades.

(v) Instructional time in second languages (and other languages) should be intensive with large amounts of time at least in the first years of instruction. Before instruction is planned for very young children (from age five to nine) careful consideration should be given to the costs in time and money for continuity through the entire school life of the child; it may be effective but inefficient.

(vi) More time should be given to musical and artistic expression, particularly in the elementary grades, within a directed and disciplined program.

(vii) More time should be given to reinforcement of moral behavior (not in terms of allocated time for a specific course but in terms of school assemblies and time out to deal with moral occasions during class).

(viii) More time should be spent on sequential development of history and geography, particularly in the later grades.

(ix) Less time should be spent on general reading and literature exercises, particularly in the later grades.

(x) Much less time should be spent on social studies and environmental studies in the early grades.

(xi) Less time should be spent on subjects that are essentially irrelevant to the culture and future of most students, certainly before grade ten, for example, geometry and trigonometry.

In general, basic skills, fitness and artistic expression should be much more developed with additional time in the elementary grades. In the secondary school, the problem is less one of misallocation of time than of inadequate organization of learning experiences in ways that will give most students a genuine opportunity to learn, i.e., time is wasted because some students have already learned what is being taught and others do not have the prerequisite skills to learn, and because there is often, in English for example, no clear sequence of learning. That leads to the second aspect of time utilization.

The School Timetable — the Mechanism for Allocating Time

If time allocation is one of the most important administrative responsibilities, the schedule is the concrete expression of that responsibility. As the functions and purposes of the lower, middle and upper grades are different, the three will be considered separately. The purpose here is not to delve into the technical minutiae of timetable construction but rather to show the principles at work.

Scheduling the Lower Grades (Grades K–4)

The timetable strongly influences without ultimately controlling the amount of time spent on a particular subject. It determines who will teach the subject. It determines where the class will take place. And it influences indirectly the kind of instruction that will take place inside the classroom.

While the paper schedule rarely reflects exactly the actual instructional allocation, let alone time on task, there is some congruence. An exception to that congruence often arises when teachers are instructed to allocate X minutes to, say, religion and if their timetables are then collected centrally and ignored. Thus it makes sense for an administrator to ensure general compliance with an agreed upon allocation, but little sense to issue a mandate that is not enforced.

The nub of this problem, of compliance with some central directive, arrangement or consensus, lies with the necessity or irrelevance of ensuring that all teachers distribute their time in an approximately similar fashion. It can be argued that as long as the teachers achieve reasonable objectives, the time allocation is entirely their business. In a goal oriented system, with regular assessment of all goals, that argument makes sense. Unfortunately, however, the school system most likely to leave scheduling to the individual teacher is the least likely one to insist on accountability or goal achievement. Another argument for leaving time allocation to the individual teacher's discretion is that the teacher knows the pupils and their specific needs. That argument has emotional appeal, but is difficult in practice to establish what is meant by pupils' 'needs.' Does a pupil who is very good in mathematics need less time for mathematics than one who is very poor? Why? What of the pupil who is very good, or very bad in everything, a not unusual state of affairs? Perhaps students whose second language is English should have more time for language; but why should that be left to the individual teacher's discretion?

There would seem to be two defensible administrative postures. One is that the teacher, as a professional, is accountable for a reasonable set of agreed upon objectives. In that case, the teacher allocates the time so that the differing pupils can best achieve the objectives. Alternatively, it is reasonable to argue that there is some relationship, at least in some subjects, between time and achievement. Therefore, if children from different classrooms ever come together in subsequent grades, it makes sense for there to be a reasonably consistent time allocation per subject. In practice, the principal adopting the first posture will probably still try to influence the time allocation by making research findings available. And the one choosing the second will allow some flexibility, if, for example, most of the class is falling behind in reading.

The schedule determines to what extent a school will operate on a homeroom basis, and to what extent it will use a rotary system. Typically, the lower grades operate as homerooms, with one teacher taking responsibility for most instruction in a particular class. The usual rationale advanced is that small children need to identify with a single person and are confused and upset by frequent changes.

Recent events make one sceptical about that argument, at least in its extreme form. Some years ago, there was a vogue for open area classrooms, with large groups of children under the tutelage of a team of several teachers. To be sure, the vogue did not last very long, but the fashion was embraced by many administrators and some teachers without much thought being given to the alleged need of the child for a single teacher. Second, there is the growth in the number of single parent families, and in the numbers of children with two parents working. These trends have led to many young children being placed in day care under a number and variety of supervisors from an early age. Third, there is the growth in the provision of specialist instruction, in French, in music and on a withdrawal basis. One New Jersey fourth grade teacher said she only saw her entire class together for fifteen minutes a day, mainly as a result of pull-out programs. Tied to those trends is the spread from the high school to the elementary school of the provision of preparation time. These trends, which have not generally been resisted by teachers, have the effect of increasing the number of teachers with whom the young child is in contact. Some of those trends are rightly controversial, for all manner of reasons, but no one seriously asserts that children suffer by having a specialist music teacher. Thus, while it undoubtedly makes good sense for a number of reasons for the homeroom teacher to teach many subjects in the lower grades, there is no satisfactory reason why there should not be a scheduled change for subjects in which individual teachers have difficulty. Indeed, it is likely that one reason why time allocation varies as much as it does is that teachers allocate less time to those subjects they dislike and in which they feel insecure. Scheduled exchanges help overcome that difficulty. It is more desirable, and sometimes more effective, to have teachers who want to teach a subject teach it than to compel the unwilling to teach it.

The schedule determines where instruction will take place. Just as scheduled exchanges make it more likely that the timetable will be adhered to, so does movement in space. One function of the specialist space, for example, art room, music room, gymnasium, is that it regularizes instruction in the subject in question. We have already described a negative characteristic of specialist space, in terms of its encouragement of indirectly regulating the time available for the subject.

The schedule may influence the organization of instruction within classrooms. There are five ways in which instruction in the class with a single teacher may take place. Put another way, there are five ways in which a pupil may be learning at any one time. The five ways are: (i) whole class instruction; (ii) instruction in homogeneous groups; (iii) instruction in heterogeneous groups; (iv) individual instruction; and (v) seatwork (which itself may be whole class, group or individual). Clearly, all members of a class do not necessarily receive the same type of instruction at the same time, and cannot do so in types (ii), (iii) and (iv). Different types of timetable will promote different types of instruction. For example, if the timetable is constructed on the premise that there will be inter-class (as distinct from intra-class) grouping, then homogeneous group instruction is virtually inevitable. In this example, classes across three grades might be synchronized for reading and mathematics. Homogeneous groups might be organized in such a way that each teacher would have either two or three groups at very different levels of instruction. Such an organizational pattern has a double effect — it guarantees time allocation in two key subject areas and virtually guarantees the method of organization for instruction. It is also highly consistent with teaching for mastery on the basis of sequential skills.

In most primary schools, however, the homeroom teacher is typically left with the responsibility for providing instruction in most subjects. Even though time allocation may be administratively mandated, teachers normally exercise a fair degree of discretion.

Scheduling the Middle Grades (Grades 5–8)

During the middle grades, the rotary schedule gradually replaces the homeroom pattern of lower grades. It has not been established that either pattern is superior to the other, possibly because organizational changes have little or no effect independently of other factors with which they may or may not be associated.

If one wants to achieve more rapid advancement in the key disciplines, then simple organizational change to rotary is unlikely to have much direct influence. However, if rotary organization is combined with a more subject centred curriculum, some improvement may be noticeable. Similarly, if one hopes to bring about a greater sense of belonging, more social cohesion, then the homeroom system is likely to be ineffectual by itself — but it may be effective if programs are introduced to consolidate the homeroom classes with their homeroom teacher. For example, homerooms may be given specific collective responsibilities within the larger school community.

An issue as crucial as the distribution of subjects among teachers is that of learners among classes. In the past, teachers have been more vocal and the reactive principal has been more aware of the former issue. Increasingly, as parents, and students themselves, become more involved in schooling, administrators are having to justify their rationales on this latter issue. Typically, parents of bright children like some segregation while parents of average and below average children do not.

Although there is much high flown rhetoric — in favor of 'open', 'democratic', common schooling for all, and in favor of selection for excellence, in order that the able and gifted are not held back to the pace of the slowest, the choice is as often pragmatic as principled. To begin with, no one really believes that selection and segregation can be postponed for ever. Even the Paideia Proposal (Adler, 1982) would have selection take place immediately after high school graduation. At the other extreme, even the West Germans postpone selection until the age of ten, and permit changes to take place later. So the operative question is when rather than whether selection should take place. The middle grades in much of the English speaking world form the battle ground for the resolution of this debate.

There are four major options available within the middle grades. They are: heterogeneous classes; setting of classes; levels of classes; and streaming. The first and fourth options are very distinct choices, the middle two attempts at compromise.

Heterogeneous classes have generally been the norm in North American middle schools, but are less universal in Europe. In Europe, there is usually some division on the basis of achievement, ability and interest by the age of twelve, and almost always by the age of fourteen. Heterogeneous classes provide all students with an essentially common experience, thus postponing until the senior grades any separation by achievement and by ability. Although middle grade teachers are often asked to group their heterogeneous classes, there is generally less grouping in the middle grades than in the elementary grades. Part of the explanation may be the greater difficulty in controlling adolescent children. Another reason may be that middle grade teachers are more concerned than elementary teachers with the academic development of adolescents within the discipline. It is important not to lose sight of the essential principle at stake. If students are to be given different instruction anyway, with different programs, the argument against streaming is obviously weakened. The most persuasive argument against heterogeneous classes beyond grade five or six is that students' level of achievement is extremely varied. This is particularly obvious in mathematics and language, in which subject students have often been grouped even in the early grades. The greater the variation among students the more difficult the instruction becomes, and the more pointless it is to keep children together. Thus the typical heterogeneous seventh grade class has children in it functioning one or two grade levels on either side of the norm in maths and three or four grade levels either side in language.

The furthest extreme from heterogeneity, pure streaming, is not well adapted to the North American grade system. In Europe, where pure streaming remains quite common in the middle grades, roughly from age ten to twelve to age fourteen to sixteen, there is comparatively little grade acceleration and repetition. Streaming functions in most European countries as an alternative to repetition. Pure streaming means that classes at a given grade level are ranged from most academically competent to least — if there are six classes there are six streams. The combination of automatic promotion with streaming, probably still normal in England, means that the least successful pupils in any given class move down a stream or two, the most successful move up stream. Streaming also accommodates the highly selective senior secondary system in Europe, where only those who have successfully survived the top streams continue to university preparatory programs. It is no coincidence that, for philosophical and pragmatic reasons, where high proportions of the age cohort enrol in post-secondary programs there is less need for streaming in the middle years. If middle stream programs in eighth grade provide sufficient training for access to university, why separate them from the top stream? In North America, where large proportions of the age cohort typically enrol in university bound courses at the beginning of high school, there is clearly little point in providing highly differentiated programs in the middle years. Streaming is quite logically rare in North America. Nevertheless, the fact that streaming is not a very satisfactory solution, does not mean there is no problem in heterogeneity, particularly when the heterogeneity is as great as it is in a typical cross section of North American 14-year-olds. Individualization is likely to result in the worst of both worlds. Instruction is very inefficient as very little time is available for each student, but there is effective separation of students.

Of the two compromises, levels of classes (or tracking) is the one closer to streaming, and is the one normally used in North American high schools. Its suitability for the middle grades is doubtfull — for essentially the same reason that streaming is usually rejected. Either the levels *are* geared to the high school levels or they are *not*. If they are, selection is necessary as soon as the levels are created, and little change from the original pupil selection will, in practice, take place. If they are not, if, for example, pupils from the middle, often called the regular, level can readily move to the advanced level in high school, what is the point of program and pupil differentiation? Typically, there are three levels — usually called advanced or enriched, regular or general, and basic or remedial. This modification does make more instructional sense than pure streaming. At least it is possible to develop three distinctive programs reasonably suited to the pupils allocated to the three levels, whereas it is quite impractical to develop six levels for six streamed classes.

A preferable compromise is the setting of classes, whereby several classes at a given grade level in a given subject are synchronized in the schedule for the purposes of differentiated instruction. With setting, homeroom classes remain heterogeneous, but differentiation takes place in one or two key subjects — language and mathematics perhaps. Just as enrichment is unlikely to be very valuable within a heterogeneous class, it is likely to be of equally dubious value in a setted (synchronized) class. Too often, special programs in the middle grades appear to have been developed mainly to keep bright children excited without leading to structured, synthesized learning. Thus, where the main purpose of setting is to provide an enriched class, the result is likely to be very similar to the enriched group within the heterogeneous class. Either the enrichment is successful, in which case advancement in reading, writing and mathematics is achieved; or it is not, in which case the purpose of the exercise is brought into doubt. The most obvious reason for introducing setting is to permit advancement, whereby children may cover a four year maths and English program in three years and then receive advance placement in high school. It is simply not possible to conceptualize a significant and valuable program of 'enrichment' in sequential subjects such as mathematics, reading and language that will not simultaneously provide the advancement required for faster movement through the grades.

These are examples of the way in which scheduling interacts with instruction in the middle grades. Scheduling change, in and of itself, is unlikely to have any independent effect on achievement of the overall group. On the other hand, if there are some other specific goals that are simultaneously being addressed, by other means, then a compatible schedule will probably be helpful. So once again we are returned to values. If rapid academic advancement for some is desired, setting is the best answer. If a total homeroom experience is desired, heterogeneous whole class instruction makes sense.

Scheduling the Higher Grades

By the time students reach the last third of their life, the idea of their having a single teacher largely responsible for their instructional program is abandoned, (except in isolated rural areas where one or two teachers may provide instructional support more than instruction itself). Specialist teachers become the rule and there are many ways in which the allocation of teachers and pupils to classes may be arranged. They may be summarized under three major types.

The traditional schedule is a complex version of the middle school rotary timetable. Time is allocated to the various subjects for the different classes. These time allocations are then fitted into the teachers' schedules. If, for example, there are to be five periods a week of mathematics, and teachers have a load of twenty-five periods per week, mathematics specialists have a load of five classes. The basic assumption is that classes move as a group, except that there may be some setting (i.e., synchronized scheduling of more than one class, to provide either options or instruction at varying levels).

This schedule has been virtually abandoned in North America where the Carnegie credit system has taken hold. It remains the norm in Europe, however, where achievement is measured in terms of final examinations passed rather than numbers of courses successfully completed. The advantages of the traditional schedule are: (i) time allocations vary among subjects; (ii) classes stay together and develop a sense of community; and (iii) double and triple periods are easily arranged in some subjects, i.e., physics and automobile repair, without providing them in other subjects and without changing the required amount of allocated time. The disadvantages are: (i) comparatively little variation of course choices is possible for a single class; (ii) except for limited setting, it is extremely difficult to provide instruction in different levels of the same subject within one class; (iii) teachers' workload may be variable, in that a geography teacher may have eight classes for three periods a week whereas a mathematics teacher may have only three classes for eight periods a week. The effect of these disadvantages is to make traditional systems not particularly well suited to the credit system.

The modular schedule in contrast is highly flexible. It permits the utmost freedom of choice for students together with great flexibility of period length. It is based on a chosen module of, say, fifteen minutes. Periods can then be arranged for any multiple of fifteen minutes. Its great and usually fatal disadvantage is that, if it is constructed within the limits of a normal school day, it requires approximately thirty per cent flex time, when the individual student is not scheduled. Typically, students therefore receive about two-thirds the instructional time they would receive in a traditional or block schedule. Apart from problems of efficiency, there are problems of control and custody during the unscheduled time. It is possible to provide a full instructional load for all pupils by extending the school day by about one-third. But that introduces a new set of problems. Teachers and students are likely to resist the inconvenience of early starting, late finishing and considerable 'down time' during the school day. Discipline and attendance can also be a problem. Consider the example, extreme perhaps, where a 16-year-old finishes one class at two o'clock and is supposed to wait until four o'clock to begin the final thirty minute class in an optional subject. In practice, most American schools that adopt modular schedules confine them within the traditional day. The modular schedule was never widely adopted in Canada.

The block schedule, an ideal partner for the credit or Carnegie unit system, is almost universal in North America. The variants of the block schedule are many, but the principle is the same. In essence, the day is first divided into a number of periods of equal length. A cycle, usually of one to five days, is selected giving a number of periods equal to the product of the periods per day and days per cycle. The chosen factor of that product is the maximum number of course/credits, including lunch, a cycle. A simple example provides six fifty minute periods per day plus passing time between periods. In a year, that example provides a maximum of five full credits or units with 150 instructional hours per credit. Another variant provides eight credits in a four day cycle, with seven forty-seven minute periods per day and 106 instructional hours per credit. Those examples both assume that credits are earned on an annual basis. Some schools give credits twice a year by combining half the number of credits with double the amount of instructional time per cycle. The term semestering is often used to describe half year courses and credits. Some American schools reschedule even more frequently still, but the administrative burden increases. The advantages of the block schedule, apart from its congruence with the credit system, are its flexibility and its efficiency. It makes subject promotion quite straightforward in a typical four grade, thirty-four section (during one block) high school with 1000 students. It also allows for a considerable number of options. As instructional hours are, nearly always, equal in all subjects (half credits being difficult to schedule), the allocation of credits or units on the basis of a given number of instructional hours is administratively straightforward.

If one assumes the desirability of a credit system, and it is certainly an efficient means of providing benign custody for the adolescent, the block schedule is unparalled. Nevertheless, it has significant drawbacks. The most obvious disadvantage is the need to allocate the same amount of time to every subject. While double to triple credits are possible in vocational subjects, one cannot decide to give six periods in mathematics and three in geography. There are usually ways to get round a particular problem but those ways create other difficulties. The basic principle of the block schedule is that the same amount of time per cycle is allocated to all courses. Coupled with this disadvantage is the uniform length of all periods. Periods of thirty minutes may be desirable in French and physical education, sixty minutes in English and two hours in cooking and sewing.

Another disadvantage of the Carnegie unit system is symbolized in the often used cafeteria metaphor. Because credits are based on minimum instructional hours and only rarely in terms of defined standards, it is very easy to assume that credits are interchangeable — they all constitute some roughly equivalent currency. Thus the Carnegie unit system can lead students to concentrate on putting in time and choosing soft options rather than attaining particular levels of achievement. Many American states have introduced competency tests, hoping that they will raise graduation standards. Other states oblige schools to build standards into their curricula. Certainly there is a problem with levels of academic achievement in American and Canadian high schools, compared with more successful schools on the Pacific rim. The causes of the superiority of many Asian countries are many and complex. But the pressure to meet the demands of an external examination may well be one.

The importance of the schedule goes beyond the mechanism of time allocation. It provides the single best composite picture of what the school is trying to do. Do students have free periods? What percentage of the school population takes physical education? What percentage takes art? How many students are preparing for work, how many for college and university, and how many remain rudderless in the middle? Administrators have no greater apparatus for the exercise of administrative discretion. Strangely, that discretion is often delegated to vice-principals and even to department heads, at the same time as principals complain that the latest collective agreement robs them of their authority.

Conclusion

This chapter has been about time and space. Schools are often said to be about people. While that is true, the cliché amounts to little. If the implication is that administrators will be most effective in bringing about change by directly attempting to change teachers we are sceptical. The next chapter looks at the principal working with teachers. If the implication of that cliché is that time and space do not matter, are part of the 'administrivia' of administration, we disagree. Time is not a sufficient condition for learning, but it is a necessary condition. And where instruction can be shown to be purposeful and effective, time is one of the most significant variables. Of course, if little learning is taking place, doubling the instructional time will be ineffectual. Space, while much less potent than time, is also important. Too often it becomes an unrecognized block to learning. One has open classrooms because there are open spaces. There are thirty periods of physical education in the schools because there are thirty periods in the week and one gymnasium. And so on. One should be first deciding what it is one wants to do, how long it will take, and what resources and organizational patterns are needed — and only then should one go about doing it. Principals should avoid changing scheduling patterns or room allocations or instructional groupings because of a passing fad or someone's good example in the next district. Instead, all available wealth should be devoted as efficiently as possible to the school's chosen goals.

Further Reading

This is a neglected area for research. One of the very few serious attempts to analyze and interpret the effects of elementary school organization is to be found in Barr and Dreeben (1983). An old but still generally valid study of streaming at the elementary level is found in Jackson (1962). The effects of semestering school terms are interestingly researched by Raphael, Wahlstrom and McLean (1986) and Raphael and Wahlstrom (1986). Murnane (1975) examined the impacts of 'school resources' — but the resources are mainly human. Facilities are included in effectiveness surveys by Walberg (1982) and Bridge, Judd and Moock (1979). Coleman's classic study of school effectiveness (1966) first empirically established what is now generally accepted — differences in concrete aspects of quality in resources (both human and material) have comparatively little impact on the learning of students in the developed world.

Chapter 4

The School Staff:
Working with Professional Teachers
and Other Adults

The Relationship Between Teachers and Principal

Chapter 2 dealt with the fundamental issues of power and authority and described the different roles that schools and principals adopt. Although principals may, consciously or unconsciously, choose one of those ways of exercising authority, the working environment usually constrains total freedom of choice. Chapter 2 stressed the constraints of the broad, social environment. Chapter 3 examined the physical context, emphasizing opportunities more than constraints. This chapter focuses directly on the working relationship between principal and teachers. Increasingly, as Chapter 2 implied, as traditional authority wanes, the principal requires consent from the governed. This means that, very often, nearly always in urban schools, the working relationship is not ordained by custom and tradition. The principal should think carefully about the relationship with other administrators and with teachers.

In reaction to the often autocratic behavior of the traditional principal, there has been a trend in the last five decades towards giving the administration a more 'human face', towards more 'democratic' decision making. This movement was given major impetus by the famous Western Electric studies in the early 1930s when the Hawthorn effect was discovered. Factory workers improved their productivity as a result of the interest demonstrated by management rather than as a result of objective changes in the working conditions. The move to humanistic management, in business and in schools, has had mixed effects.

Organizational Climate

At best, humanistic management trends have led to: a recognition by school administrators of the professional and personal concerns and interests of teachers; increased consideration of those affected by decisions; more careful and appropriate delegation of responsibility; high morale; and an emphasis on cooperation rather than bureaucratic hierarchy. At worst, it has led to: psychological manipulation of teachers, a form of totalitarian control whereby conformity is ensured by group pressure; extreme delegation and dilution of authority so that the principal is left with responsibility without authority; absence of accountability; and an inward looking self-absorption that leads to indifference or condescending attitudes to students and, particularly, parents. This assumption of superior knowledge is particularly displeasing to colleagues who do not share the 'faith.'

By 1960, McGregor had codified two approaches in his famous Theories X and Y. Theory X was bureaucratic, hierarchical and, according to McGregor, outmoded. Theory Y was based on the importance of stimulating individual initiative. Most people have interpreted Theory Y as meaning that the administrator should be 'democratic', warm, outgoing. Yet McGregor (1960) wrote, '. . . the climate is more significant than the type of leadership or the personal "style" of the superior. The boss can be autocratic or democratic, warm and outgoing or remote and introverted, easy or tough, but those personal characteristics are of less significance than the deep attitudes to which his subordinates respond . . . (what is important) is to create a deep and satisfying emotional certainty of fair treatment' (pp. 134–5). It is understandable that McGregor has been interpreted in a more superficial way. While he is probably right that employees (and students) like 'a deep and satisfying emotional certainty of fair treatment', there remains the question of how that salutory state of affairs can be brought about.

Halpin (1966) pioneered the application of the idea of organizational climate to the school. He developed eight factors (four from teachers' and four from principals' questionnaires) and derived six school climates ranging from open, not unlike Theory Y, to closed, akin to Theory X. However, numerous studies have been unable to find any relationship between Halpin's climate and student achievement. The appropriateness of applying industrial models, where workers are producing widgets, to the school where professionals are teaching pupils is very much in doubt. Widgets are passive receivers. Students are full participants in the process. Teachers, too, are very different from factory workers.

Feldwebel (1964), one of the researchers who failed to discover a relationship between climate and achievement, noted dryly that people who are happy in their jobs are not necessarily hard workers. The real problem is more fundamental. Waller (1965) shrewdly observed the tension that exists between teacher and principal (as well as between teacher and student, and teacher and parent). Where the responsibilities are unequal, the social relationships are asymmetrical. A principal's amiability and supportiveness should not be confused with friendship by either party. True friendship (according to Aristotle) is the bond between people working together in the face of obstacles to achieve a good end. But the principal has responsibility for much of the teacher's work. There are limits to loyalty, much looser than those between friends and the steel fist of hierarchy lies, necessarily, behind amiability's velvet glove. A social anthropologist observing a typical school would observe the frequency of the joking relationship between principal and teacher, particularly when there is a male principal and predominantly female staff. A joking relationship is characterized by teasing. Tension can be resolved by humor. Remarks and criticisms can be made and received half in jest, when stated seriously they would cause considerable resentment.

The ambiguity of the principal/teacher relationship is important. It is underlined by the high degree of variation in administrative style outlined in Chapter 2. The ambiguity can be reduced in a large school run on bureaucratic lines — but even there it is rarely eliminated. There are too many workers and too few bosses in schools for bureaucracy to run completely smoothly. The prevalence of the benevolent despot, even in times when experts and most practitioners talk freely about the evils of 'top down', 'authoritarian' control, is a sign of the uncertainty at the heart of the role.

Of Halpin's (1966) eight factors, the principal's thrust and consideration are identified as being most important (p. 174). But there is no strong positive relationship between the two. It is perfectly possible to be very considerate, and at the same time to have very little thrust, and vice versa. Indeed, it may often be extremely difficult to be both considerate and at the same time to possess a tremendous drive to *change* people. There is some inherent contradiction in setting out to change in some major way the person whom one loves and admires. Consideration, if genuine, stems from affection, feeling, emotion. Thrust, if professional, stems from a policy informed by reason and philosophy.

Hoy and Miskel (1982), in their text on educational administration, describe research which suggests another reason why the social climate between teachers and principal is not a good indicator of student achievement (p. 193). That research suggests that thrust is likely to be the most important factor where the context is either particularly easy or particularly difficult, but consideration is more important when the context is moderately difficult. The interpretation given is that, without a strong leader, schools can be overtaken by hostile external forces in difficult times. In very easy times, the strong leader can afford to thrust ahead to make necessary changes. But in moderate times, the external threat is not sufficient to consolidate the staff behind a strong principal; yet at the same time, the staff is not secure enough to be unthreatened by change.

Research by Brookover and Lezotte (1979) illustrates the point that high morale among teachers and consideration by the principal are insuffient to guarantee high achievement levels among students. They identified two sets of elementary schools, one set with improving levels of achievement, the other with deteriorating levels. They first assured themselves that neither improvement nor deterioration was attributable to changes in the schools' clientele. They then studied the individual schools to find distinguishing characteristics between the two sets. Staff morale was not one of them. Indeed, one of the deteriorating, middle class schools had very high morale with teachers unaware that levels of achievement were in fact deteriorating. (This is very easy to happen in situations where students are doing quite well in terms of national norms; no one bothers to find out how well the students are doing taking their favorable backgrounds into account. In the reverse situation, where students from poor backgrounds are known to be doing very badly, educators are more willing to share the blame.) In contrast with that middle class school, tension between a demanding principal and a staff was observed in more than one of the improving schools.

Blau and Scott (1962, pp. 68–9) made a distinction between 'professional', meaning client-centred, and collegial, meaning colleague-centred, social workers. If the same distinction is applied to principals and teachers, it is easy to see why measures of relationships among the teaching staff are unlikely to be satisfactory proxy variables for the health of the entire organization. It is possible that high morale in industrial organizations generally does lead to high production of widgets. Even if that is true, it does not follow that the finding will prove equally true for social organizations where the 'product' is a changed human being. Clearly, there are times when the interests of teachers conflict with those of pupils and parents, just as the interests of nurses and social workers are not always coincident with their patients'. Waller (1965) observed how teachers will sometimes band together in solidarity against pupils. But solidarity may be used to promote high standards of behavior and achievement. Thus, in a good, consensual school, teachers all apply equally rigorous rules with respect to the tidiness of work and punctuality and reliability in its completion. The rigorous teacher does not have to begin from scratch every year, as is the case in mediocre schools where a consensual sense of purpose is lacking. In the same way, in a secure family environment, father and mother band together to apply the same judgments to children. But high morale and solidarity in a school staff may be negative. A staff may resent and resist a high social class group of parents making demands for more rigor for their children. 'The parents are too pushy'; 'They drive their children too hard'; 'They think that just because they have been successful their children will be successful too.' Thus, poor work habits and mediocre achievement, considering the students' ability and social advantage, can be rationalized and protected. Similarly, in a low social class neighborhood, where traditional educational values are neither clearly understood nor supported, a staff may rationalize poor achievement levels by blaming the neighborhood, and may work to develop an informal, pleasant (but unproductive) climate in a school. Staff may rationalize that children must feel happy in their environment before they can learn; in fact many children learn quite adequately without feeling totally happy in their environment and subsequently feel happy as a result of the satisfaction achieved from having learned. The solidarity of teachers in such cases may insulate the school from potentially productive reforms.

Social Exchange

The relationship between principal and teachers may be usefully examined through the prism of social exchange theory. In Chapter 2, this theory, as applied by Blau (1964) and Clark and Wilson (1961), gave one focus for the examination of the use of the principal's authority. The French anthropologist Marcel Mauss (1954) developed the concept of the gift and its social function. Some west coast native Indians used to humiliate their rival chiefs by making gifts they knew could not be reciprocated. The humiliation was completed by the potlatch, where wealth could be ceremonially burned. Even in modern societies, we have seen leaders so powerful that they felt they could afford to shrug conspicuously at concerns of their citizens. Social intercourse can be seen as a series of exchanges, each of which sets up its own terms of trade and sets of obligations. Blau (1964), going beyond the definition of exchange discussed in Chapter 2, argues that the value of a gift is indeed important, but that the genuineness of the donor is an equally important factor. A gift which is seen to be intended to purchase has, ironically, less purchasing value than a genuine gift which is given without calculation of its exchange value.

Once again the precarious ambiguity of the principal's role in relationship to teachers is evident. If the principal is seen to be carefully calculating gifts (amiability, flattery, confidential information) in order to receive dividends, the gifts lose their potency. The popular, good looking, affluent 12-year-old sometimes achieves high status by burying peers in gifts of all kinds (varying from material gifts to gifts such as social invitations and acceptance within the charmed circle of admirers). But that social hierarchy is precarious, based on the continued acceptance by others of their low status. The charismatic principal may do the same thing to teachers. But generally, calculated gifts are easily disarmed. Suppose a principal gives a teacher, with high status in the informal organization, special attention or a concession. The response may be a cheery, half-joking, 'Oh, thanks so much. But if you think I'm going to take on that low group of maths students that Bill can't handle, forget it.' All with a smile — to the chagrin of the principal who had exactly that possibility in mind. Thus gifts have to be accepted to be reciprocated. The humiliated, spurned lover is unlikely, even in these material times, to achieve reconciliation by dispatching an outrageously expensive gift; and if it is accepted, the acceptance could well connote high status, a condescension on the part of the recipient! But if the principal is to rely on genuine spontaneous gifts, it requires an unusual openness of heart and convivial personality. More bluntly, it is unlikely that a principal will find frequent occasion to genuinely reward and praise the least liked and least competent member of staff. And any such gifts will certainly be remembered during grievance procedures concerning transfer or dismissal.

In any given case, the motive behind a gift is usually neither completely genuine nor completely calculated. Indeed, Mauss argued that there can be no such thing as a genuine gift — there is always some expectation of some form of possible return. Further, the more one introspectively examines one's motives, the less spontaneous and genuine they are likely to become.

Despite the ambiguities and contradictions, careful consideration of social exhange leads to some common sense conclusions:

(i) The school administrator should recognize both the fragility of administrative authority and the meagre supply of incentives and rewards for teachers that are actually under some administrative control.

(ii) The most potent gifts to teachers are those involving purposive incentives — whereby teachers receive a reward recognizing their success in terms of the school's goals.

(iii) Gifts quickly lose some or all of their force if
  (a) they are rejected;
  (b) they are believed, rightly or wrongly, to be manipulative in intent, i.e., not genuine;
  (c) they are given routinely to all;
  (d) they are so frequent or so overpowering that no reciprocation is possible.

(iv) In all but the most bureaucratized schools, continuing informal social exchange among teachers and between principal and teachers is crucial for the health of the organization.

In sum, it makes sense to give time, help, assistance and support genuinely, without expectation of commensurate return or 'loyalty.' It also makes sense to receive and welcome gifts, and to ask for help even when there is risk of a negative response.

Working With Teachers

There is no evidence that there is one right way to address relationships with teachers. The social structures and environments of schools are so varied as to make a golden recipe unlikely in the extreme. That variation in context is compounded by variation in administrators.

An invariate solution is unlikely to solve variable problems. Table 5 shows a two-way classification of dimensions of administrative activity and types of decision making style. The table illustrates a conceptually defensible choice from a number of potential combinations.

Table 5 *Principals and Teachers: Who Does What?*

Types of Decision Making	Student achievement and evaluation	Formal program	Teacher supervision and improvement	School systems relations	Parent and community relations	Student behavior	Daily administrative tasks	Instructional methodology	Extracurricular activities
Dimensions of Administrative Activity									
Strong individual leadership	+ +	+ +	+ +	+	+	+	+ +	0	0
Strong team leadership	+	+	+	+ +	0	+ +	0	0	0
Cooperation	0	0	0	+	+	0	+	0	+ +
Delegation	+	0	0	0	+ +	+	+	+ +	+

Key: + + = Major emphasis
  + = Some emphasis
  0 = Little emphasis

Note: The above example is most suitable for elementary schools. The secondary principal is likely to give less emphasis to teacher supervision and improvement and to daily administrative tasks, more to student behavior.

The choice is neither random nor absolute. It is intended to be a reasonable guide for application in a large number of schools, elementary and secondary. To ensure that the three-point scale (major, some and little emphasis) is applied evenly, extreme points have been used in all nine areas of administrative activity. Obviously, some areas will receive much more overall attention than others and thus a 'little emphasis' in one column may mean much more time and attention from the administrator than a 'little emphasis' in another. The purpose of table 5 is two-fold. One purpose is to show the implications of Chapters 1 and 2 in terms of relationships with teachers. To this extent, it is somewhat prescriptive. It suggests that principals should, in general, take leadership roles with respect to program, student achievement and evaluation — those areas that lie at the heart of the school's purpose. The pattern of recommended types of decision making in table 5 is most consistent with benevolent despotism and consultative bureaucracy — the two leadership styles generally most compatible with contemporary circumstances. A second purpose behind the development of table 5 is more general. Whether or not principals are able to choose to adopt benevolent despotism or consultative bureaucracy, whether or not they are able to choose to emphasize the dimensions suggested in table 5, whether or not they are able to choose to exercise a variety of decision making styles, as the table suggests, it is important for professional administrators to think through how they deal with the various aspects of school life and how they work with their professional colleagues.

Heavy emphasis on the decision making type 'strong individual leadership' suggests that the administrator wishes to or must influence direction within the dimensions listed. In the case of 'daily administrative tasks', even in a very large school it is not possible to delegate most of these below the level of administrators. In 'parent and community relations' and 'teacher supervision and improvement', administrators have little or no choice; thus it is no surprise that studies show that principals spend most of their time in these three areas. Table 5 implies they should try, where it is possible, to give major attention to program and evaluation. 'Delegation' implies principals relinquish most or all of their authority (but not their informal influence). Thus instructional methodology should be the domain of the professional teacher. 'Strong team leadership' and 'cooperation' are likely to require more time to bring about change than strong individual leadership. They also imply some delegation of authority. Team leadership involves the use of formally designated leaders, typically department heads or teachers formally selected by teachers. Team leadership is particularly useful where central, strong consensual agreement is required and where the principal also wishes to retain major influence. For example, the principal (or delegated vice-principal) will typically play an important role in committee meetings and the administrative right of veto may be clearly evident. Cooperative leadership may exist with the principal's presence, but the right of veto will be very rarely exercised. Thus, although the principal may participate widely in extracurricular activities, their operation will be left in the hands of *ad hoc* committees, volunteers, and individual teachers.

Also implicit in table 5 is the idea that principals should not try to lead everything. Once again, as always, there are exceptions. In a small school, a dynamic benevolent despot may well provide excellent leadership in all areas. The usefulness of the prescription varies with the type of influence the principal chooses to use, with the size of the school, with the nature of school's problems and with the principal's personal characteristics. Thus, if a principal has little interest in program and evaluation, if there are strong system-level programs in effect or if there are strong leaders within the school staff, then it is appropriate for a principal to provide strong (but informal) individual leadership in, say, extracurricular activities or even in instruction instead.

We are not at this point dealing directly with the mechanics of decision making. Such questions as program development and implementation and teacher supervision are addressed separately later. What we mean by 'individual leadership' here means minimal delegation of authority, while 'delegation' means maximum delegation, with the other two terms, 'strong team leadership' and 'cooperation' falling in between. However, strong individual leadership does not imply that the school administrator simply announces decisions in areas of 'major emphasis.' In the first chapter, we stressed the importance of the development of consensual goals. Once those goals are established, objectives required for the achievement of those goals require definition and specification more than discussion and debate. Even where individual leadership is strongest, decisions may be made in a number of different ways. But, as one example, the principal of a traditional Catholic high school with clear religious goals would not encourage lengthy discussion about whether the school should be open minded about abortion. In program areas of high thrust, such a principal would ensure by direct involvement or by supervision that school objectives and evaluation are tied closely to the agreed upon goals. Table 5 suggests there should be major emphasis on strong individual leadership in program and some emphasis on strong team leadership, with little emphasis on delegation. That does not mean that teachers should not be involved in program but that the administration would take great care to ensure that the objectives, substance and evaluation were all consistent with the school's overall purposes.

This section of the book will doubtless be puzzling to some readers. We have claimed there are few empirically justifiable generalizations that can be made about the principal/teacher relationship. On the other hand, table 5 gives some prescriptive advice about principal/teacher relations in the most important areas of school activity. There is no inconsistency. Firstly, it is clear that table 5 is not a blueprint applicable to every administrator in every situation. Secondly, and more important, the recommendations derive from conceptual ideas about what is important in administration and what is important in education. If the reader does not accept the premises in this book that schools ought to be about bringing about fairly specific changes in students and that administration is concerned with discretionary decision making in a professional manner, then he or she will not find table 5 valuable.

So far we have made two major points: careful thought must be given to the incentives available to teachers and to integrity in their utilization with fellow professionals; and delegation of authority to teachers or groups of teachers must be made thoughtfully, with school administrators retaining some authority over important goals for which they are likely to be held responsible. These ideas are grounded in ideas about ethics and about educational principles.

Selection of Teachers

Teacher selection is a paradoxical exercise for the administrator. On the one hand, 'everyone knows' that teachers make all the difference to pupils. Some teachers consistently achieve better results, in terms of student gains on standardized tests, than others. To be sure, there is some inconsistency when a variety of criteria are applied. Some teachers are well liked by pupils — and that group of teachers will not be identical with the group achieving the high test gain scores. Others are liked by administrators and parents. Once again, although there will be some intersection of the various sets, they will not be coterminous. Nevertheless, one might reach a consensus among administrators, parents and students about a group of good teachers and another of not so good teachers. However possible it may be to identify good teachers after the fact, it is quite impossible, with existing knowledge, to identify in advance the characteristics of good teachers and hence to predict with accuracy who will become good teachers. When picking experienced teachers, the best predictor of future behavior is past behavior.

The research does suggest that people with high verbal ability tend to make effective elementary teachers and that those with advanced specialized training in the subject matter at hand make good secondary teachers (Coleman *et al*, 1966; Summers and Wolfe, 1975). In the light of such evidence, some school systems choose those candidates with strong academic records. There is no evidence that prolonged periods of teacher training or advanced degrees in education are conducive to teaching effectiveness and there is considerable variability in the personalities of effective teachers. None of this should be too surprising. A cliché among experts in personnel is that one is doing well if one-third to one-half of one's appointments are successful. And most jobs are much less complex than teaching.

A further paradox is that administrators usually believe that they can select good teachers. Although the interview is a notoriously ineffective way of selecting personnel, it remains the predominant method of personnel selection in education. Research on interviewing suggests that those conducting interviews tend to select people like themselves. This fact may help build a happy team, depending on the characteristics of the people doing the interviewing, but it will sometimes be unrelated to teaching effectiveness — depending on who conducts the interviewing.

As teacher selection is seen as a key part of the educational process, there has been some jostling for increased participation on the part of elected officials, parents' groups and teachers themselves. What is not understood is that genuine concern that better teachers be appointed is no indicator that better teachers will actually be appointed as a result of people acting on that concern. Given the finding that interviewers tend to select people like themselves, a good bet might be to rely on teams consisting of good teachers (including ex-teachers), but we are unaware of any research to test such interviewing arrangements. By the same token, it seems likely that the addition of representative spokespersons of a variety of special interest groups (be they teachers' unions or ethnic groups) will be counter-productive (i.e., they will use irrelevant criteria).

The creation of interview teams is more likely to be a political than a pedagogical exercise. The term 'political' is not used with any pejorative connotation, except that, obviously, we are concerned that teaching effectiveness be the first criterion for teacher selection. By 'political', we mean 'pertaining to issues of policy, of decision making in the public domain.' Thus concerns over power, authority, territory and representation are likely to be significant considerations in the selection of panels of interviewers. As such considerations are likely to be costly and are unlikely to improve teaching effectiveness, we are generally unenthusiastic. It may be argued that beginning teachers will only have the opportunity to become effective if they are seen as legitimate by students and their parents. Thus within some school cultures, white teachers may be unacceptable in black schools, and middle class teachers may find it hard to teach students in inner-city schools; alternatively, they may forsake their educational mission in an attempt to become accepted.

There is no simple answer to a problem that has complex political, moral and educational elements. If indeed there is angry concern in the community, then political considerations will have to be taken into account. If they have not already done so, they are likely soon to be interfering with the educational process in the school. On the other hand, if there is tacit acceptance of the principal's authority, the principal may reasonably feel disinclined to waken a sleeping tiger.

The central issue should be the best educational interests of students (as developed in Chapter 1), but that presupposes some agreement about educational goals and the principal's legitimate authority. Ideally, we believe that there should be consensus about goals and that the principal should represent (model, stand for, support) those goals.

A possible approach in a divided community is for the principal to set up an advisory committee for teacher selection, comprising good teachers in the school and representatives from the minority community. Once formed, it should become normal for the principal to accept the recommendations of such a committee. Alternatively, the principal may chair the committee and thus influence its choice directly (but thereby lose the vestigial right to veto).

The last illustration raises the question of decentralization to the level of the school. The discussion so far assumes that the authority to select teachers has been delegated by the school district to the school. In practice, in many large bureaucratic systems, that power is not delegated, particularly to the elementary school. The usual arguments against delegation are: (i) a centralized search and placement agency is much more efficient; (ii) central hiring ensures that the system does hire exceptional prospects, as and when they become available; (iii) local hiring often leads to undesirable practices such as nepotism, favoritism, hiring of community people associated informally with the school, and hiring of local supply teachers who are known to the principal; (iv) centralized hiring ensures that routine, bureaucratic procedures are followed, e.g., references and credentials are routinely checked. These arguments lose weight when centralization is applied only at the elementary level; administrative convenience would appear to be the strongest argument for application at one level rather than the other. The central administration is open to no less pressure from community groups and individuals than is a principal. In fact, it may be harder for the chief executive officer, who owes a few favors to a local politician, to refuse to hire the politician's son, than it would be for the principal, who can hide behind bureaucratic rules and policies and the in-school committee. In general, we favor decision making at the level of the school provided there is clear accountability.

One aspect of teacher selection needs mention because it is so often overlooked. Most discussions of teacher selection, like this one to this point, assume there is a specified vacancy to be filled and the task is merely to select the best person — whether it be for senior physics or third grade. What often goes unconsidered is the determination of the vacancy. This is particularly so in stable situations, where there is little change in staff numbers over the years or where there is the occasional addition. If enrolments are increasing, principals enjoy the luxury of determining which area most needs an additional teacher, although they rarely stop to consider if some areas are already overstaffed. If enrolments are declining, the loss of three teachers and authorization to hire one replacement assures deliberate decision making. It is in the stable situation where it is particularly important to give consideration to whether the place vacated is really the one that most needs filling. In Chapter 3, we mentioned the advantages of inter-class grouping, whereby classes at several grade levels are sychronized in English and mathematics, possibly in combination with the setting up of homogeneous groups within each class. That kind of arrangement makes it much easier to hire a specialist in French or music or physical education instead of a second third grade teacher, particularly if the specialist is also able and willing to teach some other subjects. Similarly, the departure of an English teacher in high school does not mean necessarily that an English teacher must be hired. Even from the point of view of mathematical 'fairness', there may have been changes in enrolment patterns that have given some other subjects a more inappropriate teacher/pupil ratio. Or if the collective agreement permits, a teaching vacancy provides a rare opportunity for the principal and school staff to determine school policy. There may be some vocational subject, for example, nursery management and market gardening, banking and insurance, computer operation and maintenance, not currently offered, that could become a viable program offering for a significant number of students now mired in a rudderless general academic program. There may be an academic area that could be built into an area of real strength. It is easy to maintain an existing pattern without considering whether it best suits one's hopes and policies, simply blaming 'them' for not providing the extra teachers for the program one wants. Mediocre schools and principals wallow in such helplessness — happy always to have someone else to blame.

In general, it makes sense for teacher selection to be carried out at the school level if: (i) the school has a set of consensual goals; (ii) the school is being held accountable in a formal way for progress towards the agreed goals; (iii) advertising is widespread and there are established procedures for making equivalent information available to the selection committee with respect to all candidates. It may be valuable for a school district person to provide background advice or to sit on the selection committee. There should be a clear understanding of the respective roles of the committee and the principal. The greater the consensus the easier it should be for the principal to make a decision, and for that decision to be both accepted and welcomed.

The Supervision of Teachers

Teacher supervision, or, euphemistically, the improvement of instruction has been the stuff of school administration for a number of years. Most progressive school systems pride themselves on having evaluation policies for teachers and principals, and the most progressive include policies for all senior administrators as well. Yet, there is no empirical evidence that 'improvement of instruction' actually improves instruction; many principals dislike supervising teachers, and teachers, while they do not dislike being visited, strongly resist the application of any tough model of evaluation. It would probably not be unfair to say that teachers tolerate supervision amiably as long as it is not a means to threaten them or to bring about major change.

If it does not work, if principals do not like it, and teachers subvert it, how is it so persistent? Here are two related suggestions. Firstly, the development of educational administration as a business, and a practice, as a 'profession', has coincided with the growth of the psychological and sociological study of administration. In a psychological era such as ours, it should not be surprising that a new area of study should concern itself with leadership; decision making, morale, team building, and supervision. The premise that we live in a psychological age may be questioned. Yet schools are so imbued with psychology, admittedly from various and incompatible camps, that to question many common assertions is to assume the mantle of heresy. For example, the transparently false statement that all decisions in schools must be made in the best interests of the individual child is widely accepted as an uncomplicated truth. Educators and lay people alike persist in this transparent falsehood even though it should be obvious to all the school is a social institution and that, for example, the safety of the many must come before the welfare of a single individual. Incredible mental gymnastics are performed to persuade oneself that quite reasonable actions, such as suspending an unruly child or making a lazy, unimproving child repeat a grade, are committed in the best interests of the individual, leading oneself no recourse but 'unreasonable' action when the falsehood is revealed. Thus the provision of 'help' to the individual teacher is quite in keeping with the cult of the helping professions. These are therapeutic times.

Secondly, the development of educational administration has led to bureaucracies looking for activities that are unthreatening. Most texts discuss the methods by which teacher evaluation should be carried out, without worrying about justifying the activity itself. Little consideration is given in public school circles to the anomaly that in most countries independent schools are considered superior to public schools; yet they manage quite well without much supervisory bureaucracy.

The dichotomy in teacher supervision is widely but not universally recognized. The modern fiction that administrators are mainly helpers is well served by the idea that the first reason for teacher supervision is to help teachers improve. There are two assumptions: that it is appropriate for administrators to help teachers and that administrators can in fact help them. The appropriateness of administrators acting as helpers is discussed later. On the second point, it is worth noting that there is no evidence that administrative help actually works. Certainly, most teachers and administrators know, from their own experience, of odd occasions when administrative intervention has solved problems and improved teaching effectiveness. Those cases of successful intervention have, almost without exception, two characteristics: (i) the teacher involved is very inexperienced and is, in fact, receiving help from a senior colleague or mentor, and (ii) the intervention is not unwelcome. Neither of those conditions is universal or even common. The other and less talked of purpose of teacher supervision is the maintenance of minimum standards. Administrators are expected to develop a case for dismissal against incompetent teachers. Now, helping teachers is a very different matter from proving them incompetent, even though the administrator is expected to help a possibly incompetent teacher reach minimal competence before attempting to build a case for dismissal. The juxtaposition of those two expectations of the administrator is a delicate one. For example, strong rigorous advice on how the teacher should proceed, which is first followed and subsequently found ineffective, may not be the best foundation for a court case examining the subsequent dismissal of the teacher. In practice, administrators tend to work in two phases — an initial helping phase followed by a despairing case-building phase. Naturally, the administrator hopes that either the advice will be taken and minimal competence achieved or the advice will be spurned and a case for dismissal can be solidly built. The circumstance where the advice is followed unsuccessfully is unwelcome. Not much talked about, this second purpose of teacher supervision is universally accepted, even though strong advocates of administrators as helpers like to ignore or downplay it.

The gate-keeping role of the administrator includes a helping role within it. It is not considered fair labor practice to dismiss an employee for cause without giving reasonable prior warning, except in an extreme case. And the warning should normally be accompanied by an offer of assistance.

Even so, the administrator should keep a humble and respectful distance. Teachers succeed, and fail, in countless different ways. If the principal has a fail-safe recipe, why has it not been published and adopted universally? Even a young teacher, once pronounced qualified, is a professional. Young doctors and dentists are not given summary and binding advice by their senior colleagues. Perhaps teachers, like doctors and dentists, should experience serious, supervised internship. In the meantime, they should be treated as the young, qualified professionals they are. The principal should help but it should be very clear that acceptance of the advice is voluntary — they will not be dismissed for not following the advice, but they will be dismissed for failing to teach effectively. Thus, there is no questioning the value of the school administrator, preferably working cooperatively with others, determining a minimum level of accepted competence, primarily as a gate-keeper for new entrants into the profession, but also for the maintenance of minimal competence in senior teachers.

Much more doubtful is the appropriateness of the role of the administrator in formal evaluation of teachers for purposes of 'improvement of instruction'. It is difficult to oppose something so self-evidently good as improving instruction. Nevertheless, one must be sceptical about the effectiveness of improving instruction by means of the activities usually referred to as supervision, normally within a plan for formal evaluation. Principals are encouraged to be free with praise. Teachers naturally enjoy praise as does everybody else and it may be useful, providing that it reinforces genuinely good work. Unfortunately, principals have little or no sound information on the methods of achieving school goals. Hence their praise is likely to be random, directed towards some superficially appealing novelty, or insincere.

Of particularly questionable value is the regular, annual formal evaluation of competent teachers. We have read hundreds of these evaluations and they are remarkably uniform. They are all positive, usually glowing. Frequently, the things praised are characteristics not associated in the literature with gains in pupil achievement. For example, teachers today are much more likely to be commented on favorably for grouping and individualization than for whole class instruction in the achievement of mastery of skills.

This is not to assert that administrators should ignore teachers or fail to take an interest in their work. It is just that bureaucratic plans for formal supervision usually assume that much more is known about good teaching than is actually the case, that administrators are generally up-to-date in their understanding of pedagogical research, and that they know how to change teachers' behavior. For reasons not to the discredit of the average administrator these assumptions are not sensible ones.

There follow some suggestions which make sense at the conceptual level and which are not inconsistent with research findings:

(i) Supervise closely teachers whose performance is marginal or worse. Teachers are usually dismissed for inability to control the class. Teachers whose students learn very little should also be monitored closely and dismissed if they fail to improve.

(ii) Check regularly what children are achieving in all subjects at all grades by regularly sampling good, average and poor examples of work.

(iii) Praise teachers whose students do particularly well — academically, morally, aesthetically, socially, physically. Try to assess progress also in terms of improvement over time and in accord with the students' own personal characteristics stemming from natural intelligence and cultural support at home.

(iv) Make sure that teachers recognize that the administrator cares first about what students are doing and learning.

(v) Provide direct help to teachers who are not doing something well, i.e., whose teaching outcomes are only adequate or less than adequate. The administrator should be always able and willing to provide help to those who directly or indirectly indicate they want help. This requires that the administrator know good sources of help, making as much use of the informal network as the formal network.

(vi) Confine negative comments to areas where there is clear evidence of failure, for example, advanced or poor groups of students ignored; inadequate patterns of student evaluation; things not learned; poor behavior or rudeness on the part of the class. Avoid commenting negatively about the teaching process just because it happens to be uncongenial to the administrator.

(vii) Make clear that the central concern is what students are learning, not what the teachers are doing.

Three legitimate purposes for supervision emerge from this discussion: (i) to dismiss teachers who are unable to maintain a minimum standard of competence; (ii) to maintain a vigilant eye on the mediocre so that ineffectual teachers, even though they may have adequate control over their classes, either improve their teaching effectiveness or are dismissed; and (iii) to provide incentives, encouragement and assistance to good teachers to keep up or improve their professional practice.

The most common approach to teacher supervision and evaluation is the use of a schedule of evaluation by the principal and other administrators. The administrator visits the classroom for two or three periods, in different subjects and grades as appropriate, and writes up an evaluation report covering such aspects as: the teacher's preparation and lesson plan;

the atmosphere in the classroom; presentation of the lesson, for example, is there review, a statement of purpose, an exposition, question and answers, an assignment, a conclusion?; the students' behavior; the students' work as evidenced by their books and by their oral questions and answers. The final evaluation includes comments from the lesson reviews together with the general comments on the teacher's professional comportment and involvement in extracurricular activities. That method of evaluation, which, in practice, is frequently reduced to little beyond a few class visits, does meet, to some degree, the first criterion in a very limited way. But it is inordinately inefficient. It involves the recording of many details on paper, of which the audience — the teacher — is well aware.

This method, broadly applied, does weed out extreme imcompetence but it does not meet at all satisfactorily the criteria listed later — the day-to-day provision of help and encouragement; the emphasis of students' work rather than teachers' behavior and the limitation of negative comments and 'suggestions for improvement' to incontrovertibly bad teaching outcomes or unethical behavior.

This very typical approach serves in a random manner as an incentive to effective teachers. In the event that the supervisor knows what effective teaching looks like, it may reinforce good pedagogy. More often, ignorance does not prevent administrators from believing they know what they are looking for. Their predilections are idiosyncratic, a matter for humor or irritation in the staffroom. Overall, the effect on good teachers is likely to be neutral to negative, negative if teachers half heartedly make methodological changes they do not like just to keep the principal happy. It is important to emphasize again that administrative ignorance is not a matter for which principals themselves should be blamed. Partly, knowledge about good teaching practice is extremely limited; and what knowledge there is is considered irrelevant or uninteresting by many educational 'experts' whose own philosophies make it irrelevant.

Another fairly common method of evaluation, which melds imperceptibly with the first, is the informal method. On paper, it may look the same. In practice, the principal tends to await some exceptional circumstance before conducting an evaluation. Most usually, the exception is some form of negative evidence. The principal receives complaints from parents, students or other teachers and decides to find out what is going on. The evaluation policy, if there is one, lies fallow until it is activated by a problem. More rarely, the administrator may evaluate an excellent teacher, to provide encouragement and support to someone making an exceptional effort who wants a good reference for a promotion. The process of evaluation is similar to that used in the first method. However, it tends to be more *ad hoc* in style and less comprehensive.

In many ways, this method is preferable to the first. It is much more efficient and, if pursued diligently, just as effective in meeting the first two criteria. It lacks the negative effects of the first approach to a significant degree. However, great care has to be taken if dismissals for incompetence are not to be rejected on legal grounds. As regular supervision and 'improvement of instruction' become normative concepts, however false the assumptions on which they are based, the courts are coming to look unkindly on evaluation procedures that are transparently *ad hoc* and not highly bureaucratized. This may be unduly alarmist in some school districts, but, within a bureaucracy, the advice of the 'experts' carries considerable weight. Many 'experts' are likely to tell a court of inquiry that regular supervision and evaluation are necessary for effective administration.

It should also not be overlooked that there can easily be substance behind such apparently legalistic complications. The *ad hoc* evaluator, even more than the regular evaluator, may well determine, in advance, on the basis of complaints, that a teacher is incompetent and then go after him or her. A series of closely spaced classroom visits resulting in lengthy negative comments after years of neglect are understandably suspect in the eyes of external arbitrators. If the teacher has been ineffective for a long time, why was the poor performance not noticed before? If poor performance only began recently, should not the years of good teaching count for something? Is the problem only a temporary one? Even if this informal method proves legal, as it well may in less bureaucratized school districts, the burden of demonstrating fairness to colleagues remains with the administrator. In a traditional school in a stable community, that may not be difficult. The community, particularly the school community, recognizes the incompetent teacher, and the dirty job of removing that teacher receives tacit support from nearly everyone concerned, including most teachers. However, in a large urban high school, with prevailing disaffection among teachers and students, a perception of fairness will be difficult or impossible to establish. Unionized teachers will see a move against one of their members as a threat to them all. They are also likely to be less aware of the teacher's real deficiencies and a sudden evaluation will quickly be characterized as arbitrary and capricious.

A third approach to teacher evaluation is to change the focus of the evaluation from the process to the product. Instead of looking at teaching, plans and classroom walls, the administrator looks at the changes brought about by the teacher in the learners. Measures of outcomes include: standardized test scores; teacher made test results; manners and civility of students under and outside the teacher's surveillance; attitudes and level of participation in class activities inside and outside the regular program. The emphasis here is on the changes of pupils' behavior for which the teacher can take some responsibility, i.e., the value added. At its crudest, there may simply be a comparison of teachers' test results. In the most sophisticated form, a prediction is made of the pupils' performance based on their past performance, with which the actual performance, under the teacher's direction, is compared.

There are several objections to this procedure. It is claimed that our ability to measure student achievement is poor, and that any measurement of gains is equally unreliable. In Chapter 3, we noted the lack of relationship between instructional time and achievement in English after pupils reach the age of about twelve. An average improvement of little more than zero among adolescents would be perfectly normal in that subject. The answer to that criticism is that standardized test scores, where available and where appropriate, should form only one portion of the measure of achievement. In English, the reading and writing understood and accomplished while under instruction by the teacher is all part of the outcome. Further, one of the reasons why there is so little improvement in some subjects may well be precisely because no one is interested in the outcome — the emphasis is almost solely on the process. The second objection is that if teachers are evaluated according to results they will become overly results oriented and goals which cannot be expressed in easily quantifiable terms will be jettisoned. There are two answers to that. One is that good teachers will continue to work towards a complete set of goals, as they do now. The other is that a sound evaluation scheme will emcompass all outcomes, not only those easily measured. The third and most potent objection is that, on the whole, teachers do not like it. This third method of evaluation introduces a measure of accountability that neither of the others does. Clearly, the measures of process can only pick out the extreme deviant, who cannot control the class, or the deliberate obstructionist who openly defies legitimate orders (which modern administrators are loathe to give — it is one thing to describe the implementation of a new curriculum as mandatory, quite another to order a teacher to teach concept X inductively rather than deductively). With measured outcomes, however, it is possible to set a zone of acceptability, and warn all teachers whose students, on average, fall below the acceptable minimum gain.

Some combination of the second and third methods is probably the least evil, more bureaucratized where necessary, a minimal bureaucracy where possible. At first sight, the second and third methods may seem polar opposites. Is not the second method a *laissez-faire* approach? And the third an attempt to bring science to bear on human problems? To the contrary, a good case can be made that a careful record of student progress should be kept for instructional purposes and for communication to parents. The subsequent use of it for evaluative purposes (in terms of teachers) is incidental and secondary. Thus with this combination there need be no regular, formal evaluation scheduled for teachers and no undignified race to get the best standardized achievement test gain scores. But the results will be available in the case of a teacher who appears to be unsuccessful and unprofessional. In the same way, careful records are kept of patients' progress in hospital. The main purpose is not to evaluate the competency of the attending physicians but to provide the best care to the patient. Even so, if Dr. Owen's patients keep dying because swabs are left in peritoneal cavities, then allegations of malpractice will surely fly and careful records will be a valuable aid to a reasonable judgment. Certainly, the combination of the second and third methods is likely to provide the best incentive for effective teaching. The third approach alone might work for a period of time in some circumstances. However, human beings have a number of ways of responding to threats — and they are not always the ones administrators anticipate. For example, it is possible that teachers would consensually work towards some mediocre central level of achievement, to avoid odious comparisons. Others might simply be content to sit back once the minimum level of competence was assured. Others might deliberately set out to focus on different goals, and thus challenge the legitimacy of the administrators' criteria.

Most supervisory practices effectively ignore what students achieve, except in the most extreme cases. For that reason, they have almost no value beyond their function of very occasionally getting rid of the extreme incompetent unable to control a class of students. It seems probable that most principals can help their schools more by other activities than by time-consuming bureaucratized plans for teacher supervision and evaluation. However, we have made some common sense suggestions for administrative supervision. Any formal plan for supervision should focus on a broad review of the changes teachers bring about in students. It is professionally and pedagogically undesirable to focus on the teacher's delivery of the lesson.

Informal Relations with Teachers

We have expressed considerable sceptism about most formal plans for teacher evaluation, at the same time recognizing that some system is necessary for the two basic purposes we mentioned. We are not alone in this scepticism. Ryan and Hickcox (1980) write of the commonest form of evaluation, classroom observation, that it is ' . . . beset with such difficulties that one could even argue that it is dysfuntional to the achievement of better teaching and learning' (p. 113).

The fact that there is some obvious incompatibility between evaluation to 'help' teachers improve and to determine whether or not they should be fired, and the lack of evidence that regular evaluation improves effectiveness do not combine to demonstrate that teachers can be 'helped' to improve informally. It should not be overlooked that in-service training within other professions is only mandatory in the most obviously and conceptually necessary circumstances. Most professionals, sensing the need for help in difficult and changing areas, will take reasonable opportunities for additional training if those opportunities are reasonably supplied. Further, employees generally may respond to genuine interest by the employer. People work better, it is claimed, if they feel their work matters, if they feel it is appreciated. Such major corporations as Volvo and Saab, in Sweden, have instituted alternatives to the traditional assembly line whereby teams of workers take responsibility for the entire production of a vehicle, instead of each individual having responsibility for only one monotonous and meaningless job on the line. One of the reasons for Japanese industrial success is said to be the sense of corporate belonging that employees develop in Japan — with employer and employees working together in harmony, rather than in constant tension. This forms part of the rather vague Theory Z sometimes claimed to succeed McGregor's Theories X and Y. However, industrial analogies, like medical analogies, must be treated with care. Would a physician feel more rewarded by receiving a letter of commendation for her medical skills from the hospital administrator or from seeing her patients make remarkable recovery after a difficult and unusual operation? Would a teacher feel more reward from a letter of commendation from the principal about preparatory work for the Christmas concert or from seeing children read avidly who had previously been unable and unwilling to read? But neither the industrial nor the medical analogy is always applicable. Schooling is not a factory and principals, unlike hospital administrators, are professional colleagues of teachers.

On balance, letters and comments, approving and disapproving, outside the framework of formal assessment schemes seem to make much sense. However, they can be easily abused. At one time, teachers in training used to be told of psychological research into the allocation of grades and favorable comments. Apparently, even when grades and comments were distributed randomly, the future performance of the recipients improved. The implication of the research was that praise serves as an incentive and therefore should be provided freely; the more frequent the praise, the less the criticism, the better the product. The same principle is being applied to relationships between principal and teachers.

Put in terms of exchange theory, the psychologists are suggesting that by giving frequent gifts (praise), supervisors are pressing employees to reciprocate in the form of better work. (Put in those terms, the manipulation seems, as it is, rather crude.) But exchange theory suggests, as already noted, that there are two circumstances that disarm the potency of the gift — one is where the recipient is indifferent to the gift (and any related sanction); the other is where the giving is not seen as being genuine. Indifference to the gift of praise of a supervisor is difficult to predict. However, teachers who strongly dislike a particular principal are likely to be indifferent to praise from that individual. However, such dislike is not evident in many situations and even where it is evident it is often transitory. If a teacher believes a principal is incompetent in the area where praise is bestowed (for example, a principal's praise of art produced by students when the principal is well known as an artistic philistine), indifference is also likely to be the result. If a supervisor provides equal praise to all or nearly all the employees, indifference is almost certain to be the result among the more accomplished as they coldly assess their colleagues' contributions. (That fact, by itself, does not invalidate the manipulative force of praise — those who have made few contributions may feel encouraged.) The second weakness of gifts, lack of genuineness and spontaneity, is more fundamental. Indifference is often caused partly by a suspicion of calculated Machievellian manipulation. The indifference resulting from praise by an enemy has as a source of origin the fear that it is calculated for some evil purpose. To disorient the employee? To disarm the employee's antagonism? To make it more difficult for the employee to attack some future plan?

Suppose a boss gives every employee a Christmas bonus of $1,000. In the first instance, all will be pleased and are likely to work harder as a result. Suppose this happens regularly. There is likely to be some diminution in the effect with each recurrence — as the gift becomes expected. It is no longer seen as being spontaneous and genuine; it becomes part of the normal set of expected rewards. Thus, in a short experimental period, there is likely to be a positive response to an increase in praise, but that response is unlikely to persist. Now suppose that, at the same time as the superior gives everyone $1,000, it becomes known that the dollar has lost its value to inflation. Clearly, the employees will not only be less rewarded — they will be resentful that the gift has not maintained its previous value. Perhaps they will ask the boss to index the Christmas gift. In the same way, suppose the teachers who are to receive increased praise realize that it no longer has the currency it used to have — they will need more and more praise just to maintain their previous morale. Their response is likely to be resentment at being used. In other words, once praise is seen as being a mechanism for manipulation of behavior and as being hardly or not at all related to the act being praised, it loses most of its value.

Hence our emphasis on genuine, sincere, spontaneous praise. 'Genuine' is not a synonym for 'sincere.' If one pays one's grocery bill with a forged $50 bill, one's sincerity does not affect the validity of the transaction. Sincerity is a part but by no means the whole of social exchange. Sincere praise is certainly to be valued, but the sincerity is insufficient. A principal may sincerely praise, through an excess of ignorance or enthusiasm, bad art, bad writing, bad singing and bad soccer. The praise is soon seen as worthless when 'the best team in town' loses to every other team in town.

We suggest that informal praise should be provided as much as possible outside the formal supervisory procedure. It will be said in a highly bureaucratized system there can be no such thing as informal praise and criticism. At the time of a grievance hearing, all is grist to the mill. A few casual words of praise, it is said, will come back to haunt the principal who has subsequently sought to dismiss or reprimand the previously praised individual. There is no good answer to that criticism. Every informal administrative act, whether spoken or written can become evidence in a grievance. One cannot avoid all problems, but one can avoid those caused by empty rhetoric and insincerity. In a highly bureaucratized system, there is in fact danger in any informal activity. But the danger is far greater if the praise provided is insincere, and greater still if it is invalid. We do not want to give the impression that the major objection to insincere and inauthentic rewards is unfortunate bureaucratic consequences. Throughout this book, we argue that the principal should represent the moral and ethical behavior the school seeks to teach, not because of any contractual commitment, but because it is right.

Friendship with Teachers

No line can be drawn between informal supervision and other informal interaction between administrators and teachers. It is a great mistake to assume that informal interaction outside school and formal and informal interaction inside school can continue independently without one interfering with the other. This is not to suggest that the principal must wear the administrative hat on social occasions. From the point of view of exchange theory, within an organization, the function of social interaction is the same as that of other gifts — such as praise. Indeed, the genuine, spontaneous involvement of administrators in social occasions may be one of the most potent forces affecting teacher/administrator relationships. The gifts, obviously, are reciprocal and mutually reinforcing. Friendship between superordinate and employee, like any other type of friendship, constrains the freedom of both parties. It also, at the same time, permits some activity that otherwise would be unacceptable.

Suppose that a principal is expected by the school district to implement a new history program. The principal is an ex-history teacher and a close friend of several teachers in the department. The principal genuinely approves of the new program and wants to see it implemented properly. The department members like their existing program and are reluctant to change. The principal has three possible courses of action: (i) give the implementation full support; (ii) persuade the department that the new program is to be implemented because the school district mandates it all the while shedding crocodile tears; (iii) side with the department and oppose implementation. All three choices have consequences. The first and obvious course of action may lose the principal, at least temporarily, friendship and important support (the support of the history department is the principal's only constant source in the organization). The second course of action is hypocritical and manipulative and therefore unethical. It is also unlikely to lead to sound implementation. The third course of action is cowardly and means the sacrifice of the students' best interests (as interpreted by the principal).

Consider the situation where a department head is to be appointed and one applicant is a staff member who is also a personal friend of the principal — but the applicant is recognized by the principal as being second or third best. The issue has ramifications beyond the immediate friendship of the two people. Loyalty to friends is a virtue, and the choice of the best applicant may have reverberations throughout the staff, particularly in the case of other friends. This is not to suggest that the friend should get the job, merely that there are unpleasant consequences of his or her not getting it. Yet remoteness and distance also exact a price. After all, the exchange of gifts (and exchange of friendship and support is one of the most influential gifts) promotes social cohesion. Imagine a 'family' where there is almost no social exchange. It would not in fact be a genuine family. Once again, it is the spontaneity rather than the contractual gift that does most for social cohesion within the family and within the school. The staff will be pleased that the schedule is prepared on time, that the school is kept clean, that buses run punctually, and that duties are assigned fairly and efficiently. Those are all contractual gifts. But if the principal jokes with teachers, teaches a class for them so they can get away early in an emergency, and steers angry parents first to the administrative office instead of the teachers' classroom, in short, does things for which there is no assumed legal contract, then there is the foundation of a social relationship with mutual bonds. Remoteness entails an absence of feeling and therefore a reluctance to help beyond the bounds of the legal contract, precisely because the reciprocal bonds are thereby strengthened beyond the legal contract. Even amiability, once it is reciprocated, can be a negative force if it is seen to conceal an underlying unwillingness to provide genuine help.

There are dangers in either extreme — strong ties of friendship and remoteness and distance. Close social relationships and family ties incur obligations whose fulfilment is likely to create major professional difficulty. Absence of social ties promotes a barren legalism whereby everybody goes exactly by the book, by policy and by the collective agreement. A major side effect of growing unionism in schools is just such a resort to legalism. As more and more administrative areas of discretion are challenged, more and more policies and rules are developed, leaving very little room for spontaneous social interaction and the provision of genuine gifts. On balance, with all their potential dangers, positive social relations are to be preferred. A true, deep friendship (itself increasingly rare in modern society where social and geographical mobility together with increasing individualism make it difficult) should survive a case of pedagogical disagreement of non-promotion; with less strong forms of social relationship there may well be greater resentment precisely because, 'I thought you liked me and you always gave the impression I was doing a good job.' The principal knows both those statements to be true — but they do not make that teacher the best candidate for the job.

It may not seem very helpful to say that moderation is the answer — neither too many ties of social relationship nor too much remoteness and distance. The truth is that genuine, transparent honesty and integrity can make that middle way possible. The good principal will enjoy good social relationships with all or nearly all teachers in a positive way. There will be stronger relationships with some teachers, and not necessarily always the most competent. At the same time, there will be a clear understanding that the school is to be run in the best interests of students and that educational decisions will be made on that basis and not on a basis of comradeship or friendship. One of the problems is the lack of clarity in our use of and thinking about language. We use 'friendship' to denote the deep, lasting bonds described by Aristotle but also to describe the weak bonds of day-to-day amiable camaraderie.

Dealing with Unions

Bureaucratization based on collective bargaining can grow in either climate — where the administration is cold and aloof and where it is warm and friendly. The roots of unionism rarely reside in a single school. A warm and friendly climate, particularly if staff are only slightly unionized, i.e., the collective agreement only deals with workload in a cursory way, permits the exercise of administrative discretion. But use of that discretion is fraught with danger when unionism is strong in the surrounding environment.

Teachers may occasionally want a half day off to visit a daughter's graduation or to visit a sick relative. The principal may choose to fill in, even though the authority is not granted by policy or by the collective agreement. Let us suppose that a kindly principal accedes to a number of such requests. Then, one day, a teacher asks permission to leave early to go home and see a sick child. The teacher in question has a record of poor attendance, late arrival and early departure about which the principal has said nothing, not wishing to compromise the high morale of the staff. So the principal refuses. The teacher may well take the matter to grievance or the matter may be taken up by some form of union management committee within the school, if such is allowed for in the contract. Either way, the process of unionization is accelerated and administrative discretion is curtailed. Every decision favorable to employees becomes a precedent and the variable use of disc- retion can readily be seen as being unfairly discriminatory. The union may well be able to show that the kindly principal has been very friendly with those teachers who are given time off, and not with the teacher who was refused. That is quite likely to be the case; in general, school administrators are likely to get on better with the more competent, the more industrious, the more supportive than with the less. Where there is disagreement or ambiguity about the principal's motives, a tribunal is quite likely to resort to precedent — what is given to one should be given to others unless there is a clear, public record of qualitatively or quantitavely different behavior with respect to public, legitimate school policies.

In a situation where the administrator is more remote there is likely to be little discretionary activity, but, 'going by the book' may still turn out to be unfair. Beginning teachers may receive more difficult and larger classes than senior teachers — not by deliberate policy, but because consultation with department heads leads to situations reflecting the prevailing power structure. First year teachers are not there in the spring to be consulted. The union may decide this prevalent practice as an issue to run with, with or without a formal grievance, particularly if the administrator decides to let go one of the beginning, probationary teachers (who of course were not consulted about the assignments) and if the senior department heads are weak supporters of the union.

The most elaborate policies and collective agreements require interpretation. Indeed, the more elaborate the clause the more definitions and subclauses required. As the complexities of human behavior in schools cannot (and ought not to) be adequately captured in manuals and collective agreements, ambiguity and manifest unfairness may result from the application of a ruling designed to solve one problem without consideration of others not appreciated at the time.

The earlier examples illustrate the commonest issue leading to labor relations problems with teachers: the discriminatory (not necessarily unfairly discriminatory, although that is the union's charge) use of discretion; the abuse of authority. The more mistakes made by administrators the more their authority is rolled back. Note also that a single minor mistake by one vice-principal can lead to the roll back of authority in all schools in an entire school district.

An important point here is that unionization does not affect school administrators only through the formal, bureaucratic framework, i.e., through collective agreements and grievances. The threat of a grievance, even one that is clearly ill-founded — and it is rare that either side can be completely sure of the outcome of any particular grievance — soon becomes a potent threat to the administrator, who is in time likely to retreat to a bureaucratic style.

It follows that a lengthy collective agreement does not necessarily determine a unionized bureaucratic school. Just as teachers may use a flimsy agreement to threaten administrators with more, so collective agreements, like any other policy documents may gather dust in a closet as the benevolently despotic head continues to work happily with teachers who like it that way. The social structure in that latter situation is always precarious — a small group of hostile teachers may activate the available mechanisms at any time.

As administrative discretion is steadily rolled back in most unionized situations, issues arise from interpretation of collective agreements and from alleged breaking of the terms of the collective agreements. Sometimes these issues stem from one side or other trying to bend the agreement. Very often, they arise from genuinely different understandings by the two parties, each being guided by its own mind set during negotiations. Often they arise when the agreement is applied to situations which had not been fully envisaged when the aggreement was made. Agreements tend to be hammered out in the heat of battle — and every possible future contingency is not foreseen.

The movement towards unionization tends to become self-reinforcing. If administrative discretion remains, inevitably there will be some dissatisfaction with its use. If it is eliminated, the application of detailed rules and policies inevitably leads to interpretive problems. Concessions by the legitimate authority are seen as signs of weakness and admissions of previous wrongdoing. A firm stand by the legitimate authority is seen as obduracy and a determination to 'save face' whatever the circumstances.

One way for school administrators to deal with the problem of growing unionization is to change from a reactive to a proactive stand. When faced with growing militancy, the tendency of administrators is to lie low, hoping that things will quieten down and work themselves out. They are gradually forced into a situation where they merely react to problems and accusations — unless they happen to work in a quiet backwater uninterested in the collective agreement in the first place. Agendas of union management committees are replete with complaints on every conceivable issue. With forethought however, the administrator can see many of the problems before they arise and take them to the parity committee or to the union representative for advice. This amounts, in practice, to a degree of co-management as it is inconceivable that a principal can ask for advice and then proceed to ignore it every time it conflicts with prior wishes. There must be a zone of tolerance for parity committee recommendations. The administration thereby overtly accepts some loss of discretionary authority. But regular administrative contributions to the agenda do give the administration much more control over the field of activity — and forces the union to accept some of the consequences of unpleasant decisions.

The union is in a position of particular strength as long as it can use the collective agreement to advance a barrage of complaints, grievances and even personal attacks. The principal loses more and more authority by reacting and by waiting for the next onslaught than by openly bringing issues to the union so that its recommendations become public. In terms of the styles described in Chapter 2, the reactive principal becomes a bureaucrat, the proactive principal a consultative bureaucrat.

In the long term, it seems improbable that a trend to unionization can be reversed within a closed system. There are times when unions make no progress and other times when a satisfactory co-existence appears to work quite well. It seems likely, however, that the decline of unions only comes about by means of external pressure or intervention. Thus, over the last three decades the proportion of Canadian workers in unions has increased, while the proportion in the USA has declined. The difference is usually attributed by labor analysts to two factors: the deliberate 'union busting' tactics used by some major corporations in the USA and the move of industry from the unionized northeast to southern states where unions are weak and 'right to work' is strong.

In education, the growth of private schools, particularly in combination with some form of state aid or voucher system poses the greatest threat to the unionization of school staff. In England, legislation was introduced in 1987 to permit schools to leave the local school system and receive direct funding from the state. The proposal, although widely attacked by educators, has received strong public support probably because the schools are seen as being overly unionized and working too much in the interests of employees rather than students.

It will be evident from the above discussion that we are unsympathetic to strong union structures in schools, although we do recognize that in some situations they may be a lesser evil than the alternative at a particular moment in time. An assumption throughout this book is that the principal is a professional educator who ought to have significant influence on the running of the school. That does not mean that authority should be either total or unfettered. It by no means excludes cooperative administration involving representative school committees in different forms. In Chapter 1, it was argued that all schools should have a focused sense of purpose; it is from that sense of mission that the principal's authority over teachers derives. To be sure there is also some managerial authority required to keep the organization going — but the exercise of that particular form of authority does not require a professional educator. The principal as professional educator embodies, models and symbolizes the school's purposes.

A frequently heard response to our position is that the principal can still exercise influence without a great deal of legal authority — adopting the role of bureaucrat or democrat for example. Thus, the principal's authority becomes informal rather than legal, earned rather than announced. By this account, the principal is more consultant than boss.

In the context of and generally in opposition to that widely held notion, the argument here in favor of hierarchy is based on two propositions. First, influence is often dependent on or enhanced by legal authority. The principal ought to be ultimately responsible for some aspects of the behavior of teachers: (i) managerial matters — attendance, completion of records etc.; (ii) the goals and objectives towards which they work; (iii) the evaluation of students and program; (iv) sequence and significant content in curricula. That formal responsibility requires some formal authority. The principal should not have to rely on informal influence, which may not work. Second, the existence of significant formal authority by no means excludes informal or moral authority; indeed the two easily go hand in hand. Without legitimate authority, principals may change teachers by persuasion, unethical manipulation or by charisma. As persuasion often does not work, principals without much legitimate authority often either provide little leadership or resort to manipulation. It is not suprising then, that some of those quite opposed to hierarchical authority appear to implicitly accept Machievellian manipulation. This theme is continued in Chapter 6.

The Teacher as a Professional

As well as having a managerial relationship with teachers, the principal also has to cope with the even more difficult 'professional' relationship. We have already noted the difficulties inherent in the managerial relationship. The proportion of employees (teachers and other staff) to managers (educational administrators) is high and teachers often disparage what is derisively called 'administrivia.' But hierarchical relationships among professionals are always particularly delicate. Among physicians, the notion of hierarchy is generally avoided; specialists, although better paid, are not considered hierarchically superior — merely specialized, in the same way that teachers do not recognize any hierarchical superiority in a senior maths teacher over a first grade general subjects teacher. Engineers and architects frequently supervise the work of other professionals in a hierarchical organization, but that too differs from the principal/teacher relationship. If a mechanical engineer supervises a chemical engineer, the supervision will be essentially managerial, not professional. A principal, who may be a specialist in physical education, or who may have no specialization at all, is assumed to be a professional leader of specialists in history, English, mathematics, physics and remedial reading. The assumption is broadly accepted, as least nominally, in the elementary grades but there is much more scepticism as one reaches the senior high school levels.

If there is one cliché to which all principals and teachers will agree it is that 'principals should treat teachers as professional colleagues', but what does the term 'professional' mean in this context?

Frequently used defining criteria of the professional, as distinct from the technician or manager, are: (i) long period of required, specialized training or education; (ii) the work requires specialized skills; (iii) payment is by fees for services rendered; (iv) the occupation is self-governing; (v) a high level of discretionary decision making.

Definitions are often developed to capture the notion we already believe. Thus a definition that excluded architects and physicians would quickly be discarded. The third and fourth criteria can quickly be put aside. Many professionals of all kinds are not in fact fee paid, and the desirability of fee paying is a matter of debate. Further, many professions in many countries are not self-governing.

The first two criteria are a part but not all of the definition. After all, highly trained technologists and technicians are not professionals. Thus the last criterion — professional discretion — becomes the key. If we compare the most obvious professions, medicine, law, ministry and the church, with some of the least obvious and least accepted professions, nursing, pharmacy and teaching, the crucial role of discretion becomes clear. The discretionary choices and the consequences of making wrong discretionary choices are much more evident in medicine, say, than in nursing. (It is important to distinguish the importance of discretion from the importance of practice.

The consequences of a bus driver making an error are enormous, but that does not make bus driving a profession.) The bus driver, and to a lesser extent the nurse, is expected to follow a clear set of procedures.

Thus, to treat a teacher professionally is to accept a zone of professional discretion. Previously, the argument has been made that it would not be appropriate for schools to allow individual teachers to select educational goals (any more than doctors should choose the goals of medicine). Similarly, teachers should not be the sole judges of the quality of their work. In the latter respect, it may be argued that teachers should set up tests of all areas of achievement in school — evaluative measures of all goals of education. If all students were regularly assessed and if exceptional performances of teachers, good and bad, were recorded, the profession would be making a significant contribution. But of course that does not happen. Teachers should therefore not be allowed to proscribe external evaluation. While it is true that a doctor might refuse to use laboratory tests, the client can easily choose another doctor. In practice, no doctor does refuse as a general principle to use external laboratory tests. As a general rule, neither parents nor students have the option of choosing another teacher if the teachers in a particular school refuse to accept external evaluation of students' performance.

Professional discretion therefore principally resides in the area of instructional methodology. A case can be made that even here discretion should be drastically limited, in effect that teaching is not or should not be a profession. In the same way, pharmacy has lost some of its professional status as increasingly the filling of prescriptions consists largely of distributing manufactured drugs and providing the physician's and the manufacturer's directions. There remain important professional aspects of pharmacy, but they are arguably much less significant that they once were. Some will argue that as we learn more about instruction, teachers should too be given less discretion. Many school districts do in fact provide most explicit instructions about how to teach almost everything, instructions, incidentally, which are often ignored.

However, in general, we do not know very much about what constitutes good and bad instruction, and there is little evidence to suggest that teaching will become increasingly effective if it is more highly organized, synthesized, programmed and standardized. There is strong evidence that teachers are both successful and unsuccessful in a variety of ways. Thus for the foreseeable future most teaching should remain professional in character, and that means teachers should be left considerable discretionary room about how to teach.

This solution goes part way to addressing the problem of a principal supervising a physics specialist who knows far more about physics than the principal. There is good reason why principals should be involved in the checking of the content of the physics curriculum, what is taught and what is not taught, and in checking student and program evaluation. Principals are only required to learn about the nature and purpose of physics, not to learn the discipline of physics and/or how to teach it.

Use of Non-Teaching Adults

There are two ways of introducing additional help into the school — by paying non-teaching adults, such as psychologists, teachers' aides, social workers and counsellors, and by inviting volunteers, usually parents. Whereas in most areas of business the first method is normal, in schools the use of volunteers is more common than widespread differentiated staffing. Differentiated staffing sometimes means a way of providing different rates of financial return and different amounts of responsibility to teachers; we extend the term here to the use of non-teaching staff. Most secondary schools employ counsellors. Even here, the typical counsellor is a trained teacher, paid on the teachers' salary scale and often combining both counselling and teaching. True differentiated staffing is unlikely to be popular with unions, as it implies that some jobs previously done by teachers will be done by non-teachers. Many school systems employ social workers and psychologists, but they are usually not attached to a single school and, when they are, their role is strongly differentiated from the teachers'. Librarians are most commonly 'teacher/librarians'; if they are not, their instructional responsibilities are minimal. As for teachers' aides, they are always hierarchically subordinate and additional to teachers. No matter how gradually and painlessly the plan might be phased in, there is little chance that teachers' unions would approve any plan whereby a school staff of one hundred teachers was replaced by forty teachers and one hundred teachers' aides.

As the very idea is so radical, we have no idea whether such a plan would lead to more or less effective instruction. There should be little surprise at teachers' opposition. No union welcomes a reduction in its membership. What is rather more surprising is the almost complete success of teachers in defeating even experimentation with the differentiated staffing model. Hospitals have an elaborate hierarchy of nursing aides, nursing assistants, registered nurses, degree nurses, medical technicians, interns, general practitioners and specialists. Schools typically have teachers and a principal and occasional adult visitors. The persistence of the egg crate model (one teacher with thirty pupils in one box) cannot be attributed entirely to teachers' natural conservatism and to the power of their professional organizations. The same pattern persists in private schools. Even the newer private schools, set up to serve the special requirements of children with physical, neurological and psychological disabilities, differ only in the relative generosity of their teacher/pupil ratios. There may be good, functional reasons for the prevailing structure, but it is unfortunate there is so little experiment.

Order in a school, particularly in a secondary school dealing with difficult and rebellious adolescents, is delicate and precarious. Without clearly established hierarchies, norms and patterns, the continuing authority of the teachers becomes threatened — a topic dealt with more fully in the next chapter.

Existing patterns should not be quickly or arbitrarily changed. At the elementary school level, to the age of thirteen or fourteen, there is much to be said for the stability of the traditional class. However, given the enormous expense of reducing class size and the lack of evidence of effect of reduced class size, except in the early grades with drastic reduction, careful thought should be given to the possibility of maintaining or even increasing class size, given a selection of very effective and well paid teachers, and increasing the amount of auxiliary support provided them. At the secondary level, where students group and regroup frequently already, the experiments could go a little further, with much larger classes in some subjects compensated for by reduced teaching hours and/or increased non-professional assistance.

Given this lack of experiment, it is surprising how widespread is the use of volunteers. As Waller (1965) pointed out many years ago, parents and teachers are natural enemies. Both have authority over the child. They are rivals for the child's obedience and, sometimes, affection. Their patterns of approved upbringing rarely coincide exactly, with the parent likely to be more particularistic, the teacher more universalistic.

This natural and usually inevitable rivalry is augmented in many situations by two other fundamental factors. Teachers are middle class in orientation. Teaching has been a traditional means of upward and social mobility — so many teachers actually come from lower middle class or respectable working class backgrounds. But the culture they represent conflicts with that of the majority of their pupils. Most pupils come from lower social class backgrounds. The tension created when parents feel their children's manners are being commented on unfavorably is well known. Less well studied is the tension created when teachers have to deal with children who assume that their home culture is superior to that of the teacher. This phenomenon is becoming more common. Teachers are generally unaccustomed to being treated as servants or nannies. Private schools for the well-to-do have traditionally dealt with this problem by establishing fiercely enforced, rigorous standards of control and social interaction. The English public school boy, son of a duke though he may be, no more patronizes his house master than does an army recruit, from the best of families, the sergeant major. The rigorous development of role differentiation is one way in which natural, underlying resentments can be masked.

As well as social class differentiation, there tends to be functional differentiation. To parents, their children tend to be individuals, particularly in the psychologically oriented modern world. It is easy to forget how, less than a hundred years ago, families tended to be considerably larger and children enjoyed, in relation to adults, a common and inferior status as little adults.

Today, children without any or with only a single sibling are more than ever likely to be treated predominantly in a particularistic fashion. That is to say, they are dealt with differently according to their own apparent qualities, predispositions and wishes. They are encouraged to develop in their own ways and to develop differently. In the classroom, even those based on 'progressive' philosophies, children are expected to do many of the same things and to accept common school norms. Universalism is the predominant guide to interaction with the teacher. Indeed, the teacher who treats children differently, unless such difference can be justified by some factor very obvious to the children, is likely to be condemned as unfair, as having pets — one of the most heinous crimes a teacher can commit. A hierarchical ratio of one to thirty is extremely unusual outside school; its stability is direly threatened if some individuals are perceived to be favored.

All this makes the introduction into the classroom of other adults without a clearly subordinate role, particularly if they happen to be parents, a perilous exercise. The danger to social cohesion is that much greater if parents are interested in helping their own child's class and by inference their own child. Even more threatening is the parent of high social status who, intentionally or not, assumes a high profile in the classroom. There are cases where teachers and parents work very closely together in harmony, so perhaps the enmity is not natural, but contrived and based on misconceptions. However, even dogs and cats can become friends, but no one therefore believes they can easily be kept together in large communal kennels.

In general, the prevailing circumstances appear to support Waller's thesis, although the causes of the disjunction are open to question. Most parents are not in fact regular, willing and welcome visitors to their own children's classrooms. The fact that parents of young children visit much more often and much more willingly than parents of adolescents suggests that they go principally to hear good news of their prodigy's progress, not to share in the task of a difficult and exciting upbringing. After all, parents do not regularly claim that the problems of upbringing are all solved by the time their offspring reach adolescence. Quite the contrary. Although there are many exceptions, teachers typically do not look forward to parent interviews. Although most parents are friendly, polite, courteous, discreet and even grateful, a few dissipate the existing tension in aggression and angry criticism. Very likely, pupils themselves understand the tension intuitively — without being aware of the cultural inhibitions which tell adults that parents and teachers ought to be partners in harmony. Pupils rarely want parents to visit their teachers, particularly as they reach adolescense, even when there are no guilty secrets to be revealed. They feel uncomfortable mixing the two very different worlds where their roles and behavior are different. Children frequently live very different lives in school and home, the perfect child at home sometimes being difficult and rebellious at school and vice versa. In contrast, students usually welcome parents in the simple role of spectator, when they take part in plays, sports events or concerts — either in the community or in school. In this case, the parent's role is unambiguous, not in any way confused with that of the teacher. Young people want parents to appreciate their work and progress, but not to enter into and disturb the social world of the school. In the same way, most parents do not have a ready and easy entrée to the company of their child's adolescent peer group, which has set up its own patterns and norms, although they often communicate easily with the same adolescents as individuals when familiar role patterns can be quickly adopted. Young adolescents are acutely aware of their parents' foibles, and fear the derision of their peers.

If one accepts the premise of tension between parent and teacher, it can be understood why one should hypothesize that two conditions are likely to be conducive to greater permanence in a parent volunteer program. Firstly, parents particularly and also other adults should be given a very clearly defined and inferior role. It is perfectly acceptable to have a visiting expert teach something esoteric like string instruments or potting, but a regular visiting expert teaching mathematics or reading poses a real threat to the teacher's authority, far more so if the expert happens to be a parent well known to many children in the class. The more frequent the visits, the more important that the role be inferior. Typically, volunteers help in the school library, mark student work, prepare materials, read aloud to small groups and help with remedial work — all under the direction of the teacher. Secondly, parents should not normally be allowed to work in the same classroom as their own child. The conflict between particularism and universalism is likely to be most acute in that circumstance. An exception would be where a child has such severe and recognizable learning problems that particularistic treatment is obviously necessary, evident to all other children in the class.

There are several reasons why volunteers are much less common in secondary than in elementary schools. Parents generally show less overt interest in their children's schooling, at least they visit schools less often, as their children grow older. Even highly interested parents feel they are less able to influence either their child or the school. The teaching task becomes more complex, the young people more difficult and more threatening. One other important reason may be that the social structure within the secondary classroom is even more delicate than that in the elementary school; the climate in a significant number of secondary classrooms is insufficiently robust to tolerate interruption and uncertainty — witness the difficulty in conducting school trips, the difficulties faced by supply teachers and the problems inherent in any other deviations from a standardized routine. Of course there are many teachers with complete control and many schools where students are generally tractable. But it is not uncommon to find tacit agreement between a worn teacher and some non-producing students that neither will interfere with the other's lives — there is a cautious truce. (See *Horace's Compromise*, Sizer, 1983.)

If teachers and parents are natural enemies, the question must be raised as to why one would bother to bring them together. Again, if one accepts the premise, a volunteer program will require continuing rather than one short administrative effort — travelling uphill requires expenditure of energy. In modern society, characterized by extreme division of labor, there are countless examples of similar reservation, tension or hostility — between police and defence lawyers, between police and social workers, between workers and bosses, between unionized teachers and administrators. None of the pairs is exactly analogous with the parent/teacher relationship, but they will serve as illustration. There are several ways of dealing with natural tension. One is separation, as in the case of police and defence lawyers whose hostility is structural. But note how the natural hostility between police and defence lawyers normally exceeds that between defence and prosecution, who are often friends outside court. Both defending and prosecuting lawyers are concerned with 'justice' as defined by a set of arcane rules. The police are concerned with protection of the public. To some degree, the division between particularistic lawyers and universalistic police reflects that between parents and teachers. Another way of resolving tension is by teasing and joking, but this requires some familiarity, not always possible between parent and teacher. But joking is sometimes adopted by individual teachers and parents in small communities. The most common resolution is role differentiation. Hostility between workers and bosses can be contained if both follow an agreed upon but not necessarily written set of rules. This is relatively easy on an industrial assembly line, much more difficult where there is frequent interaction. Another method is to set up an exchange of gifts, both formal and informal gifts with counter obligations — a system already discussed in the context of the relationship between the principal and the teacher. Another solution is to cooperate in joint effort for some larger cause. The threat of foreign invasion, for example, causes traditional enemies to cooperate. Loyalty to a paternalistic employer sometimes has similar effects — as attested to by companies such as Xerox, IBM and Shell, and by the Japanese industrial giants.

Segregation has been the traditional solution in the case of most teachers and parents. If the interaction of parents and teachers is frequently troublesome, then, perhaps, like police and defence lawyers, they are as well kept apart. Many successful private schools adopt this posture. Role differentiation appears to be the most easily applied solution if segregation is unacceptable. However, role differentiation is not easy when there is considerable social interaction and when there is no guarantee of superiority in terms of education and skill on the part of the teacher. The possibility exists that the volunteer, trained or not, is simply more knowledgeable and more competent than the teacher.

The involvement of adults, particularly parents, in the school is justified on two grounds — that it is self-evidently a good thing to bring more people together to work cooperatively in a worthwhile enterprise; and that it will benefit the pupils. There is some evidence that consensual involvement of the community in support of the school is extremely helpful, (Coleman and Hoffer 1987) but there is little evidence that simply introducing more adults into the school will by itself produce better results. Indeed, if some of the adults are unsympathetic to the teachers' and school's goals, intentionally or not, the effects may be negative.

A stronger case can be made for involving the community in an ongoing supportive, working relationship with the school than with involving a few individuals, probably parents, outside the school with a few possibly reluctant individuals inside the school. A successful school is likely to be one with strong consensual values shared by teachers, parents and students. If those values are lived on a daily basis in the community, so much the better. Note that this kind of communal sharing is much less likely to be troubled by the natural teacher/parent enmity that is found within the individual relationship within the classroom. Teachers as a group and parents as a group, or, preferably both together, can work towards a consensual end based on shared values. Fall fairs, jumble sales, teas and lunches for senior citizens, whist drives and fund raising campaigns for school activities (library books, school travel, etc.) all bring those interested in improved education together in a common cause. Thus the home and school and parent/teacher associations, often criticized because they do not get involved with controversial curricula and program issues, have survived as well as they have precisely because they work in consensual rather than divisive programs. There is no suggestion here that communal activity can keep a school going that is totally divided on fundamental philosophical issues. Rather, a school that is unified on basic issues can become stronger by bringing the community together in a common enterprise. This community involvement should not be confused with the involvement of a select group of parents in day-to-day activities within the school.

Conclusion

Many texts on administration assume that supervision and working with teachers will be the major task of the principal. But researchers in teacher supervision agree there is little evidence it helps, although most are prepared to suggest ways in which they believe it might become more effective. There is a simple and good reason why most supervision of a formal nature has not worked very well. Principals, like teachers, have ideas about what works and what does not work in teaching. Usually, these ideas are based on their own experience of success and difficulty. But different administrators' ideas are usually contradictory and are seldom based on large scale empirical research.

Thus it makes sense for principals to concentrate their supervisory time, which should not be a substantial portion of their working life, on (i) attempting to raise incompetent and modiocre teachers to levels of competency and, in the event of failure, in moving to dismiss them; (ii) helping teachers in a supportive, non-directive, informal way. More time should be spent on activities outside the teachers' discretionary zone, on program development, on the assessment of student progress, and on the evaluation of the program itself. Chapters 5, 6 and 7 will address these issues.

Further Reading

A good picture of the North American teacher is given by Lortie (1975). Jackson (1968) gives an interesting view of everyday life in the American elementary classroom, although it lacks the penetrating insight of Waller's classic written fifty years ago (1965). Gross and Herriott (1965) reported some empirical research on the principal-teacher relationship at a period in time when there was widespread belief that school effectiveness was essentially a function of principal/teacher relations. It provides a good set of references, but the work itself is inconclusive and the later development of school effectiveness research has shown that the principal/teacher relationship is only one minor aspect of a much larger problem. The classic study of the pre-school effectiveness era remains Halpin (1966).

Chapter 5

Working with Students

Students, Teachers, Parents and Administrators

Books and university courses on educational administration do not give much direct attention to students, whose education is the justification for the administrator's existence. The explanation is that, supposedly, everything educational administrators do is for and about pupils, directly and indirectly. Therefore, by that account, addressing them separately isolates only a few factors of importance to them. The problem with mainstream approaches is that discussion of organizational theory and principal/teacher relations provides little evidence or argument to the effect that a particular approach will benefit students. Students are central in our conception of the school. This chapter emphasizes the point by stressing some of the instances in which administrators have direct responsibility.

In Chapter 4, the distinctive professionalism of the teacher was located in discretionary authority. It was argued as well that there are pragmatic as well as intrinsic reasons why professional discretion is desirable. Generally, there is a lack of research evidence to show that teachers can be usefully and effectively persuaded to adopt a particular methodology. That is not to say that there is never a case for uniform methodology and it is certainly not to say that any methodology is as good as any other in any circumstances. But an important theme of this book is that informal, discretionary relationships (between principal and teachers, between teachers and students, etc.) are important glue for cohesion and stability — and these depend on discretionary authority in all professionals.

One might infer therefore that pupils should merely be left to teachers, once the educational goals and the methods of evaluation of their achievement are settled. The separate treatment of the student in the life of the principal may appear to be contradictory in two ways: (i) if students are the purpose, teachers are being treated only as means, hence as objects, yet the treatment of people as objects has been described as unethical; and (ii) the by-passing of teachers implicit in the importance of principal/student relationships serves to invade the discretionary authority of the teacher.

The school is a very complex social system; the teasing out of roles and responsibilities is a delicate task. Teachers are and ought to be professionals with a degree of professional authority; but parents have a legitimate relationship with the school, even the school district, as well as one with the teacher. The unethical treatment of teachers, as will be illustrated in Chapter 6, lies not in their direction or persuasion or in policy limits, but in their dishonest manipulation. Professional treatment of teachers does not imply total autonomy, but it does imply freedom from manipulation. The specific hierarchical principal/teacher relationship within a profession is unusual; but it is not at all unusual for more than one professional to have ongoing professional relationships with a client, for example, orthodontist and dentist, surgeon and family doctor, family and criminal lawyer. So while it is perfectly possible for the principal to undermine the professional relationship between teacher and student there is no reason why any involvement on the part of the principal must have that effect.

The allocation of time and space is one important way in which administrators may influence students; the supervision of teachers is another. Those issues have been dealt with. The next two chapters look at student program and evaluation, both bearing important implications for students. Chapter 9 addresses directly the significance of the school's moral climate and its importance for student life and growth. This chapter emphasizes more general issues of climate and particularly the question of discipline.

One thing that makes schools so different from other organizations is the complexity of interrelationships among administrator, teacher, parent and pupil. The natural tension or hostility between school people and parents (Waller, 1965) discussed in the last chapter has important implications for the discipline of students. Teachers asked by the principal to meet a parent of one of their pupils with whom they are having problems invariably wonder on whose side the principal will be. The assumption of sides is a given. Meetings of three supposed partners, usually precipitated by a 'problem', are fraught with misgiving on all sides. Parents only rarely ask for a meeting of teacher and principal to provide congratulations or in a spirit of general inquiry. The meeting more usually arises in one of three ways: (i) a request from the teacher who is concerned about the child's behavior, academic progress or appropriate placement; (ii) a request from the parent who is concerned about the teacher's behavior or the child's progress or placement; or, much more rarely, (iii) a request from the principal with a much less predictable purpose (the principal may wish to take strong disciplinary action not approved by the teacher, for example;) whatever the purpose, the principal then becomes the initiator rather than the judge/mediator, a more normal role. Adding the child to the meeting increases the complexity of the relationships. If the parent is particularistic, the teacher universalistic, the principal mediating and judging, the child is the *object* of discussion — like a disease in a doctor's office, an engineer's bridge, or an architect's building, (but an object that is also the real client). Partly for that reason, and partly because some or all of the participants genuinely feel it would be better for a young child not to hear some of the good or, more usually, bad things being said, elementary aged pupils are often excluded.

The above picture is overly simplistic. As Waller (1965) and Dreeben (1968) have said, the elemental distinction is between parents' particularism and the teachers' universalism. But consider the case where parent and teacher both take a particularistic position that the child be transferred to another class — the parent because the child does not like the teacher and is not progressing satisfactorily, the teacher because she does not get on with the child and feels she lacks support from the home. Often, a sensible principal will be only too happy to please both parties. Sometimes the principal, without being able to adopt a mediating role, will rule against both parties. It may be that the principal's professional concern for the child demands that she insist that the three (parent, teacher and pupil) sort out their differences because the alternative placement would be academically unsuitable. Thus all three may make particularistic judgments but disagree. The principal in this case may appear to be impugning the professional judgment of the teacher; but the principal not the teacher is responsible for judging the appropriateness of the alternative placement. (Now, of course, the principal may have less professional reasons for rejecting the joint recommendation — she may be terrified of a row with the teacher of the other class who does not care for the increased workload; or the extra body may contravene the collective agreement of school district policy or the school staff's recommendation.) The more common situation where the principal will not support a joint recommendation is where the principal considers universalistic principles. After application of school policy with respect to progress, assessment and ability, a child is designated for non-promotion, i.e., he must spend three rather than two years to complete elementary school. A complaining parent persuades the teacher to support his request for promotion, 'I don't really agree with grade repetition myself and I'd like to see Tony go ahead, but it's school policy, you know.' Principals often give way unprofessionally in situations like this, which are not uncommon as the whole question of 'failure' becomes a matter of controversy. It is serious enough to have a policy that non-promotion is subject to parental approval; but simply unprofessional to give way to complaints and break one's own policy. What results in the latter case is the reinforcement of the tendency for low social class pupils to repeat grades — their parents have insufficient knowledge and clout to make influential complaints.

This is not to suggest that the principal should be a rigid slave to policy. After all, the principal, like the teacher, should be able to exercise professional discretion. In some cases, the principal may even exercise particularism against the universalism of the teacher. A teacher may refuse to make any allowance for a hard of hearing child in spelling dictation, for example. In some cases, the principal may exercise what Dreeben (1968) calls 'specificity', to override teachers' universalism. (Specificity is when universalism is applied seperately to different groups, for example, to boys and girls.) A frequent scene in middle and junior high schools is the grade promotion meeting. The passing average may be sixty per cent. So the homeroom teacher may argue that Don has failed, with an average of fifty-seven per cent, and should repeat. Other teachers provide valid reasons why it would be unwise for Don to fail. Fair administrative policy demands that the other students between fifty-seven per cent and sixty per cent also pass. In other instances, the principal may make special exemptions for senior students or members of a school team.

The examples used so far involve extra-class considerations. The principal justifies the use of hierarchical authority on the basis of responsibility to the school as well as to teachers, pupils and parents, individually and collectively. A parent may object to his child being compelled to use a 'profane' book in language class or to being compelled to learn about evolution. The parent is asking for particularistic treatment within the program. Certainly there are implications for other parents and other issues, but, for the moment, no one else is directly affected. But the decision is particularly difficult when the principal must consider conflicting views of the student's best educational interests — outside a context where universalism is of overbearing moment. The good administrator should be prepared to put the individual before the law, the rule or even the collective agreement. But to ignore laws, rules and collective agreements is to abjure one's legitimate authority and responsibility. The key to this type of particularistic respect lies in Chapter 1. The greater the agreement on consensual goals, the less difficulty there will be in dealing with particularistic requests of this kind. A Catholic school should not have much of a problem dealing with a request for the inclusion of abortion as a form of birth control within the curriculum. However, even a Catholic school may still have differences when it comes to dealing with a request for exclusion from communion or mass. Suppose an adolescent declares himself a non-Catholic (or a 'Catholic' who does not believe in traditional practice). We would judge it unethical to compel him to participate fraudulently in a religious ceremony; one might differentiate between attendance at mass (which implies no necessary commitment) and communion which surely does. The classic film, *Au Revoir les Enfants*, shows how a principal in wartime France defies the legitimate authority, partly for the benefit of threatened Jews for whom he has no legitimate responsibility, and partly out of Christian duty. Thankfully, such moral situations are rare and legitimate authority is not to be flouted lightly. But the students should feel that the principal is actively promoting their best interests, collectively and individually in that order.

Just as the informal relationship between principal and teachers provides the glue that binds professional colleagues, even within a hierarchy, so the discretionary behavior of principals towards individual students gives the principal authenticity. More importantly, the pattern of decisions, including the way they are made as well as the actual decisions themselves, should reflect a philosophical direction which is not anti-teacher, anti-parent or anti-student but which gives body and meaning to the school's ultimate moral goals, which policy, rules, laws and collective agreements reflect at best imperfectly. Nearly all rules must occasionally be broken. It is a bad rule that is frequently broken or whose underlying principle is transgressed.

Discipline

The first responsibility of the principal, not the most important but the first, with respect to students is the maintenance of order and safety. Beyond that essential requirement, the way in which the issues of control, discipline, punishment, deportment, dress, punctuality, obedience, courtesy and industriousness are addressed both underlies and symbolizes the school's role in the moral domain. For that reason, the distancing of the principal from what can often be a distasteful set of tasks is unfortunate. One possibility is that vice-principal is seen as the real authority, the one who makes the important decisions. The principal who delegates all the day-to-day tasks of control misunderstands the substance of legitimate authority. The vice-principal is particularly likely to become the *de facto* leader if genuine power is delegated. If the principal delegates responsibility, but not legitimate and moral authority, the vice-principal comes to be seen by pupils as a mere punishment machine. The principal's remoteness is either interpreted as lack of interest, or lack of courage, or as a means of currying favor with students. Further, where there is more than one vice-principal, there is a real danger that vice-principals will use discretion in quite contradictory ways. In one case studied by a student in Chicago, one vice-principal made dispensations (i.e., developed informal specificity) for students who received *strong* support from *good* homes, rationalizing that the combined efforts of home and school would help the student get on the right track without much exemplary punishment. The other vice-principal made dispensations for students who received *weak* support from poor homes, rationalizing that such students had not had sufficient opportunity to internalize the school's standards. The situation in that school serves to highlight the problem inherent in excesseive discretionary behavior in the interpretation of very general rules. There is much to be said, in a consensual environment, for a minimum of written rules. In the absence of such consensus, specific rules are required. Another possible consequence of delegation is that the vice-principal, resenting or tiring of the distasteful tasks, will become casual and slack, hoping to be seen, against the odds, as the 'good guy' despite the unwanted role. The hidden message given students is,

'Don't blame me. I'm just following orders. I realize all this is nonsense and is quite unfair.' It is not unusual for one vice-principal to adopt a 'pastoral' approach, another a universalistic approach — the one announcing to students, 'I am really on your side', the other announcing to parents and teachers, 'Despite the lack of support I get, I am trying to maintain some semblance of standards in this place.'

Two principles stem from the argument so far: (i) the principal should be centrally involved with school discipline; and (ii) there should be a consistency of approach to discipline. Central involvement does not mean that principals should spend most of their time dealing with individual miscreants, a trap into which many middle and high school principals fall. Central involvement does mean that principals should share in the maintenance of day-to-day discipline and should be symbolically involved in policy setting and in the exercise of authority in extreme cases. One excellent principal is often teased because he is so often seen picking up minute pieces of litter in his large high school. That school, an old one, is exceptionally well maintained. The principle of direct involvement in the school's policies and rules is fairly uncontroversial and many principals, particularly in elementary schools, accept the role unthinkingly. It is in large bureaucratic high schools, with intense division of labor, that the principle is often ignored. We are not implying simple cause and effect (the well known problems of large, urban bureaucratic high schools are enormous and complex), but it is schools with those problems that are in particular need of strong, involved, symbolic leadership. Principals' withdrawal is often a result of failed involvement rather than the cause of the problems — but that withdrawal stands out as a strong symbol which leads quickly to further deterioration as the teaching staff follows suit.

The principle of consistency requires more discussion. Few will argue for extremely inconsistent treatment of the same individual student by different teachers and administrators. But there is considerable disagreement about the amount of discretion administrators should allow in the treatment of different students; in practice the two ideas are not easily separated.

Rutter *et al.*, (1979) in an effective school study of secondary schools in London, England distinguished pastoral discipline from universalistic discipline. Pastoral discipline is particularistic. It operates under the assumption that individuals will respond best to very different treatment depending on the cause of their misbehavior. It assumes a psychological rather than a sociological ultimate cause of deviance. Rutter's work and effective schools research generally (for example, Coleman, Hoffer and Kilgore, 1982; Coleman and Hoffer, 1987) show that effective schools are generally associated with clear rules, clear consequences and uniform application — they are orderly schools. Wynne (1980) shows how universalism works in practice in a series of case studies carried out by his students. The disagreement about approaches to discipline mirrors differences about approaches to education in general. Progressives usually prefer pastoral discipline; traditionalists universalistic discipline.

One's concept of punishment also affects one's approach to discipline. The goals derived in Chapter 1 include the notion of virtue. Truth is to be preferred to dishonesty, and not just because the consequences of dishonesty are often unpleasant. Similarly, courage and compassion are virtues in themselves. (In contrast, others would see values as arising purely from the context — truth generally makes sense much of the time, but sometimes it does not. They would argue that everyone should determine values individually.) With this book's assumption, it becomes axiomatic to assert that ideas of punishment and of morality are closely related. Lying should be punished because it is wrong; not because it is inconvenient or troublesome in the particular context. If there is good and bad behavior (in this absolute sense), then punishment is the word being used to describe the appropriate response of a person with moral responsibility for another, for example, a caring parent or a caring educator with responsibility for a child. Consider a good mother who believes in good and bad. From an early age, she would teach her young child the difference. Suppose a young girl beats her young brother. Such a mother's response may be a verbal reprimand, 'Don't do that. That's *bad*.' It may be a slap, 'Don't do that again.' It may be removal, 'If you can't behave well, you can't play with Andrew.' In some cases, the mere absence of praise or approval (rewards), constitutes punishment. Note that in these instances the level of punishment is only slightly related to the level of consequence from the misbehavior. An unsuccessful attempt to hit Andrew is just as much a cause for reprimand as the unsuccessful attempt that causes him to fall and hit his head (if one assumes equivalent intent).

Thus, if good and bad are believed to exist in real terms, and not just as descriptors for appropriate and inappropriate behavior in the context, then punishment, as distinct from negative reinforcement, becomes a requirement. In practice of course, the behavior denoting punishment is often identical to the behavior denoting negative reinforcement. And belief in punishment does not indicate disbelief in negative reinforcement. Many principals adopt codes of behavior and appropriate consequences for failure to adhere to them for the sound and practical reason that they work, i.e., they achieve the desired consequences. However, the daily practice of those principals is likely to be somewhat different from those who use punishment for moral as well as practical reasons. For example, the practical principal will: (i) try to codify every possible misdemeanor so that as many negative consequences as possible can be avoided; and (ii) overlook inappropriate behavior that is not observed or that does not lead directly to negative consequences to the organization.

In contrast, the moralist will: (i) limit the categorization of misdemeanors in the hope that students will come to understand the nature rather than the definition of bad (as distinct from inappropriate) behavior; (ii) emphasize the wrongness of the behavior more than its immediate consequences. Thus it is as wrong to mimic and make fun of a blind student for the entertainment of others as it is to mimic and make fun of a deaf student. Teasing and bullying are all the more reprehensible if there is likely to be no resistance from the victims themselves, their acquaintances and their family.

Thus the practical principal, as compared with the moralist, will deal more harshly with the student who steals a friend's car at lunchtime and becomes involved in an accident involving a prominent local politician than with the student who steals $5.00 from a very poor, learning disabled student's purse; and more harshly with the student who has not completed assigned work by a stated date than with the student who lies about work allegedly left at home. The moralist will try to restrict rules to the minimum denoted by moral, courteous and civilized behavior. The practical principal will attempt to cover all those offences likely to affect unfavorably the smooth running of the organization. Both principals however are behaving in universalistic as distinct from particularistic ways.

In most situations, the moralist and the practical principal are unlikely to be as distinguishable as those distinctions might suggest, partly because even the most practical of principals usually retains some traditional sense of right and wrong and partly because the factors leading to codes of discipline go well beyond the two philosophical rationales described. School district policies, senior administrators, parents, teachers and students all legitimately influence discipline policies. Futhermore, the greater the lack of consensus among them the more rules that are required — irrespective of the principal's moral or consequentialist preferences.

To the believer in pastoral discipline, these distinctions will appear superfluous. What both the moralist and the practical have in common is an assumption that the punishment should fit the crime. Both believe in the universalistic application of sanctions for particular offences. Both will make occasional discretionary variations from the rules, but for different reasons. In contrast, pastoral discipline implies fitting the punishment to the criminal. Strong, rhetorical argument can be made for this approach too. Reasons why children are late for school are infinitely varied — some are lazy, some want to challenge authority, some are not wakened by their parents, some miss the bus, some do not have a parent at home to wake them, some are tired and hungry, some are frightened. The practical response is straightforward. Empirical research shows that consistently applied discipline works well in the vast majority of cases, exceptions breed exceptions. The moralist's position is slightly more qualified. Young people ought to learn to take responsibility for their own lives and should therefore not be punished for offences whose nature they do not understand or for behavior over which they have no control. Once again, in practice, the moralist is going to be close to the practical principal, holding that children without caring, nurturing parents must learn quickly to accept responsibility for their own behavior. Neither of those positions satisfies the pastoral administrator. The pastoral, particularistic principal will insist that treatment (as distinct from punishment or negative reinforcement) of each child should depend on the child and the circumstances. The problems with this approach are many: administrators can rarely understand all the circumstances surrounding a particular child — they are often easily misled; they all have slightly differing standards and values; their feelings will vary from time to time and from day to day depending on their personal circumstances. The extremely varied outcomes of particularistic treatment are seen simply by students as signs of weakness and unfairness, as evidence that the principal has no genuine standards. Many principals of course fall somewhere between the pastoral and the universalistic archetypes. Few are going to analyze the causes of every minor misdemeanor; and few are going to refuse to consider such reasons for absence as a break-up in the parents' marriage or a traffic accident. Moralists will spend more time with the unusual extreme problems that reflect moral weakness. Concern for the virtue, as distinct from the appropriate behavior, of the students is likely to move them some way toward the pastoral but not to a completely particularistic approach.

On balance, it seems likely that school administrators spend too much of their time on discipline, and not enough on more general aspects of school program. The idea embraced here that punishment is necessary and desirable does not mean that more is better. Punishment should symbolize bad, just as praise and rewards should symbolize good. Either one, punishment or praise, loses its value if (i) it is used too freely; and (ii) it is used indiscriminately.

Opponents of punishment frequently comment that ineffective schools are riddled with punishment. To some extent, this state of affairs is logically necessary. One would expect schools where many bad things are done to have more punishment than ones where good things are normally done. Beyond that obvious truth however, the frequent use of punishment denotes failure not success. The purpose of punishment is to teach the right behavior; if it is used continuously, obviously it is unsuccessful.

All this seems obvious enough, but the logical truths about excessive, unearned praise are often deliberately flouted. For example, teachers are often exhorted to praise freely, even when work or behavior is not particularly valuable (on the demeaning grounds that it is somehow good for the student concerned). The advice is based on the finding that people respond more to praise than to threats of punishment. What is overlooked is that the response only continues as long as the praise is believed to be genuine. One may get away with lying for a time. One may get away with being genuinely indiscriminate for a time (i.e., some teachers honestly cannot tell the difference between good and bad writing), but eventually students are sensitive to both insincerity and incompetence. More important, such behavior on the part of teachers and administrators destroys the good school's own standards and purposes. Thus, discipline is difficult to maintain in a school where there is no appeal to high standards and where praise and rewards have been inflated — and devalued.

An obvious practical question arises. It is easy to find good schools in operation where good work and behavior are the norm and where punishment is respected, even feared, but rarely applied. It is easy to find bad schools with poor standards of work and either frequently applied but ineffective punishment or little attempt at punishment. But how does one turn a school around? If a school is indisciplined and is resorting both to frequent punishment and to frequent indiscriminate praise, how can a change be brought about? It there were a magic cure, there would be few such schools. And it must be borne in mind that the existence of a problem is no guarantee of a cure. If the research findings and the philosophy outlined above are valid, then the road to recovery, if there is one, will look something like this:

(i) Find and refine a community consensus about goals and more specific objectives — including all domains;

(ii) Develop an organizational plan involving staff to reach those objectives;

(iii) Refine a community consensus about a clear, very distinct, detailed code of conduct and consequences (making sure that students themselves are included as it is developed);

(iv) Foreshadow the beginning of a new school year with significant, symbolic changes, for example, school uniform, a spotless, newly painted school building, super-vigilance on the part of staff and administrators, signed consent of parents and students;

(v) Enforce the code rigidly from the beginning — with no warnings about 'next time';

(vi) Be prepared to suspend considerable numbers of students in the first few weeks and to recommend expulsion.

The last point is crucial. If a school has no power to remove students from membership, its only logical alternative is to become a jail (if it wants to maintain order); that is what we call institutions of compulsory confinement. Suspension and expulsion take administrative courage as senior administrators and elected officials often see these actions as failure on the part of the school, as, in a sense, they are. But that does not mean that the school without expulsions is successful. Once a well-disciplined school is off and running it should be characterized by less rather than by more punishment. However, to establish that state takes time, patience, firmness and courage. Many schools avoid suspending and expelling students by a type of Horace's compromise (Sizer 1983), whereby the staff ignores minor misdemeanors, poor attendance, poor work habits, rude behavior in return for the absence of more aggressive disturbance. A blind eye is turned to increasingly poor attendance which eventually turns into non-attendance.

It is that kind of compromise that leads to the mediocrity of many urban high schools, where it is considered normal for several students in most classes not to be working and for student attendance rates of ninety per cent to be considered quite good. To carry out a plan for renewal without strong initial support from the school district is extremely difficult, which is one reason why it is rarely attempted. The lower the level of school district support the more important it is to develop strong, united support from staff, parents and students before beginning. If most parents oppose the suspensions and expulsions, the chance of their being upheld is slight.

But turn around can be made. Lightfoot (1983) provides a graphic description of one such school in *The Good High School*. An inner-city school in Atlanta, Georgia provides remarkable testimony. In Holmes' (1988a) New Jersey study of a school improvement project he came across another example, a middle school in the centre of Newark. Of the seventeen diverse schools in the study, this one was the best disciplined with the most difficult school population. The incumbent principal had taken over the school several years earlier and had turned the school around from a black-board jungle.

Praise is of course the other very important side of the coin of discipline. A discipline code will probably only work effectively in difficult circumstances if it is accompanied by a comprehensive set of reward systems. The development of a positive, moral framework for student lives is developed in Chapter 8. The point made here is that there should be frequent, genuine rewards for the behavior that is desired and desirable. There should be group rewards as well as individual rewards, rewards for effort and improvement as well as for achievement, rewards in the moral, social and cultural domains as well as in the intellectual. It is in the context of right behavior that deviant behavior can best be seen as being wrong and legitimately subject to disipline. Thus it is of crucial importance that students be consulted about the development of discipline codes. In a traditional school, formal involvement is unnecessary because there is general consensus among parents, students and teaching staff about what is desirable and undesirable. In modern, bureaucratic schools, none of this can be assumed and therefore the codes should be subject to discussion and possible revision. The aim is for students to internalize what is good within their community; not that students will become perfect but that they will know and appreciate right and wrong.

Group Punishment

It is fashionable to discredit any form of group punishment. The argument against it is straightforward — no one should be punished for an offence he or she has not committed. Implicit analogy is with adult life: no one would be convicted merely for being involuntarily present during the commission of a crime.

However, the analogy falls down in two ways. Firstly, school misbehavior is not usually criminal, any more than is a child's misbehavior at home. When tenets of criminal law are applied unthinkingly to the school's social system the school becomes inoperable. Consider the following not unusual case. A 14-year-old boy, Brian, has been warned and punished many times for shouting rude comments behind a particular teacher's back. Eventually, Brian is sent to the principal for more serious punishment. Brian denies the accusation, admitting that a rude comment was made but not by him. The principal talks to the teacher who is certain it was he, although she did not actually see him. She asked the rest of the class when Brian hotly denied it, but no one would confirm definitely one way or the other. All witnessed the event, but no one said who did it. Two of Brian's friends told the teacher they thought it was someone else, the rest of the class grinned knowingly. There is insufficient evidence perhaps to satisfy a court of law, but the principal also takes into account two other factors: (i) the teacher may lose control of the class entirely if she does not get the support she expects, and (ii) Brian has a record of flatly denying all guilt in the face of the most damning evidence. The wise principal may be able to find some happy compromise, perhaps transferring Brian to a different class. But no wise principal will simply return Brian, triumphant, to the class just because the case is not proven beyond all reasonable doubt. If the principal decides to punish Brian in some formal way, the 'verdict' will go something like this, 'I am almost certain you are the guilty party. You have done this many times before. It is unlikely Mrs. Stratten is mistaken. I put little faith in your own denial because you have lied to me so frequently before. If this punishment is a mistake, I am sorry, but you must think of all the other occasions when you have unfairly escaped.' Thus the social context of the offence becomes much more important than in a court. The principal implicitly recognizes the unwritten code often found within classes that no one 'squeals'. Similarly, within the family a parent will punish a child for stealing some cookies based on circumstantial evidence alone, increasing the punishment if the child concocts an unbelievable story that a strange man came in and ate them.

One of the reasons for lowering standards of evidence in the school and in the home is of course the fact that the consequences of guilt are so much smaller. No children go through family life, and few students through school life, without being punished, and routine acts of punishment for minor common offences are soon forgotten; at least they are considered normal. In contrast, a criminal record is a much more serious matter. The case of Brian involves an individual, but it should be noted that even the individual case cannot be considered outside the social context. If a strange boy hurled the same abuse at Mrs. Stratten miles away from the school she would probably not dream of mentioning it to the boy's (unkown) parents, the police or anybody else. What made Brian's offence (if he was guilty) significant, as he and the other students understood as well as Mrs. Stratten and the principal, was the social context.

Secondly, it is not true that there is no collective punishment in adult life. Entire communities are frequently punished (as distinct from being convicted) for the behavior of some members. Senior levels of government frequently punish lower levels of government for their bad spending habits. Communities are punished for voting for the wrong political party. An entire work force is laid off because excessive wage demands are made by the majority. Sports teams are regularly punished because of behavior of some members. Countries are invaded or bombed because of the behavior of their frequently unelected and unpopular leaders. There is no collective punishment in the judicial system, but the school, like the family, is not part of the judicial system. Courts themselves generally recognize the need for a great deal of administrative leeway in the running of schools.

In some instances, collective punishment is necessary and fair. Groups, classes or the entire school may be rewarded, or punished by lack of reward, for their performance with respect to a variety of criteria. Entire classes are rewarded or punished for their participation in keeping the classroom or school tidy. Such cases are generally uncontentious. More contentious are cases where something is stolen and nobody is allowed to leave until the thief confesses. Particularly if most members of the group must know who the thief is, the punishment does not seem inappropriate, if applied carefully and reasonably. Young people must learn that there are times when right behavior and civic responsibility in the larger society must come before loyalty to the sub-group and even before loyalty to a friend. At an extreme, witnesses to a violent assault by a friend should be prepared to give evidence. (This extreme example is given to illustrate the moral force of the argument. In the case of a violent assault, however, one is dealing with potentially criminal behavior and care must be taken in such cases to ensure that the rights of the accused are not in any way infringed.) In the case of theft, criminal prosecution is usually not an option under consideration. Most thefts within schools are of personal belongings or school equipment not carrying high commercial value. The weight of group disapproval is brought to bear on the thief who will learn a valuable moral lesson, as will the entire group. The good of reinforcing the importance of honesty far outweighs the slight inconvenience to some. It should be noted that there is symbolic value even if the thief is never discovered. Teachers and administrators should handle such situations with enormous care.

The situation is entirely different if there is no reason to believe that anyone other than the thief knows the thief's identity. In that case, only the threat of a physical search is likely to elicit a confession as the incentive not to confess (having to face the humiliation of being identified and disliked by the rest of the class) increases with time. In the former case, the chances of the tactic being successful are very high and at least there is important symbolic effect. In the second case, there is still some symbolism in the action but its likely futility and more questionable fairness more than offset it.

Perhaps the most frequent collective punishment is that given to a class as a consequence of misbehavior by certain members of the class — perhaps a minority. Once again, in the context of social life, that is not unfair. A number of similar events occur in adult life although they are certainly more common and more obvious in the intense, more closed social milieu of the school. Planned trips may be abandoned if the class frequently misbehaves and gives the teacher or the administrator reason to believe that it cannot be relied on to behave on the trip. The entire class may be kept after school, in some circumstances, if the behavior of some members has made the completion of a reasonable amount of work impossible. Additional homework may be given. All these punishments are not only acceptable but in reasonable conditions are desirable, because they symbolically reinforce the purpose of the school in terms of academic achievement and civilized behavior. Young people must learn that they have collective as well as individual responsibilities. To the extent that school, group and class solidarity can be developed for the achievement of desirable educational ends by means of group rewards and group punishments, the practice is, within reasonable limits, desirable. However, in situations that are likely to be contentious, it is very important to talk through the underlying principles in advance with students and parents.

The increased bureaucratization of schools leads to the concentration of disciplinary action solely on the maintenance of the day-to-day operation of the school. Safety and order are indeed of fundamental importance. But it should not be forgotten that the school has important purposes beyond the custodial. It is necessary for young people to live together in an orderly and peaceful way, but that is not sufficient. Both rewards and discipline should be used to emphasize the significance of the school's central, for example, moral goals. Writing grafitti on school walls is not merely offensive because the consequence is that the custodian has to spend time erasing the marks. It is also offensive because the school should be attractive, pleasant and aesthetically appealing. Finally, it is offensive because it indicates disrespect for the community of the school. The following generalizations summarize this discussion:

1. An orderly school is prerequisite for effectiveness.
2. Punishment is morally desirable and necessary to express community disapproval of bad and inappropriate behavior.
3. As the frequency of bad behavior should be low, punishment should itself be infrequent.
4. Punishment and praise (rewards) are part of the same scale.
5. Punishment used indiscriminately, unreliably and very frequently denotes failure.

6. Praise used indiscriminately loses its value and obscures the model of good behavior.
7. Legitimate, genuine praise should be used very frequently but its object must be extremely clear — there should be no confusion of achievement, effort, improvement or of the various domains (moral, aesthetic, etc.).
8. The detail necessary within school rules depends on the level of consensus within the school community; with a strong traditional consensus, few written rules may be necessary. As schools become more bureaucratized and as consensus fails, more rules are needed.
9. Punishments should be clear, unpleasant, explained, generally publicly known and sequential in their severity.
10. The moral offence to the school community evinced by the offensive behavior should be the first component in determining the level of punishment.
11. Punishment should be based on a consistent set of principles supported by all administrators and all teachers.
12. Punishment should be consistent, fair, universalistic and comprehensible.
13. Standards of proof are less rigorous than in a court of law.
14. Collective punishment is often legitimate.
15. The best disciplined school is one where activity is guided by principled incentives for good behavior directed towards the achievement of the school's goals and where discipline is open and universalistic but not a dominant part of school life. It is one where learners do the right thing because they choose to achieve the right goals and want to develop the traits reflected by right behavior.

The School Administrator: The Student and Social Issues

In this section, one example will be used in particular to exemplify a more general theme: the administrator's role in adjudicating among the individual, the group and society. In the last chapter we agreed with Waller (1965) that there is inevitable and continuing conflict between parents and school. The school's discipline is not organized only, or even mainly, for the benefit of the individual; order and safety are required for the organization, for the group and for society. An adolescent's psychiatrist may recommend that her knife-wielding behavior be ignored by the school administration — it is only an attention-getting device. Even if administrators agree with the girl's psychiatrist (i.e., that ignoring the incident is in the girl's best interests), they cannot stand by and do nothing — either ethically or, increasingly, legally.

Although parent/administrator interaction and student discipline illustrate the tension between individual and group, there is a larger tension. As societal consensus weakens, the underlying conflicts among groups and between society and group also become increasingly obvious and increasingly difficult to deal with. Coleman and Hoffer (1987) suggest that the traditional community school had consensual, assured norms despite the existence of dissent. It is not that the individual/group/society conflict did not exist in more traditional times, but rather that there was a general belief or myth that the school, and educators, acted on behalf of society. Marxists argue that the traditional schools actually acted on behalf of the rich, the powerful, the capitalist class (Hollingshead, 1949). However, whether or not or to what extent that argument is valid is not the issue here. Dissenters recognized that they were dissenters, rebels; some were from the wrong side of the tracks; if they behaved badly they were scorned by their upwardly mobile fellows as well as by the dominating classes. Other dissenters were aesthetes, artists, left-wing dilettantes — whose evident deviance was as important to them as it was obvious to conformists. There is no attempt to embellish those 'golden days.' The educational and social problems were obvious enough. Children from the wrong side of the track typically did not break free of their background (although many of them did); often the price of breaking free was the breakdown of family affiliation and community — they became 'better' than their parents. Nevertheless, the problem for the school was more straightforward. It embodied a consensual, clearly accepted social code. Dissenters recognized its force as clearly as did supporters — in the same way that poachers recognize game laws.

Recent changes in social structure are well known: the provision of educational equality for boys and girls; increased proportions of families with both parents working; increased numbers of single parent families; increased 'off hour' and shift work; increased immigration to many parts of Canada, the USA and western Europe; decreasing willingness on the part of immigrants to become assimilated, and decreased expectation that they should; increased tolerance and acceptance of homosexual lifestyle; decreased prevalance of the mainstream Christian religious denominations; increased intellectual and media articulation of 'working' and 'under' class interests; growth of fundamentalist and evangelical Christianity but not its acceptance by others. These trends are reflected in changes in the school structures over many of which administrators have little or no control, for example, increased segregation of students by neighborhood and by school program. The traditional small town comprehensive high school is almost dead, replaced by a variety of very different schools serving different clienteles with different delivered programs. And individualization of program often results in segregation of children even when nominally they attend the same school.

The most obvious outcome of these fundamental social changes, as far as the school administrator is concerned, is the lessening or even breakdown of social consensus. Thus it becomes much harder for the principal to articulate the interests of society — which are now so nebulous, threatened, and widely resisted — against the interests or even the will of the individual. Yet, we have argued that consensus, unity, a social community with strong glue, is precisely the quality most needed for success. To deal adequately with all the external problems modern society has posed for the school the principal would require a separate book. However the attempt in this book is not to lay out in detail a set of directions of how to solve every problem. What follows is an attempt to work through one particular, contentious area.

The School's Responsibility in the Promotion of Sexual Equality

In Chapter 1, a basis of moral commitment was laid for school administration. It is unlikely that a school will be successful in any domain if it attempts to be neutral in all or nearly all moral areas. Industriousness, competitiveness, respect for authority, personal responsibility, sense of control of one's destiny — to name a few qualities that are not uniformly and universally admired in educational circles — are all linked conceptually or empirically to performance in more than one domain.

As societal consensus has changed to a general acceptance that women ought to be treated equally in the workplace (for example, given the same pay and opportunities for promotion as men), schools generally have for the most part genuinely tried to ensure equal opportunity within their programs. Sizer (1983) claims that girls find greater equality within school than they will subsequently find outside. At a superficial glance then, sexual equality appears to be a problem for industry, not for the school. However, schools, where there is a turnover of students every four or five years, should be more flexible than industrial organizations, where some employees may remain for twenty or thirty years.

The practical implications of promoting sexual equality are not obvious. Feminist argument has two distinct and arguably inconsistent strands. On the one hand, there is the demand for equal treatment on the grounds that men and women are equal. Schools have generally interpreted this argument to mean that men and women are or ought to be treated the same. Thus programs remain much the same, but girls are either encouraged or compelled to participate fully in what used to be mainly or entirely male pursuits — shop programs, physics, chemistry, basketball, baseball, soccer, band, chess, debating; and to a less extent boys are encouraged to participate in what were typically female pursuits — clothing, cooking, study of the family, dance, drama, typing and cheerleading. Administrators increasingly try to ensure that, where sports remain segregated by sex, time in the gymnasium and funds for travel and equipment are equally or equitably divided.

In contrast, other feminists increasingly argue that, although men and women are equal politically and spiritually, they have different natural and/or cultural characteristics; and both masculine and feminine characteristics should be equally rewarded and catered to (Shakeshaft, 1987). Thus, the allegedly feminine, cooperative style should be supported in school as much as the allegedly masculine competitive style. Some feminists go so far as to argue that girls should therefore be segregated in separate schools, and it is noticeable in the USA how elite women's colleges are once again gaining enrolment.

Either one of these trends of thought makes administrative treatment of female adolescents and young adults difficult. For example, if the first strand, which seems close to the societal consensus, is accepted, teachers in family and social studies are likely to adopt one of two viewpoints. One is that women have been discriminated against in the past and therefore in the future should be given special treatment to overcome prevailing social bias. Intelligent girls in particular will be pressed by teachers and counsellors to 'raise' their ambitions beyond housewife, secretary, nurse or teacher — to lawyer, doctor, engineer or manager (but less likely to truck driver, plumber or electrician). A second viewpoint, adopted by those believing rather generally in male and female equality is that both men and women should be reasonably free from societal and family pressure to make their own choices about their futures. Whatever they choose is acceptable providing that the choice is grounded in a full and benign understanding of their own capabilities and the consequences of their choices. The second less radical ideology is more accommodating of the large traditional minority which will not be entirely happy even with such a level of free choice. Many traditionalists will argue that free choice should be grounded in the context of the children's cultural tradition, rather than in a metaphorical cafeteria.

Even if the school adopts the second, less radical option, but still within that first strand, the principal remains in a quandary. Perhaps the school enrols a large number of traditional, Catholic immigrant girls whose parents are totally opposed to sexual equality, i.e., the idea that girls and boys should have identical roles in the home and at work. And 'open' discussions in school predicated on a prior assumption of free choice obviously undermine the education (or indoctrination) such girls have received at home. Such parents are often disadvantaged (by lack of education, lack of fluency in English, lack of political skills) and usually do not pose a significant political threat to the principal or school district. But the moral quandary remains the same. To what extent is it legitimate for the school to intervene in a planned, deliberate manner to change a student's values (and with them their sense of virtue)? We are not here thinking of changing the morally bad to the morally good (avarice to generosity; dishonesty to truthfulness; cowardice to courage). But there is surely nothing immoral in an intelligent woman being a housewife, in believing in chastity before marriage, or putting family before employment. None of this is to imply that the public school has a duty to reinforce whatever beliefs an individual parent has. But a strong moral and ethical argument can be made that the principal should take reasonable action to avoid a deliberate, programmed attack on parental values that are not manifestly immoral. Teacher led discussions about family values should be constrained. In particular, minority pupils with unpopular opinions, for example, holding strong religious or traditional beliefs, should be protected from the power of teenage derision and scorn. Sensitive counselling should be provided to individual girls whose family's values are being overwhelmed — they should not be simply exhorted to 'raise' their ambitions. Parents, particularly less advantaged parents, should be encouraged to come in and discuss the conflicts between the school and the home and the home and the larger society. Irrespective of the school's program, there will be considerable conflict outside. The school should not be expected to drop or drastically change its consensual program. But teachers should be careful to moderate their ideological fervor and consider the interests of the parents.

The second strand, expressing strong sex-based differences, poses even more fundamental difficulties. If men and women are fundamentally different, the entire modern attempt to treat them as being the same is called into question. The problem of equality of the sexes, perhaps more than any other, strikes at the heart of what remains of a social consensus in education. Taken to an extreme, the second strand would have all girls treated differently from all boys, on the grounds that they are fundamentally distinct. At present, the principal can, politically, resist this attack fairly easily — most activists in the secular, modern school are still demanding the same treatment (and the same outcomes) for girls and boys, not different treatment (with the same or different outcomes). The former is both more logically consistent and easier to attain than the latter. But the principal who adopts the mainstream position must become sensitive to the radical claims that the reason for male dominance in certain areas, for example, mathematics and science, lies not in boys' natural proclivity for the associated skills and not in unfairly discriminatory expectations and treatment of girls, but in treatment that is unfairly discriminatory because it is the same. These subjects, allegedly, according to this assumption, are now taught in ways that promote individual competition rather than group cooperation, and which are thereby less attractive and accessible to girls.

In addressing this significant issue, school administration should reflect carefully about the meaning of professional practice. It means working through principles that have been established earlier in the book. There should be some meaningful consensus on what the school is about. There should be some vision of the genotype of the ideal society of which our current society is merely a struggling phenotype. The cultural and social traditions on which our society is based should form an organic base from which the improved phenotype will emerge. Teachers should be provided professional discretion in their teaching; but the students' interests should be put before the teachers'. The core dignity and sense of worth of the individual student should not be invaded by an educator's ideology, however sincerely held, unless that ideology, or ideological fragment, is most clearly an evident part of the school's consensus. (And that consensus, it must be remembered, embraces the entire community of parents — not just the teaching staff.) Thus an educator may legitimately, and indeed ought to, make a child feel shame and contrition about lying, stealing, bullying or racial prejudice. But the educator should not make children feel similar shame and contrition about the traditional and cultural beliefs they have learned within their families.

So where does this leave us regarding education and sexual equality? The following principles emerge:

(i) *In general, boys and girls should be given the same educational opportunities, except where established, generalizable differences make them unwise.* Modern, Western democracies accept that there should not be sexual discrimination. It does not follow that boys and girls are the same, merely that they together with their parents should be allowed to exercise choices reasonably freely. In some areas, the differences between most boys and most girls are so marked that the same educational opportunities would effectively make competitive programs unavailable to most girls (for example, in track and field, tennis, basketball and soccer from the onset of puberty). Thus, girls' teams should be maintained where their participation might otherwise be curtailed. This example illustrates a larger issue. The administrator's decision making should not be constrained by two narrow alternatives — single sex or mixed teams. Certainly, competitive excellence in sports should be promoted, but not at the expense of broad participation. Goals themselves should not be compromised, but there is no advantage in not being pragmatic about means.

In most areas outside sports, there is no evidence that most boys are better or worse than girls; i.e., there is enormous overlap between the sexes although one sex may be more successful on average than the other. So in general the question reduces to one of choosing approaches to programs that are valuable for all learners, not just for one possibly dominant group.

(ii) *A general working assumption should be that, while families with both a father and a mother are to be preferred, either both parents or just one may work, or one or both may be disabled, unemployed or retired.* Clearly, enormous sensitivity should be shown toward children of single parents, a large and growing minority. But equally, societal preference, often on moral as well as pragmatic grounds, for marriage, and its disapproval of unmarried adolescents and young adults bearing children for whom they cannot adequately care, should be expressed. We are here interpreting the social consensus, at least in the English-speaking democratic West, as valuing a loving marriage and family. The fact that society tolerates a wide variety of choices does not make all those choices equal.

(iii) *The school administrator should be careful that teaching styles in sub-disciplines are not permitted to discriminate unintentionally against girls.* For example, it may be worthwhile offering options in physics and maths with different instructional approaches. However, it would seem unwise to exclude boys from the 'cooperative' class or girls from the 'competitive' class.

(iv) *In discussions of family life, there should be a presumption of fairness and a sharing of household tasks.* For example, it is clearly unfair for a working wife to carry most of the household and family responsibilities as well as her full-time job. However, that does not mean that every individual task (i.e., cooking, cleaning must be shared equally). There must be acceptance of the fundamental equality of husband and wife, but not of equal voice in every decision making area.

(v) *Teachers should recognize that any attempt to present a value-free picture of sexual relations is impossible. They should be careful not to present their own view, which is likely to be more liberal than the general public's, as the unbiased, 'moderate', consensual view.* The danger is less from teachers frankly discussing their own views than from their presenting their own ideology as being something very close to the truth. There is much less indoctrination where a teacher says, 'These are my views, but the majority of adults believes X for Y reasons', than where the teacher asserts, 'But don't you think you should recognize that X will have negative effects while W will lead to much more happiness!' The former statement accepts personal responsibility for personal values; the second artfully argues for unacknowledged personal opinion. The only 'true' ideology within the school is that which reflects the school's legitimate goals accurately. (There is of course always transcendent truth, and we have assumed that professional educators will work only in schools with whose normative values their own are reasonably compatible. Therefore, there should be relatively few occasions when any teacher should feel the necessity of expressing a transcendent truth that runs against the school consensus.)

(vi) *Despite the above generalizations, deference should be given to legitimate parental philosophies, even though they may lie outside the school consensus.* Legitimate philosophies are those that are not immoral (for example, they do not engender racial or ethnic hatred; they do not condone lying, lack of compassion, cowardice or fundamental injustice). That deference should not extend to silence on the consensual position or the pretence that all values and cultures are somehow equal or equivalent. Rather, the importance of culture and family should be stressed and the difficulties inherent in conflict between minorities and consensual beliefs recognized.

Some other contentious areas where the school administrator should reflect carefully on students' interests include: ethnic and cultural differences; linguistic differences; racial differences; religious differences; selection of texts and readers, particularly in English; the treatment of homosexuality and abortion. Too often, educational administrators try to ignore or bury these fundamental issues which are part of the stuff of education. Formal education should not be irrelevant to important decisions in daily life, even though its influence is limited.

Together with sexual equality, the status of minority cultures is probably one of the most perplexing policy issues affecting the contemporary school. The status of minority cultures is somewhat different in Canada compared with the USA, with Britain and Australia in this case being closer to the American than the Canadian position. However, contrasts between a Canadian 'mosaic' and an American 'melting pot' probably exaggerate the differences. The USA has a history of long tolerance of its minorities, the Amish being a good example, and Canada has a not very glorious tradition of half-heartedly assimilating native Indians who became neither Indian nor mainstream Canadian. We shall not attempt to outline a cultural or multicultural consensus for any of the English-speaking countries. But even here, particularly here, it is of fundamental importance that the administrator develop clear principles to deal with conflicts among society, cultural groups and individuals.

The Principal in the Everyday Life of the Pupil

In this chapter we have dealt with some aspects of the principal/pupil relationship; other important aspects are dealt with less directly in other chapters. The next two chapters are indirectly concerned with students in terms of the enhancement of their programs. Chapter 8 deals with the development of a moral climate.

There are four occasions when the principal is most likely to deal directly with a pupil: (i) where a problem is raised by parent or teacher; (ii) where there is a discipline problem; (iii) within extracurricular activities; and (iv) in both chance and structured meetings about special school events — year book, assemblies, plays, sports events, school policy, etc.

It is unfortunate but true that in many large schools the principal is either not seen at all by pupils or is seen only as the ultimate 'punishment machine.' The answer is not to divest oneself entirely of disciplinary responsibilities. A better answer is to spend less time on discipline by making penalties for most offences routine, in which case they can often be shared, and to spend more time in curricular and extracurricular activities requiring direct contact with students. The principal should retain involvement with major symbolic activities — suspension and expulsion. The more informal social exchange there has been between administrator and student, the easier and the less necessary the disciplinary function becomes. The more students see administrators trying to grapple with serious disagreement and difficulties within the community and within the larger society, the more they will see a true educational model.

Conclusion

A number of distinctly unfashionable arguments have been developed in this chapter. The principal's relationship with the individual student is not an easy one — the principal is not merely an agent of the parent, or of the state, or of society. The principal is a model of the school's goals and should, as far as humanly possible, reflect those goals, and the societal consensus behind them, in thought and deed. The principal who profoundly disagrees with important, societal educational goals should simply resign.

There is a fundamental conflict between administrator and parent, as well as between administrator and teacher, and that is natural and to a degree healthy. If the fundamental tensions of rivalry, opposition and differing interests are not recognized, small and normal problems may become large and personal. The resolution of such conflicts usually lies not in their dissolution but in sharing, mutual support, and, where necessary, frank and open discussion.

We have argued that discipline, far from being either a desirable or an unpleasant necessity, lies at the school's moral core. It is discipline and praise, punishment and reward, that lie at the heart of the school's legitimate effort to teach moral and social behavior. This teaching should not be in the form of narrow indoctrination; quite the contrary, the administrator should always be at pains to ensure that students understand and, as far as possible, share the school's concern for good behavior and civility, only not by rule memorization but by persuasion and, ultimately, the individual's exercise of deliberate, free choice. To try to persuade students, to try to have them accept personal responsibility, is difficult, time-consuming, but also respectful. The good school uses comparatively little severe punishment (suspension and expulsion) not because punishment is bad, or because students are simply fearful, but because students recognize the symbolic value of membership and actively choose to continue their participation in a shared community endeavor. Their fear of punishment is not more than the fear of losing something valuable in itself. The ideal will never be achieved, but it should not be lost.

Openness, tolerance and value neutrality are, *if used as an educational foundation*, fundamentally antithetical to good education which must be characterized by postive attributes, rather than by the absence of some negative ones. It is the schools that stand for something, not for something else's absence, that are alive and vibrant. Nowhere is this more important than in the administrator's dealings with the students who should come to see in administration the embodiment of the school. As adolescents are frequently rebellious, unruly, undecided, changeable, moody and sceptical, they are likely to come into contact with administrators, who represent, sybolically and in fact, authority. Nothing could be worse than for them to find weakness, fear, ambiguity, uncertainty, lack of faith, lack of trust and vacillation. But it is not enough for the administrator to represent clarity, justice, consistency and predictability; indeed, those qualities can be unhelpful if they are not accompanied (and moderated) by genuineness, sincerity, authenticity and commitment. There is no other area where the principal's role is so difficult and so crucial.

Further Reading

The general approach used in this chapter (as in other sections dealing with the internal working of the school) is functional, although the book taken as a whole is couched within a context of assumed prior purposes. Thus relatively objective observation of how schools actually work may help practitioners use the school's mechanisms to more effect. But we are not merely interested in observing objectively the social functions of schools. Activities are dysfuntional if they subvert the school's legitimate purposes; but we do not see all conceptually possible purposes as being morally legitimate. Durkheim in modern translation (1956, 1961) provides a clear exposition of functional theory, within a value framework not identical to ours. Dreeben (1968) gives examples of the functional idea in a more contemporary context. Coleman (1961) provides good insights into the way schools may unintentionally undermine their own goals. Numerous books have examined aspects of the school's social culture. Good examples include Stinchcombe (1964), Hargreaves (1967), Lacey (1970), Metz (1978), and Peshkin (1986). The implications of divisive policy issues such as gender and education, sex education, multiculturalism and religion for administrators in comprehensive, public schools have not been well developed in the literature. Although there is much commentary from a general curricular and philosophical point of view, only rarely are administrative implications developed. Some useful sources are; Delamont (1980) on gender issues; Holmes (1978a) on ethnic issues and Wynne (1988) on sex education. *Ethics in Education* (published by OISE Press) has published in Volume 7 (1987/88) a number of articles on these issues including a special issue on gender (Volume 7, Number 2). Multiculturalism has been discussed in Volume 7, Numbers 3, 4 and 5 (1988).

Chapter 6

Program: Structure, Development and Implementation

Goals, Program, Evaluation

Program, formal and informal, is the stuff of the school. The basic wealth of the school can be seen as consisting of: material and time, a teaching staff, a group of pupils and a program. To many observers, program should be the most important concern of the school administration. There are, arguably, enormous constraints on what can be done about the other three categories. We have argued that it is not helpful, certainly not in the context of our current knowledge, to lay out a single ideal role definition; but we have also argued that principals should think carefully about how they spend their time and that they should limit the time spent attending to daily events — to telephone calls, to complaints, to squeaking wheels among parents, teachers and students and to regular discipline problems. To say there is no one role definition towards which all principals in all contexts should aspire is not to say that any role definition is as good as any other. A central argument is that discretion is the heart of being professional.

Exhortations to principals to become deeply involved in program are often interpreted as meaning that the principal should be involved, on a day-to-day basis, in curriculum planning. Those promoting this idea usually speak from an elementary perspective; principals in secondary schools are understandably more keen to delegate curriculum development to specialist departments. However, if program is broadly defined to include all the intended experiences, both formal and informal, presented by the school, then obviously a professional principal should be concerned with program. But that broad definition includes most of what is discussed elsewhere in this book — working with students and determining a moral ethos are examples. In this chapter, program is being defined more narrowly — essentially as the school curriculum. So, it is still axiomatic that the good principal should be 'concerned' with curriculum — but that concern is by no means automatically translated into direct responsibility for curriculum development and implementation. Unfortunatly, efforts to persuade principals to become involved in program sometimes result, intentionally or not, in principals telling teachers, however benevolently, how to implement and, eventually, how to teach.

The book began with purposes. The school's purposes should underlie program in a real way. What sometimes happens is that vague statements of goals are scrutinized like tea leaves in a futurologist's teacup; fantasized patterns are built around an already implicit program framework. That is time wasting, bureaucratic nonsense. School goals should be clear enough, whether they are formally written or traditionally implicit so that program objectives can be developed fairly directly. Once legitimate, reasonable, defensible, consensual goals have been developed, it is the administrator's responsibility to ensure that programs reasonably reflect those goals. Professional, effective teachers may reasonably argue that there are other important goals, not directly or adequately addressed in the school set. Education is not an exact science; goals are not always easily separable from methods and sets of goals that truly satisfy the criteria mentioned above are rare. Thus even a fairly good set of goals is not reason to limit a good teacher's instruction in a rigid way, provided that the teacher is effectively addressing a reasonable facsimile of the official goals. It is one thing to do more, to go beyond the goals, another thing entirely to omit some because they are uncongenial. (But bear in mind the assumption that the goals are legitimate, reasonable, defensible and consensual.)

The evaluation of students and their performance in the program is left to the next chapter. That is itself a large topic and an area in which the principal should be involved in a different and even more direct way. This book necessarily runs sequentially, even though the arrangement of chapters may at times be a little arbitrary. In school life, there is neither beginning nor end. A written statement of goals rarely precedes program development and student evaluation. More usually, principals are involved in all three aspects — the discussion of goals and objectives, instruction and program development, and evaluation, all at one and the same time.

Instruction

The Professional and Teaching Methodology

It may seem a little strange to deal with instruction before program development. Instruction can be seen as a detail, a part of the finished program. Instruction is addressed first because issues relating to instruction are far-reaching, fundamental to the teacher/principal relationship and relevant to the way the principal approaches program issues. If our argument is accepted, then certain forms of written program are acceptable, others not.

Already suggested in Chapter 4 is an underlying principle that the professional teacher should have input but not decision making power over educational goals, input and interpretive involvement in evaluation, but primary authority over teaching methodology. The emphasis in this chapter is on program, rather than on the professional. Barrow (1984) argues for the teacher's authority over methodology on narrow, pragmatic grounds. Ironically, he implies an even broader base of professional discretion than we do — he includes areas of purpose and evaluation, but his rationale is based only on a pragmatic argument. Barrow surveys the claims made for a number of generalizations about teaching and finds them to be either lacking in empirical evidence or trivial, common sense truths by definition. Although Barrow overstates his argument by suggesting that there are no useful generalizations about good and bad instruction, it is important to recognize that there is not empirical underpinning for many popular beliefs about instruction, for example:

(i) That small group instruction is better than large group;
(ii) That individualization helps most children, particularly those who are falling behind;
(iii) That smaller classes are more effective than larger classes;
(iv) That inductive learning is better than deductive learning;
(v) That the more students are praised the better they learn;
(vi) That there is a single 'best buy' in teacher style for any given subject matter;
(vii) That personal and expressive approaches to reading and writing are more effective than direct instruction.

Indeed, some of the contrary statements could be better supported by empirical evidence.

In short, there is very little in the way of methodology that a principal can confidently direct teachers to use, beyond the banal or the common sense (which admittedly may still not be obvious to the beginning or extremely incompetent teacher). Students have to be quiet and attentive if they are to learn ideas from the teacher; time wasted in lengthy argument over misbehavior arising from a lack of routine is not learning time; students should be treated with kindness, as persons rather than objects.

One of the important themes concerning professionalism in this book goes beyond Barrow's argument. Even when generalizations do hold, (and, unlike Barrow, we believe some do), their imposition may be unethical and inappropriate. Part of the rationale is Barrow's: the small gains attributed to the best method are easily offset by losses attributable to teachers' loss of interest in using what to them is a 'bad' method and to their sense of loss of control over their work. We add to this an ethical assertion that goes beyond empirical argument: professional teachers ought to be given some control over their work, as it is that discretionary control that makes them professional. It is unethical for bureaucratic hierarchy to eliminate the professional element of a teacher's work without the strongest of counter-arguments (which must be made in terms of benefit to the child).

That is not an end to the discussion. It may in some circumstances be better to have some things taught by non-professionals. For example, experiments using more highly trained non-professionals in the primary grades would be worthwhile. Trained non-professionals, under the guidance of a professional, might be able to provide more effective direct instruction in the basic skills at a lower cost. Professionals often do not like giving direct instruction, partly because it is so straightforward and mechanical, in a word, uninteresting. And sometimes there are strong managerial reasons (factors that are not strictly pedagogical or educational) for reducing teachers' professional discretion. As an example, there may be no compelling instructional reason why *Macbeth* should be taught in tenth grade rather than *Hamlet* or *King Lear* — but if some students will encounter the latter plays in grade 11 there is a very strong managerial reason for the choice of *Macbeth*. This example, it is true, turns to content rather than instructional methodology but there may also be occasions when sequential methodology makes sense too. If a group of slow learners has finally mastered multiplication in fifth grade it hardly makes sense to use a different instructional method for review in grade six. In another exceptional circumstance, some schools are set up with the express intent of reflecting specific educational approaches and philosophies (for example, fundamentalist schools, progressive or alternative schools, Montessori schools). It would be unreasonable for teachers voluntarily taking positions in such schools to demand the right to use methodologies totally opposed to the eductional spirit of the school, however justifiable their preferred methodologies might be on empirical grounds.

This discussion illustrates an important point for the practitioner. Although it is fairly easy to develop conceptual distinctions among goals, instructional methodology and student evaluation, in practice the three become intertwined. A progressive teacher, who may agree to a goal reflecting the importance of learning to read, may object somewhat to that goal being emphasized in first grade and may object stridently to the goal's achievement being evaluated by standardized tests at regular intervals during the primary grades. Subject content (what is to be taught) straddles the classification, sometimes being a goal, sometimes a method.

Despite the many difficulties and exceptions, the general principle remains sound. Professional teachers ought to be given room for professional discretion and there is in most cases no intrinsic reason why a particular instructional methodology should be laid down. There are both ethical and pragmatic reasons for this principle.

Effective Instruction

Most useful generalizations about effective instruction have been developed over the last fifteen years. It is during this period that focused research, mainly in the USA, has led to the discovery of the important components underlying the teaching of the basic skills.

In summarizing six major strands of thought and research relevant to the principal's understanding of effective instruction, we neither ignore nor seek to refute Barrow's argument that we can make no firm generalization about teaching methodology. In practice, we have noted, we are generally sympathetic to the implications of Barrow's arguments, i.e., there are generally few good reasons for overriding professional discretion in the area of methodology. On the other hand, the fact there is no perfect answer, no perfect recipe, does not mean that all advice to teachers, particularly those just beginning and those in trouble, is redundant.

Six Recent Sets of Ideas About Effective Instruction

1   Bloom (1976) using some earlier ideas of Carroll, developed the system of mastery learning, variants of which enable teachers, in some subjects, in some situations, to achieve better overall outcomes with a lower range of difference between the best and the worst.

2   A number of researchers, mostly American, have developed a set of ideas that seem to be related to effective instruction in the basic skills (US Department of Education, 1986). These include: direct, whole class instruction; regular routine; division of content into small sequential pieces; intensive instruction (to a level of mastery), of each piece before movement to the next; frequent testing and regular rewards and reinforcements.

3   Several large-scale research projects confirm that, on balance, traditional, direct instruction is more effective than informal, non-traditional methods, particularly for young children learning basic skills (Bereiter, 1981; Cooley and Leinhardt, 1980).

4   The use of meta-analysis permits large numbers of research studies to be assessed simultanesouly. Once again, even opponents of direct instruction, recognize that overall the research favors this approach (Gatheral, 1979). More recently, meta-analysis has been applied to teaching one of the most difficult and least understood skills — writing. Hillocks (1984) concludes from his analysis of major empirical research in the area that the popular 'process' approach is almost as ineffective as using grammar alone. The same principles successful in mathematics and reading appear to be equally applicable to writing, i.e., students should be directly taught in a sequential manner exactly how they are expected to write — for different purposes and different audiences. Expecting them simply to transpose knowledge of abstract grammar to the complex task of writing is unrealistic. It is also unrealistic to expect that writing will improve by simply encouraging children to write reams of personal

narratives about what they 'feel' — an approach unlikely to prepare students for clear, grammatical writing for a number of purposes and audiences.

5 Over the last twenty-five years, research in 'effective schools' has flourished. This book stems in part from that line of research, which is addressed directly in Chapter 9. Claims of the 'effective schools' researchers are analogous to those of the effective instruction researchers. Conclusions from this line of research are that effective schools are characterized by: clear objectives; firm, consistent discipline; high expectations of students; careful, systematic use of incentives and rewards; and regular monitoring of achievement (Northwest Regional Educational Laboratory, 1984).

6 In the vital and core area of reading, Chall (1983) surveyed fifty years of research and concluded that direct instruction based on phonics is the single, best approach.

It will quickly be seen that the six strands of thought and evidence are internally consistent. But, some accommodation must be made with Barrow's ideas. The most obvious accommodation is this: None of the research cited shows major, substantive differences between good uses of one approach and good uses of another. For example, Chall would not deny that many children learn to read beautifully by themselves or by means of informal instruction. Mediocre teachers using phonics are less successful than good teachers using alternative methods. Many excellent writers have received little, totally inadequate or no formal instruction.

That reason, combined with the earlier argument based on teachers' professional discretion, make it inadvisable, in general, for principals to direct teachers to use a particular methodology. Even persuasion should be used with care. A good teacher who feels philosophically compatible with informal ideas may well be achieving excellent results. There is no reason to believe improved achievement would result from a change to direct instruction.

On the other hand, there are a few circumstances when strong persuasion is justifiable. The most obvious is the case of incompetent or mediocre instruction, where the outcomes are clearly unsatisfactory. Beginning teachers, too, deserve to receive the best advice from the school's professional leader, providing the advice is based on clear evidence of empirical effect (such as that summarized above) or on consensually derived school goals — not on personal idiosyncrasies and 'what worked for me.' They also deserve in-service training opportunities in good forms of teaching. It cannot be assumed that education programs in universities will be based on the latest research. For many years, many faculties of education in Canada and to some extent elsewhere, have been dominated by 'progressives' whose philosophies favor 'child-centred' methodologies — hence the prevalence of these approaches despite their refutation by the empirical research. Advice, in contrast to direction or silence, is nearly always ethical and respectful; however, the principal should be sensitive to the distinction between direction and advice and make it very clear, particularly to new employees, which is which. Many teachers are now accustomed to manipulation; they simply assume that kindly, paternalistic advice is a covert command. They are all too accustomed to administrators coming back about 'advice' not taken, more in sorrow than in anger, saying 'I didn't want to have to tell you; I was trying to be sensitive to your needs.' They are used to the manipulative deceit in the approach, 'Now, I'd like to help you change to more contemporary approaches to teaching. I know how threatening change is so I have arranged for a consultant to come in and help you through the first difficult stages over the next five weeks.' Note that the question of change is side-stepped; no order is given — it is just assumed. Advice, as we have said, is courteous, professional, respectful. Manipulation (in the guise of advice) is odious.

A difficult problem in instructional methodology is consistency among teachers. Very often principals and department heads say that teachers should use a particular approach, frequently one not supported by large scale empirical research, 'because this is how we do it in this school.' If the direction is challenged, response is likely to be:

(i) A consistent approach is necessary if children are to learn;
(ii) Children get confused if they are confronted with different methods from year to year; and
(iii) We work as a team and this is how we have democratically decided to do it.

In the vast majority of cases these arguments are simply not valid. Certainly, it is extremely important for there to be a sequence of learning from grade to grade. Indeed, one of the greatest problems of contemporary schools in the English speaking world is precisely the lack of such sequence, notably in English, junior science and history. But that problem is largely a matter of content (i.e., knowledge, skills, concepts) not of methodology. Ironically, many schools are ideologically tyrannical over teaching method, but *laissez-faire* over content (resulting in repetition, gaps and frustrated students). There is not empirical evidence that consistent teaching style is helpful to learning (although, as we have said, schools that consistently use direct instructional approaches will be a little better than those that are child centred — but that is an argument for a particular method rather than for consistency per se). Conceptually, common sense would suggest the opposite. As different students respond in different ways to different teachers, and as some informal teachers are extremely successful with some students, a range of instructional styles may well be fairest to the greatest number of students. For example, a school that is entirely direct in its methodology may get very good results overall, but may be consistently unsuccessful with a minority of students whose learning patterns and interests are less linear and analytical. If those students tend to be predominantly female (and that is not unlikely), a further problem, is introduced. If elementary instruction is primarily given by women and is characteristically child centred, linear thinkers (often boys) may be disadvantaged.

The second argument, of methodological confusion, obviously carries little weight if the first cannot be supported. Children are admittedly often confused in school. Good instruction should remove such confusion. Teachers should be accountable for their work; if children are confused about fundamental knowledge and ideas they are supposed to have learned, something has gone wrong. But confusion is unlikely to result from changed methodology. Quite the reverse, enormous numbers of students change school every year and those who are successful in one school tend to be successful in another, those unsuccessful in one unsuccessful in another. If educators genuinely believed that difficulties arising from instructional changes ought to be alleviated, they would support much more standardized programs among schools and throughout the nation (an ideal favored by the public much more than by educators). Problems arising from moving, particularly among weak students, are likely to result from their having to learn new things based on structures they had not been taught in their previous school, i.e., it is what one has or has not learned that matters far more than how one was taught.

The third argument, 'We work as a team,' is unprofessional. Some doctors like to work cooperatively, some do not. So it is with lawyers, dentists and teachers. There is no logic in arguing that because three teachers in a department choose to work together using a single methodology, so should the fourth. Indeed, a strong argument can be made for diversity. Students can only benefit from professional competition using different methods to get the best results; the more so if they are able to choose their method of instruction as knowledgeable consumers.

There are undoubtedly cases where methodological consistency is either very desirable or necessary. There would seem to be no sense in changing from the Orff method of music instruction to some other alternative after one grade. It is difficult for a second grade teacher to base reading instruction on phonics if the first grade teacher has used indirect, informal methods. In that case, the second grade teacher may well find that 'remedial' (i.e., beginning over) teaching is required for those students who have learned little but have been promoted on 'social' or other grounds.

Beginning reading and beginning number are probably the areas where the strongest case for directing teaching methodology can be made. Thus a principal might justify instruction as one criterion in hiring a new teacher. However, even in that area, the argument does not extend to forcing an existing teacher who is getting good results to change. Or there may be parallel grades using different approaches. Then parents should be consulted about the placement of their children.

One situation where it is most justifiable to demand or very strongly advise specific methodology is in a school whose philosophy includes a specified methodological approach. This is particularly the case in independent schools where parents have unfettered freedom of choice. In public schools, it is completely justifiable when and only when parents can make an informed choice among several competing educational approaches. It may also be defensible to a limited degree in schools where there is a strong and genuine consensus among administrators, teachers and parents. But today that is unusual if one excludes the situation where the staff inform the parents about all the wonderful new things they are going to do, at the same time providing abundant misinformation about the likely effects on the pupils. Educators should no more claim unverified improvements from an instructional change than should physicians from a change of treatment.

Organizing Effective Instruction

It will be useful at this point to integrate some of the ideas developed at different points in the book. In different chapters, the following points have been made:

(i) The administrator has an array of organizational choices to make in using instructional time;

(ii) Although streaming and non-streaming are often considered simply in ideological terms, although different organizational patterns are unlikely in *themselves* to make major contributions to improved achievement, it is still possible to choose a set of organizational arrangements that best matches the school's own goals;

(iii) Teachers should be left as much professional room as possible to choose their own methodologies; and

(iv) There is reasonably firm evidence that, on balance direct instructional methods work better for the teaching of skills than do less formal methods.

Taken together, those assumptions make some organizational choices at different grade levels more sensible than others. It is important to note that the following arrangements have not been adequately researched and may in fact not be readily researchable. They stem from a set of assumptions based on a variety of arguments — partly empirical, partly on a sense of what a school's purposes ought to be. The desired effects are likely to be best achieved, it seems safe to say, by combining sets of compatible strategies with matching goals. But public claims should be cautious.

Organizing the Primary Grades

The suggestions for primary organization (grades 1 and 2) are based on three assumptions:

(i) *Children entering first grade are less functionally differentiated than are children entering later grades.* This is not a testable proposition (we cannot use the same measures on fifteen-year-olds and six-year-olds), but it is generally accepted and it makes sense. Few children read and have much sense of number (as distinct from being able to count) when they begin school. In contrast, the same children beginning ninth grade vary from being almost illiterate to having reached a very senior level.

(ii) *It is more important at the primary level for children to grow in a broad, well-rounded fashion (i.e., to learn to enjoy singing, dance and art; to learn good behavior and manners and to learn about the society around them) than to compete strongly in skill development.*

(iii) *Children who fail to learn the basics in the first two grades usually fall further and further behind later and often remain illiterate.*

If those three assumptions have some validity, it makes sense for a minimum of differentiation to take place in the first two grades.

Teachers should be encouraged to help children together as much as possible, i.e., not to divide them into homogeneous groups. There will be a few exceptions. Children requiring special care who have serious learning disabilities and exceptional children whose learning has already surpassed the goals for first grade are examples. But in general, the aim is to have all children master the basic concepts of reading and number and to learn to print and count with care and accuracy.

The reader, particularly one imbued with trendy educational ideology, will probably object:

(i) That six-year-olds are very different and should be treated individually;

(ii) That introduction of mass educational ideas into first grade is retrograde;

(iii) Children learn best when freely following their own interests; and

(iv) That this section flatly contradicts the earlier assertion that it is unethical to interfere in the teacher's professional domain.

There is little further to be said about the first three points. The research seems to contradict the third point, the second is rhetorical and the first is a matter of philosophical choice — do we want everyone to become functionally literate or do we want to differentiate children as much as possible at an early age? There is no evidence we can have both. The consequences of that choice should not be lightly disregarded. To individualize is to base instruction very directly on the interests, expectations, demands and culture children bring with them from home. It is easy to understand then why individualized instruction leads to large disparities. As one purpose of the state-supported school is to give children a more equal start, i.e., more equal than if they depended on tuition at home, then outcomes-based approaches make best sense.

The last point is much more troublesome. The suggested advice does appear to interfere with the primary teacher's professional discretion. In defence of some interference, two points may be made:

(i) The research is stronger at this level than any other and justifies strong persuasion;

(ii) Although the organization of the school (and the testing program), should make it 'easy for the teacher to do the right thing', we do not advocate ordering teachers exactly how to teach. Advice, persuasion, yes; imposition and negative evaluation, no. Even though the research evidence is fairly strong at this level, it does not come close to showing that all or most teachers would do better if they switched to direct instructional methods. It merely shows that on balance direct instruction is associated with better achievement.

Although a strong argument can be made for concentrating teaching resources in first and second grade (with class sizes of twelve to fifteen), an alternative argument, derived from discussion in Chapter 4, would see class size remaining normal (say twenty-five to thirty) in these grades with the addition of a full-time technical aide, trained in instructional methods, working under the direction of the teacher. Thus the teacher would retain some professional discretion, deciding whether to exclude some children from the large group and planning instructional strategies while the aide would carry out much of the day-to-day training with most students in the class.

Organizing Grades 3 to 5

These grades may be considered transition grades. Computational and reading skills remain important and writing skills become critical (i.e., students who are not reading and writing well by the age of twelve generally have enormous problems trying to catch up later, unless they are learning to speak English as a second language, having come to it after mastering their own). Most children below the age of ten do not have well developed skills in rational thinking and they are likely to accept the teacher's authority, at least in academic areas. However, the extension of whole class instruction may be unwise as the achievement levels of 9- and 10-year-olds are often extremely varied. To what extent that variation is inevitable and to what extent is results from reluctance on the part of primary teachers to apply mastery learning in a pure form (after all, individualization rather than whole class instruction is fashionable) and from the opposition of parents with bright children to mastery approaches is difficult to say. Whatever the cause, the reality is that the achievement levels of children aged nine to eleven are extremely varied in western, modern, industrialized countries (possibly somewhat less so in the developed communist countries and the Asian countries on the Pacific rim). Thus no pure mastery or whole class approach can be confidently recommended (even though it does work in other countries).

In some academically homogeneous schools, the mastery approach might be continued through fifth grade but with growing numbers of exceptions. In extremely heterogenous schools, formal grouping should begin by third grade.

The general organizational principle should be to group when necessary. Grouping should not be seen as being desirable in itself but as being in some circumstances a lesser evil. Generally, however, it seems likely that grouping in skill areas (mathematics and language particularly) will remain normal by fifth grade. Even with good instruction, some fifth graders will still be reading at the third or fourth grade level, while many others will be reading beyond the ninth grade level. In grade level terms, the difference in mathematics may appear less (from grade level 3.5 at the beginning of fifth grade to grade level 6.5), but the gap in skills is just as or even more marked, comparisons between differences in growth in different subjects being unhelpful. The reality of trying to teach decimal fractions to children who have not yet understood the concept of decimal place value is apparent. Where grouping in skill areas takes place, it should be homogeneous, with level of achievement as measured by standardized tests being a major criterion for placement. However, underachieving bright children should be strongly encouraged to work up to their ability and placed, at least initially, in a group above their level of functioning. The reverse does not hold for slow children — if they keep up by 'overachieving' they should be encouraged — unless the extreme effort is causing evident personal and family problems. Some young people of average or below average measured ability still manage to succeed in quite demanding post-secondary programs. Perhaps their ability grows and develops with constant exercise and effort. Or perhaps they compensate for a lower level of ability by supreme concentration, perseverance and organization. Either way, a child who is functioning at a high level should not normally be discouraged.

Heterogeneous grouping is not inappropriate in all elementary subjects. The purpose here is to outline the principles on which organizational structure should be based. There is no single recipe for all teachers and all schools. And there are always exceptions. Homogeneous groups make sense in focused, step-by-step sequential curricula. Heterogeneous groups make sense in projects where children are to learn to cooperate, with different members making different contributions. They are often useful in science, social studies, drama and debating. Even within the basic skill areas, heterogeneous groups should be used, sparingly, for reinforcing drills — and spelling bees, mathematical computational contests etc. Within that context, better students will coach poorer students to achieve victory for their team, and in so doing will reinforce their own skills.

Organizing the Middle Grades

The following assumptions underline the suggestions that follow:

(i) By the age of eleven or twelve, the variation in achievement level of children is so great in sequential skill subjects begun at the age of six that whole class instuction will usually be comparatively ineffective for the most and least advanced learners;

(ii) Learning is most efficient when learners do not already know what is taught, and when they have developed the prerequisite skills to learn that which is taught;

(iii) As children prepare for the secondary grades, it is important for them to come to understand their strengths and weaknesses in comparison with others and take some responsibility for their own academic progress

The first assumption is a matter of judgment, not a matter of empirical fact. The judgment is shared by most middle grade teachers in mathematics and, to a lesser extent, in reading and language. The second point is conceptually irrefutable although defining the consequent practice is often difficult. The third assumption takes us back to the unavoidable and important distributive function discussed in Chapter 1. However desirable some commentators may believe postponement of division (or 'streaming') may be, the reality is that even in ungrouped, heterogeneous classes one can still predict future success fairly well by the age of twelve. Teachers know who are the most promising students and achievement test results reveal similar conclusions. Best students in sixth grade tend to be the best students in twelfth grade. Major reversals are uncommon. These student differences stem largely from differences in home backgrounds. In Western countries these differences are increasing and the consequences for schools are important.

In the middle grades, roughly ages ten to fourteen, adolescents should be placed in reasonably flexible homogeneous groups, based on achievement and ability, in key sequential areas — at least in mathematics, reading and writing. A common core program should be covered by all (or nearly all), but the bright and ambitious should be able to move ahead faster. The more the program is genuinely differentiated (genuinely 'enriched') the greater the danger that the groups or separated classes will become rigid streams or levels. If one student goes ahead of another in a single program, it is always possible for the other student to catch up later and perhaps even overtake the faster student. But once programs are differentiated, changing from stream or level to a higher stream or level becomes difficult. Inevitably, by the third year of the program it will be difficult or impossible for a student in a slower group to move into a faster group without the help of a special summer or extracurricular course, which should be made available where practical. In grades five and six, homogeneous grouping — whether intra-class, inter-class or inter-grade — should be very flexible. In grades seven and eight, synchronized setting of classes makes more sense than homogeneous grouping if the school population is large enought to permit it. Most courses, where sequence is less important, should be taught in heterogeneous classes, with a large common core of must know skills, knowledge and concepts, together with should know and nice to know components, which will not all be attempted by everyone. Rigid academic and social divisions should be discouraged. As the differences in fundamental skills become more pronounced, the highest homogeneous groups, or, in the case of synchronized scheduling of classes, entire classes should be moved ahead a year for advanced placement in high school. Advancement has an important quality lacking in so-called enrichment; students may work slowly and still achieve the goal (of high school graduation or college entry), but that success may not be possible if they miss sections of the curriculum.

Organizing the High School Grades

The major organizing principles used so far are:

(i) Children should be kept together for instruction as much as reasonably possible;

(ii) Separation into groups, sets, levels or streams should take place extremely conservatively (i.e., groups before sets, sets before levels);

(iii) Separation should be confined to sequential skills; and

(iv) Selection for different groups or sets should be based principally on objectively defined criteria, i.e., achievement level and ability.

These principles can be traced back to Chapters 1 and 3. In Chapter 1, a single set of goals was developed, implicitly for all. That is to say, although one recognizes that not all children will achieve at the same level, the general goals should be the same for everyone. The good school will lead even the poorest student some way within all the domains. But one goal was obviously not intended to be universal as its point of application. It referred to the preparation of young people for their futures in post-secondary education or in work. Obviously, that goal implies a high degree of role differentiation to match the very great division of labor found in developed societies. Thus while limited separation for instruction can be justified as a lesser evil within the elementary grades, at the high school level separation becomes both necessary and desirable to achieve legitimate goals.

Adler (1982) and others argue that separation should be postponed until after high school. The argument about the age of segregation of young people, although heated and often ideological, seems essentially one of practicability and economics. No one argues for segregation on the basis of future occupation at age five; and no one argues that there should be no segregation ever. The division of labor is a reality. For the foreseeable future even rich, developed countries will not provide post-secondary education for nearly everyone both because they cannot afford it and because they find it impractical to persuade all young people to participate in the absence of some significant material reward. (For those destined to less well-rewarded occupational levels, the material incentive for continuing formal education and training is much reduced.) Even in the USA, only about one-half of the age cohort enrols in post-secondary studies; elsewhere the proportions are much lower.

The high school is very different from the elementary school in one other very important respect. Principals in high schools typically have comparatively little authority to determine their organizational structure for instruction. In Canada and the USA, school districts, or provinces and states, typically determine the basis for granting graduation certificates and often also mandate the patterns of permissible programs, for example, advanced, college preparatory, enriched, academic, general, technical basic, vocational. The block schedule and the Carnegie credit system have become the norm in both of those countries. In Europe, either, separate, segregated schools prepare students for different futures or there are separate streams within a single comprehensive school serving the same function. In Europe also, the structure of external examinations serves to determine the organizational features of the school, at least with respect to the increasing proportion of students wishing to leave with some formal qualification.

It is not practical to address the enormous variety of organizational patterns required to meet such a variety of exigencies. Instead, we apply the logic of the argument developed so far to the secondary school grades. In a few schools in a few countries, the ideas may be readily applicable; in others, they may be partially applicable.

Evaluation is formally addressed in the next chapter. At this point, it is important to note that once students are destined for a particular future, as motor mechanics, college students, university students in science or applied science and so on, there is competition within that identified group for limited places. That is to say not every applicant gets into engineering school in university; not every qualified applicant gets a suitable job as a motor mechanic and even when vacancies are readily available (in employment or in post-secondary institutions) not every vacancy is of equal value. Therefore, students must be evaluated in terms of their group. Such programs should be organized in a series of sequential steps that will culminate in the best preparation for their future opportunity (which may be defined narrowly, as a motor mechanic, or broadly, as mechanical and electrical skills). At the elementary level, educators typically think in terms of development and growth; they give secondary consideration to a particular level or standard. But secondary educators have to be concerned both with the level of achievement of the incoming students and with the required standard for at least some of their graduates. Somewhere in the secondary schools, standards can no longer be arbitrary and self-selected.

On entry to high school, students should be placed on a sequential step in a sequential program in key compulsory areas. Thus the intermediate program should mesh closely with the high school program. Some students should receive advanced placement; most will be placed in the regular step but some will require special preparation before they can qualify for the regular step. Either at that time (around the age of fourteen or fifteen) or, preferably, later (around the age of sixteen) students should also be placed in a sequential program leading to their particular chosen future. Thus ideal high school programs in mathematics and language consist initially of a single structural sequence into which entering students are placed according to their achieved level of competence. Access to each successive step is dependent upon success in achieving competence in the defined core (must know) areas of the previous level. Optional courses should be available for students interested in, for example, English for post-secondary entry, for employment and for general enrichment and interest.

The argument about the age of definitive segregation by future career expectation, an issue which is less philosophical than pragmatic, should be settled in a realistic way. The choice should not be made so early that intelligent, informed choice is difficult, and not so late that good preparation for the future becomes impossible. Another reason for not postponing choice until after the end of high school is that many students, it appears, choose to drop out altogether rather than accept twelve years of fairly academic education — they understandably see school as being a holding tank, irrelevant to their future. They are implicitly being asked to forgo current income without any expectation that their later income will be higher as a result. Contrast that situation with students who go to university with the implicit understanding that future higher income will compensate them for the forgone income during the university years. In most developed western countries, the age of specialization should be around fifteen or sixteen, permitting two or three years of specialization.

Table 6 illustrates an organizational pattern in English. Each of the blocks represents a one-year program. Obviously every course could be offered in concentrated one term (semestered) blocks. Each block could also be divided into halves, with promotion every half year instead of every year. In this model, step 2 would be a common language experience for nearly all students (but not at the same age). However, a few students would advance from eigth grade directly into step 3. As step 3 would provide the minimal level for high school graduation, some students would move from step 2 into a specialized practical, everyday English in step 3 which would be their last

Table 6: Organization of a Secondary English Program

	LANGUAGE SEQUENCE (CORE)		OPTIONAL COURSES	
Step 5	Advanced reading, literature, writing	University entrance	Advanced literature 5A	Advanced literature 5B
4	Reading, writing, public speaking, debating	College entrance	Advanced literature 4A	Business English 4B
3	Formal and informal language, correspondence, reports, reviews	High school graduation	Writer's workshop 3A	Everyday English 3B
2	Entry level reading, writing, spoken language			Writer's workshop 2A
1	Prepatory reading, writing	Literacy		

Notes: 1 On entering secondary school (ninth grade, age 14 or 15), students would enter level 1, 2 or (exceptionally) 3 in the language sequence.

2 Level 1 is a basic literacy course.

3 Level 2 is a common program (but with must know, should know and nice to know components.

4 Students may graduate from level 3 in the sequence or from option 3B.

5 The remaining options may be taken in addition to the compulsory, core sequence.

6 A minmium number of credits in English should be specified (four is the number on which the model program is based).

required skills course before graduation. It is assumed also that a specified number of courses in English would be required to obtain sufficient credits for graduation from high school. It would not be possible for a bright student to move directly into step 3, pass the course, drop English and graduate with only a single course in English. The pattern in mathematics would be very similar. In second languages, there would be a single and shorter sequence. In geography and history there would be three-year sequences (steps 2, 3, 4). There could be some additional discrete options. Technical and vocational options, which might be double or triple courses at a given step, would be mainly two-year sequences at steps 2 and 3 or 3 and 4, depending on the required beginning skills in English and mathematics.

One advantage of this plan is its relative simplicity. It can be more easily accommodated in a medium to small school than can a typical three level or three track program because fewer different courses are required. At the same time, it makes the teacher's job easier because students must reach a particular level to gain entry to a subsequent level. Currently, there is usually enormous overlap in skills from level to level (track to track) and from grade to grade. The overlap is particularly evident in English where many ninth grade students are far superior to many twelfth grade students in the same level or track and where many students in a low track or level are superior to other students in a high level or track. Further, as most schools have insufficient students to offer all levels and tracks, students categorized at one level in one school are categorized very differently in another with consequent gross mismatch of students and program.

One facet of the proposed model is its organizing principle: students are sequentially developed for the futures they themselves choose. Thus there is no question of being in a holding tank — they are making progress, slowly perhaps, towards a chosen end.

Overview of Program Organization

We have suggested that principals should only exceptionally be involved in the direction of instructional methodology. Teachers should be given encouragement and support if they wish to work cooperatively to develop and share common methodologies, but there should be no pressure on the dissenter, always provided that teaching effectiveness does not suffer. The administrator's involvement in teaching methodology should generally be informal. In the same way the principal may decide to coach the soccer team, direct a theatrical production or lead a choir. None of those activities implies the principal has any special authority *qua* principal; as a professional, the principal has interests and strengths like any other professional. It makes sense that those strengths be voluntarily contributed to the good of the community.

It was argued too that school organization should be premised on minimal separation of students (except by age) during the early years. As students progress through school, and as the differences between them become more apparent and more difficult to deal with, they should be increasingly separated on the basis of their achievement levels, first by group and then by defined level in key sequential subjects where new learning is dependent on previous learning. Finally, they should be separated both in terms of their level of competence and in terms of their future plans.

Program Development and Implementation

Too often, program development begins without any clear sense of the students who will be in the program, the goals that should drive the program and what the content of the program should look like. In the past, program development and implementation were considered two separate issues. Thus programs were typically developed according to some variant of the Tyler rationale (Tyler, 1950). They were then implemented according to ideas of some of the more recent thinkers in the field of implementation. Fullan's ideas on implementation (1982) are a good example. The concern here is narrower than Tyler's and Fullan's — they were concerned with the general development and implementation of school program, typically at the level of the school district. We are concerned with the school, whose ability and freedom to develop program are limited.

However, many of the major issues are the same. Some of those issues are:

(i) What do we mean by program? What does it look like?
(ii) Which parts, if any, are mandatory?
(iii) How should it be developed?
(iv) What do we mean by implementation?
(v) How should implementation be carried out?

Before addressing the five substantive questions, we shall look at the concept of program development and implementation within the school setting.

Program development and implementation should be integrated parts of the whole. The implicit assumption has been that development precedes implementation — and that first sight appears to be logical. How can one implement something not yet developed? Unfortunately, the assumption has led to a corollary that something that has been developed must be implemented. Thus implementors see their jobs as implementing, as overcoming objections. Teachers who resist change are 'psychologized.' 'They are old; they are conservative; they are fearful of change, they are set in their ways.' The possibility that teachers may reject the new program because it embodies ideas they have tried unsuccessfully before, because it reflects a philosophy they do not share or because the new program demands an instructional methodology with which they would feel uncomfortable is not given consideration. Such ideas, according to gungho implementors, must not be considered seriously, i.e., as anything other than obstacles to be overcome, because if they turned out to be legitimate, the implication would be that implementation should cease or that the program should be massively changed. A good question for school administrators to ask when faced with a new laid on program is: Why not implement, experiment and evaluate as one goes so that one can stop at minimum cost or change direction? No other professional field has new programs to be laid on without adequate justification or testing.

In other areas of practice, medicine, engineering, dentistry, research is always the rule. Indeed, to develop a medical program (a new drug or new form of surgery) and to proceed to implement it without carefully testing along the way would be unethical, dangerous and unthinkable. Yet in education new programs are continually introduced and implemented without trial and experiment. Where there is a pre-implementation pilot, the pilot is virtually without exception planned to find difficulties in implementing the program so the difficulties may be overcome. The difficulties may be inherent faults in the program or reluctance and opposition on the part of teachers. Even if evident faults in the program are discovered, the solution is simply to paper over or eliminate the faults. There is no attempt to discover whether the program is an improvement, i.e., if students learn some different things, or fail to learn some of the old things, or learn some of the old things better or worse. As it is admittedly difficult to ascertain improvement in educational practice, one might assume that imposed program change would be infrequent, except for the necessary updating of knowledge. In fact, the larger educational bureaucracies become, the more frequent the flow of planned changes. Indeed, Fullan and others would evaluate school districts largely on their ability to implement change.

As principals are usually the receivers of new programs, and as they are expected to be 'front line' implementors, it is important for them to ask critical questions. A good set of questions to ask the promoters of a new program is the following:

(i) Which particular areas of learning will this program improve? In what precise ways will children be changed as a result of the program?

(ii) Could you let me have the large-scale, research evidence showing the impact of this or a similar program?

(iii) Have evaluators checked to see if there are any areas of knowledge, skills, concepts, attitudes, appreciation or expression that are harmed by this program, i.e., are there undesirable side effects?

(iv) How is the program to be evaluated in this district? Have we base line data on the old program with which to compare the new? If not, will such data be collected before implementation?

(v) Is implementation mandatory for all schools? For all teachers? Will there be pilot (treatment) schools and control schools that will be compared?

(vi) If a teacher who fails to implement a mandatory program is fired, will the school district be able to produce enough compelling evidence to convince a court adjudicating that teacher's alleged wrongful dismissal that it is reasonably evident that the students suffered as a result of the teacher's decision not to teach the new program? Are there experts who will give contrary evidence?

There are very few recent program innovations on whose behalf favorable answers could be given to those questions. That is an indictment of recent innovation, not an argument against asking the questions. The success of the bureaucratic implementation game, which gives undeserved credit to 'innovative' administrators and consultants, depends upon the bureaucratic compliance of principals, some of whom place getting along with superiors ahead of the interests of the students.

What would be the likely result of such questions being reasonably addressed in advance? The number of national, state, province and district-wide innovations would be greatly reduced. The level of imposition on schools and teachers would also be reduced. The changes by individual schools and by individual teachers would continue and both they and the large-scale changes they go through would be much more carefully monitored.

Decision Making

In Chapter 2, we examined the different ways in which principals could use authority. This book is based on the assumption that, in general, the principal should be an active leader, although not necessarily in all areas. The principal should be an agent for the maintenance of that which is good and the improvement of that which is not so good. This includes the implementation of program changes and the introduction of more desirable content if there is a genuine probability of enhancing student achievement. It also means improving the things that are already being done. The benevolent despot and the consultative bureaucrat are the two types of administrative style that appear to permit active leadership and at the same time remain practical options in the contemporary world. Benevolent despots who decide to take an active role in the program area are likely to be more forceful and more directive than are consultative bureaucrats. But both are likely to consult   the latter on most issues by policy or principle, the former on major issues; the latter with a formal stucture of committees, the former by means of informal conversations with the interested and affected parties.

Contemporary wisdom in educational administration is that decision making within a zone of acceptance can be made fairly freely, but that decision making outside that zone should involve those who have a stake in the decision and those who have expertise (Hoy and Miskel, 1982, p. 282). The problem with this idea is not that it is wrong, but that it is misleading. Administrators are led to believe that there is one effective way of making decisions. But that is incorrect; if one stops to think it through there is no reason at all why it should be. Consider the question of organizing the secondary school on a semestered (term) or non-semestered (annual) basis. Expertise (research) suggests that there is a difference in the value of the two systems; achievement in some subjects is better in non-semestered schools (Raphael, Wahlstrom and McLean, 1986); (Raphael and Wahlstrom, 1986). The application of the idea of stake (among teachers and students, perhaps parents) will certainly favor the semestered plan. Teachers teach fewer sections, meet fewer students in a day and allocate homework less frequently. Students have more flexibility (many can finish school several months earlier) and probably get more of their homework done within the longer class periods. Extensive genuine consultation with all three affected parties might lead to disagreement between teachers and pupils on the one hand and parents on the other. Limited and superficial consultation with parents and full consultation with pupils and teachers, the normal practice, will almost certainly lead to a semestered school. In the Province of Ontario, the vast majority of secondary schools are now semestered. So, consultative decision making is ineffective if we are primarily concerned with student achievement; on the other hand, it is effective in reaching a peaceful decision if some interested parties are consulted and if important information is unavailable. Obviously, there is no particular reason to believe that consultation among people with different ideas and different interests should lead to either a good decision or a peaceful process; and it does not.

If we want a pragmatic generalization, the following is a truth by definition: to make an effective (as distinct from good) decision, one should consult all those with sufficient clout to prevent its implementation. That is crass but true. Some of the people with clout may not qualify under the criteria of expertise and stake. For example, a fundamentalist preacher in a neighboring town with no involvement in the school may have sufficient clout to prevent the implementation of a new sex education program.

Thus there is no simple recipe for achieving the right decision. The recipe for achieving an effective (i.e., acceptable) decision means brokerage politics.

The ethical issue is clearer. It is ethical to consult those people who have expertise and those people who will be seriously affected. There is an enormous difference of course between what is ethical and what works and a confusion of the two may easily lead to decision making that is neither effective nor ethical.

The benevolent despot is in a stronger position than the consultative bureaucrat when faced with the semestering decision. Even in the context of wide consultation, the benevolent despot leaves room for the exercise of administrative authority. Thus, when the decision is announced, the benevolent despot merely notes: most teachers like the idea of a more flexible schedule, but some worry about the consequences for their program; most pupils like the idea of possibly finishing school a few months earlier, but some wonder if they would miss some interesting courses and most parents are concerned about achievement levels. The consultative bureaucrat, who must count votes in a formal setting, is more constrained. To go against a vote of the staff of seventy to fifteen would be an act of conspicuous courage, or of foolhardiness.

This is not to endorse the style of benevolent despot, merely to point out that in some circumstances it may lead to better decisions. But to return to the point made in the first chapter, the quality of the decision is dependent on the principal using traditional authority within the context of consensual goals. Without consensus, or if the principal acts in areas beyond traditional authority, the principal is likely to be soon in trouble. The decision to favor achievement would be morally legitimate.

Does it make sense to consult teachers affected by very minor changes of program? There appear to be two principles to apply here. One is the triviality test, the other is the control test. Teachers do not usually enjoy long periods of time discussing trivial issues in staff meetings. This is one of the truisms underlying the notion of a zone of acceptance. There is tacit agreement in most organizations that certain decisions should be made by the boss. However, an objection to the zone of acceptance concept is the implication that whatever has proved acceptable in the past remains acceptable; the obverse holds true — if the zone is very constricted, there is almost nothing the principal can do without consultation. Thus the democratic leader tends to constrict the zone of acceptance, the despot to broaden it. There is obviously no single 'right' formula; but equally, whatever happened in the recent past is not necessarily 'right' either. The triviality test suggests that teachers should be involved in decisions, whether or not they have been recently, in areas involving their professional discretion. The control test concerns the eventual influence of the principal and staff on the decision. Normally, if an unambiguous decision has been made by a central government or the school government or the school district there may be information to disseminate, there may be a need for discussion, but consultation is not appropriate, unless the external directives appear to be professionally, morally or ethically objectionable. In the same way, teachers ought to be consulted about program matters if the proposed change is neither externally mandated nor trivial. Past practice and current organizational norms should be taken only as very general guides.

An additional test to be applied, particularly in major decisions, is the moral test. Are there moral or ethical implications in the decision? A decision to teach Latin America before Australia rather than vice versa is not considered moral. However, a decision to abandon a study of Africa and replace it by a study of apartheid in South Africa would certainly have a moral (and ideological) component. The presence of a moral component makes extensive consultation much more necessary, because moral concerns are often rightly at the centre of people's lives. Thus while most parents are somewhat interested in the teaching of beginning reading, not at all interested in the detailed content of a course in the history of the middle ages, they are very interested in a new program in, say, sexual awareness.

The principal should consider five aspects of the decision before beginning consultation:

(i) Who has sufficient clout to overturn any decision in this area? The answer to that question should temper the entire process. This criterion is practical.

(ii) Is the decision trivial? If so (and if the answer to the first question does not cause alarm), then any consultation should serve purely practical, *ad hoc*, purposes.

(iii) Has the decision already been made? If there is little or no possibility of changing the decision, a semblance of consultation is likely to be dysfunctional and, very possibly deceitful. For example, weak principals often love to consult on such decisions because they can then join with their colleagues in complaining and hand-wringing, giving them a short-lived sense of collegiality. Despite the temporary solace, they become further weakened by the process. Their inability to affect the school's direction becomes more and more evident to all and their informal authority thereby weakened.

(iv) Does the decision have a moral or professional component? If it does, then consultation should be exhaustive. If the problem also involves educational substance, parents as well as teachers must be involved. As moral decisions often arouse fierce sentiment, care must be taken to consider again all those who have sufficient clout to overturn the decision, even if they are not directly involved.

(v) Who ought to be consulted? At this point, notions of expertise and interest (stake) should be considered.

Decisions in the area of program are numerous. Some concern content, some concern elaborative approaches to instructional methodology, some concern materials, some concern sequence and some concern implementation. For the remainder of this chapter, we shall concentrate on two of the most important types of decisions: program development and program implementation.

The Tyler Rationale

In North America, most program development follows a model very similar to the Tyler (1950) model. Although schools only rarely develop complete programs from scratch, one should be aware of the basic components of the model. Tyler begins by asserting that three sources should be used for the development of ideas about objectives:

1 Study of the learners;
2 Contemporary life outside the school;
3 Subject specialists;

Two external disciplines of knowledge should then be brought to bear on those three background components:

4 Philosophy;
5 Psychology;

At this stage, useful, behavorial objectives should be developed:

6   Behavioral statements of objectives;
    These objectives should be stated in specific terms, describing how students will be different as a result of the instruction.

Next, learning experiences should be developed to ensure the objectives are achieved:

7   Learning experiences;
    The learning experiences should focus on: (a) thinking; (b) information; (c) social attitudes; and (d) developing interests.

The experiences should be organized within a program:

8   Organization of learning experiences;
    The organization should assure: (a) continuity (from term to term, year to year); (b) sequence (development of the idea from simple to complex); and (c) integration (among subjects).

Finally, achievement of the objectives should be subjected to:

9   Evaluation.

Results of the evaluation loop back to begin the process again.

The widespread use of these ideas, and variations of them, speak to their utility. They at least provide a set of criteria for the program developer to apply. Three major considerations lead to a somewhat different approach.

Problems with the Tyler Rationale

Most important, all program should be rooted in the school's goals. Ironically, the Tyler rationale will be least harmful in those schools with the most rooted and clearest philosophies, i.e., the direction is so clear that they can afford to begin with learners in contemporary life.

More generally, however, program development based on Tyler's ideas has often proved to be characterized by superficial contemporary trends. For example, beginning readers have often excluded myth and legend because they are 'irrelevant' to the lives of inner-city children. Stories of courage and romance are replaced by uninteresting but 'relevant' stories, written to a formula of multi-ethnic representation and equal participation by sex. Ironically, such stories end up being far more remote from everyday life than the truths of sibling rivalry and intergenerational conflict reflected in traditional myth. Children's ignorance becomes, perversely, a rationale for not teaching them. Indeed, much of the force of the 'effective schools' research (discussed further in Chapter 9), stems from the widespread existence of poor programming based on thoughtless application of ideas by well-meaning people inspired by people like Tyler and Dewey. (The philosophy underlying Tyler appears to be Deweyan, modified by some Skinnerian behaviorism.) Some of the undesirable features of badly applied Tyler are:

(i) There is a loss of substance, as every experience is made 'relevant' or fun.

(ii) As some learners fail to learn, there is a downward spiral of expectations justified by such unauthenticated and often meaningless rationales as: 'Children have not yet reached the age of abstract thought, i.e., they cannot understand science at age 10'; 'Children have to be at the right stage to be taught X and Y'; 'Children have to be motivated before they can learn', 'Children are only interested in what is directly relevant to them.'

(iii) Learning experiences take precedence over learning.

(iv) There are no built in checks on the program until the final evaluation.

(v) Evaluation takes place only of the specified objectives, so there is no consideration of whether children are learning what they really could or ought to learn.

A second problem is with behavioral objectives. Little will be said of them as they are not widely used today. Indeed, today there is probably a much greater problem with vague, meaningless goals and objectives than with overly precise ones. It is still worth noting the following standard objections to behavioral objectives:

(i) They are generally less easily applicable to the more holistic subjects such as advanced literature, advanced history and to expressive goals.

(ii) They focus teaching and evaluation narrowly on what has been precisely captured in the objectives, rather than on a broad conception of what children ought to learn and become.

(iii) They direct teachers' methodology and inhibit their methodological freedom.

(vi) They imply that subject matter can be ordered most appropriately in uniform, bit-size pieces developed outside the context of instruction.

(v) They are often too numerous for the teacher to keep in mind at one time. (How can students be expected to learn bite-size pieces which even the teacher cannot remember?)

(vi) They make useful synthesis of learning very difficult for students.

We are not advocating vague, nebulous statements of intent with only indirect bearing on how children will actually change as a result of the instruction. Objectives should clearly indicate the kind of changes one wants to see in children and intelligent, objective observers should be able to agree reasonably on whether the changes have in fact taken place.

194

Before mentioning one further objection to the Tyler rationale, taking the form of an external critique of what it excludes, we present a modified Tyler rationale consistent with the philosophy and approach of this book.

Stages of Program Development

1 *List and interpret the relevant school goals.* If the school has no written goals or only vague ones, then relevant goals must be inferred (if the school has a clear philosophy) or developed (if it has not).

2 *Develop objectives by grade or by term.* The objectives should be sufficiently detailed to guide evaluation. However, there should only be as many objectives as are necessary to describe the learning requirements of the students to an interested observer — such as an average parent. This probably means between ten and twenty-five objectives per course per year (fewer in art and musical appreciation, more in language and the social sciences).

The objectives, directly derived from the goals, should be developed in conjunction with:

(i) Content — the 'stuff' of the program over the grades surveyed should be summarized and put in sequence;

(ii) Levels of competence — the 'stuff' of the objectives should be considered in terms of must know, should know and nice to know. One alternative is to develop the objectives themselves in must, should and nice components. For example, a must know objective for a tenth grade course in European geography might be (a) students must know: the geographical situation of major European countries (Great Britain, France, West Germany, East Germany, Italy, Sweden, Norway, USSR, Poland) and their capitals; the climate and agriculture of Mediterranean Europe, Atlantic Europe and the North European Plain. In contrast, a nice to know objective in the same course might read: (c) For honor standing, students will appreciate the influence of the Iron Curtain on different types of economic and social development on either side of its border.

(iii) Learners' prior level of knowledge and understanding: the principle of taking students from where they are is a sound one providing it is not used to limit expectations of growth.

3 *Activities, materials and teaching techniques.* This section may be as detailed or general as one chooses, depending very much upon the wishes of the teachers involved. This section, unlike the objectives, would be advisory rather than policy.

4 *Program and student evaluation.* This important issue is left to the next chapter.

Program Implementation

Two problems with the Tyler rationale have been dealt with — the secondary status it, probably inadvertently, gives to fundamental educational purposes, and the impracticability of detailed behavioral objectives. The alternative approach emphasizes grounding one's educational program in a consensually derived set of goals, which does not encourage the removal of programs of proven educational value in the name of fashionable trends, which focuses from the beginning on minimal standards as well as on more difficult, should and nice to know objectives and which reduces objectives to a manageable set.

A third problem with the Tyler rationale is equally applicable to the modified model. Program development and implementation should not normally be separated.

Fullan (1982, p. 56) argues that four fundamental factors affect program implementation:

(a) Characteristics of the change (including its need, relevance, clarity, complexity and quality);

(b) Characteristics of the school district (including its history of innovation, administrative support and community characteristics);

(c) Characteristics of the school including the principal, teacher-teacher relations and teacher's characteristics);

(d) External characteristics (including government and other external influences).

Although the four headings do summarize the kinds of things educators should consider as they think about changes and innovation, the mainstream, contemporary approach, typified by Fullan, has several shortcomings. Among them are:

(i) Going further than Tyler, the mainstream approach encourages the bypassing of fundamental educational goals. Frequently, new educational innovations are not tied to explicit goals that have been carefully thought out and agreed upon. For example, the rush to place computers in elementary classrooms has been generally accomplished by hype (based on a few individual cases) about what children can do with computers — and notably not about important eudcational purposes which computers can help fulfil.

(ii) Program implementation usually ignores moral and ethical problems. Thus, types of persuasion are implicitly endorsed that see teachers as objects; teachers are to be given a 'sense of ownership' of programs which have been externally developed. Fullan makes no mention of this kind of abuse and indeed makes no reference to moral or ethical principles in implementation.

(iii) Although Fullan and others recognize the continuity of program development and implementation, their implementation plans generally assume that implementation is a good thing, the more the better. The possibility that a new program (which apparently meets the criteria of need, relevance, clarity, quality, administrative support, hierarchical support etc.) *ought not* to be implemented is not considered. Yet there are reasons why this may be the case: the program may be extremely offensive to a significant minority of parents, for example, a new sex education program; the program may not address important goals, for example, an elementary computer program; the program may be extremely inefficient in terms of staff and material costs; the program may have negative side effects, for example, language immersion programs such as French immersion in Canada which has served to segregate children on social class lines; the program's effects may not have been adequately measured or the program may simply be a bad program; for example, value clarification programs are based on the assumption that all values are up for grabs and that adolescents should choose their own in consultation with their peers.

Although the current literature emphasizes the importance of the principal's role in providing leadership, the assumption is usually that the principal's task is to take what comes down the bureaucratic ladder and implement it. Occasionally, some recognition is given to school level innovation but never to the principal's responsibility to monitor, question and even refuse innovation. If educational change had been subject to the rigorous testing given prescription drugs, then the principal's role would in fact be one largely of implementation, although we should always bear in mind responsible physicians adopt a very conservative stance with respect to many controversial and high risk drugs. But, it is almost unknown for educational programs to undergo external testing under closely monitored conditions before general implementation. Indeed, many never get adequately evaluated despite widespread implementation and general approval or disapproval. Fullan does endorse the idea that innovations should change as they are being implemented. But that is a very different consideration indeed. The point made here is that in many cases innovations should be rejected not changed. Indeed, recent research on implementation suggests that sound innovations should not be changed during implementation; as they change they lose their effectiveness (Huberman and Miles, 1982). Thus, if one does have a highly effective new program it ought not to be changed to suit the convenience of the administration and the teachers; the change many very well remove the effective components.

Thus several strands of thought developed earlier come together as the principal considers the implementation of a new program, which may be developed within the school, or more likely, is being sent down by the school district:

1 The question of the value of the program, its appropriateness in terms of the school's goals;

2 The problem of decision making and the involvement of teachers and parents;

3 The professional authority of the teacher and the conditions under which it may be legitimately invaded; and

4 The problem of integration of program development and implementation.

Current Practice

Principals often become enthusiastic about a new program they hear about. Often the motivation is seen as suspect by other principals and by teachers. As schools are frequently not evaluated in terms of their actual effects on their students, principals believe, not unreasonably, that being visible and being first to implement a new program are criteria of success and promotion. Thus although a degree of enthusiasm by educators of all kinds is a *sine qua non* for success, fervent enthusiasm, redolent of conversion to a new religion, is often harmful in two ways: the principal's suspension of disbelief makes it all the more likely that problems and difficulties in the new program will be ignored or overridden; and, senior teachers' cynicism about the latest fad is reinforced by what they see as, at best, child-like naivety and, at worst, Machievellian manipulation, on the part of the principal. Such enthusiasm often leads to more form than substance — to computers purchased in all manner of ways but rarely used, or used only in superficial programs with little discernible educational content.

Principals sometimes deal with programs in a neutral, bureaucratic manner. They provide information and act as go-betweens, and avoid personal involvement. This approach is better than enthusiasm for ill thought-out innovations; it is not very helpful to ones that are potentially useful. Strong teachers easily resist school district consultants, who typically have little power. The principal's bureaucratic neutrality is not seen by either party as support for the innovation.

Occasionally, principals are more negative. New programs are delivered with a knowing wink or a lighthearted jest ('Here's another package for your closet'). This approach is unfair to teachers, who are left with the responsibility of deciding whether or not to do anything at all about the new program without knowing where the principal will be standing if there is trouble from the senior administration.

Those three undesirable treatments of change are probably not the norm. They are just examples, familiar enough to experienced teachers, of how principals can avoid their professional responsibility. Only the neutral approach can be defended — in some circumstances. For example, suppose an innovation arrives to which the principal is unsympathetic. It appears to be similar to some used unsuccessfully earlier and it involves teaching methodologies which the principal has found unhelpful and certainly has no wish to impose. On the other hand, the program has been partially re-searched and there has been some local, limited success. The principal feels strong support would be insincere but has no strong grounds or principle on which to reject. Neutral, bureaucratic handling makes sense. But unbridled enthusiasm is never fair — at least there has not been an educational innov-ation over which unbridled enthusiasm has proved justified; and dissent by innuendo is cowardly.

A Plan for Program Development and Implementation

The following steps form a sequence reflecting the thesis developed in this chapter. There is no suggestion that the principal should take personal re-sponsiblity for all the steps. A good program passed by the school district should already have gone through the initial steps before it reaches the principal. The principal's responsiblity is limited to checking the results from these early steps.

1 *Identification of the innovation or change.* The new program may be based on philosophy (young people ought to learn more about economics and sociology in school), a good idea (if chil-dren learn to enjoy being read to in the elementary grades, they will think more positively about reading), a new technology or methodology (a video tape may be used to teach and test observation and listening skills) or on a problem (many sixth grade children have not learned the basic skills). But the basis may be a hare-brained, badly researched idea.

2 *Development of the idea.* The idea should be developed in suf-ficient detail for it to be rationally assessed. If the idea is signifi-cant but not entirely original (and few ideas are) then the ques-tions about the past research on its effectiveness listed earlier in this chapter should be directly addressed.

3 *Decision about continuation of development and trial.* The decision should be made by the legitimate authority, for example, the principal, the district chief educational officer, elected school board, after appropriate consultation. The decision should take into account: the program's fit with major goals; the current program; currrent levels of achievement; research findings on the same or similar ideas, if available. If the program involves a replacement of a current program, careful research should be carried out on: objectives not being achieved by the currrent program; appropriate but missing objectives; redundant objectives and areas of possible weakness. If the

program is a new add-on program, for example, AIDS education, the overall goals must be carefully considered by all concerned. If the program is deemed desirable but does not fit the organization's goals, then the goals themselves should be changed — and that should not happen lightly.

4 *Development and implementation plan including decision making.* In general, the plan should cover the steps that follow. Particular emphasis should be placed on who is responsible, who has a right of veto and when 'go' and 'no go' decisions will be made.

5 *Formal decision on development and mode of implementation.* At this point, it must be clear whether the program, if successfully developed, is to be mandatory for all affected grades and teachers, optional or limited in some specified way, for example, as a trial in one out of three fifth grade classes. It should be clear by now that in most cases new methodological approaches to old objectives should not be mandatory.

6 *Program development.* The steps were listed earlier in this chapter:
    (i) Reconciliation with schools goals;
    (ii) Development of objectives;
    (iii) Activities, materials, techniques;
    (iv) Evaluation (student and program).

7 *Pilot implementation.*

8 *Program evaluation.*

9 *Decision on further implementation.* The feedback may lead to a change in the original plan. For example, the outcomes of experience may be so negative as to abandon the entire change. But they may also be so positive as to warrant speedier and fuller implementation.

10 *Confirmed implementation.*

11 *Further development of materials, in-service training and policy.*

12 *External program evaluation.*

Those steps are difficult and time-consuming. Common sense suggests that they should not apply to minor, consensual organizational changes. However, even if they are only applied to major program changes in substantive subjects, not mere updating of knowledge and terminology, they will tax the resources of most districts and schools. There are several competing explanations of the discrepancy between the plan and current practice: (i) this plan is hopelessly unrealistic; (ii) schools and districts are understaffed; (iii) educators do not know how to evaluate programs efectively; and (iv) many programs are unnecessary. If the last one is valid, the first and second are irrelevant. It is very rare for schools or districts, or even states, provinces and countries, to measure carefully what is and is not being learned before deciding that an existing program is inadequate. The most optimistic observer of current educational patterns in the developed English-speaking world would not claim that much improvement in average achievement has been made in the last twenty years — yet the program changes have been countless.

It is sometimes argued that change is good in itself. It forces teachers to think about what they are doing. That hypothesis should itself be tested, because it seems improbable. Certainly it is a specious argument for forcing those professionals to change who are getting good results already. Most good teachers do in fact continually change and update their programs — trying different approaches and materials. There is an important difference between (i) a thoughtful professional learning about different approaches and choosing to apply them, and (ii) a bureaucracy compelling or engineering changes within professionals' pedagogical domain.

Implications of Program Change for Decision Making

Earlier in this chapter, several principles were developed for decision making, with particular reference to the involvement of teachers in curricular change. The power relationships must be taken into account. It is usually sensible to consult those who have the clout to veto the decision, at least if there is some possiblity they may use their power. Decisions that are trivial should be made without or with very limited consultation, even if predecessors have consulted widely. But the decision to change that pattern should itself be the subject of consultation. Decisions with an important moral component should be treated with extraordinary sensitivity, i.e., parents and, possibly, students should be involved in issues where they would not be but for the presence of such a component. It is ethical to consult fellow professionals about any possible change that may affect their working lives, particularly in areas where discretionary behavior is or ought to be important.

The precise methods by which consultation takes place, informally, in staff meetings, in formal committees, are not a matter for discussion here. Partly the method will depend on circumstances — the size of the school, the historical pattern of committees, partly on personal choice and partly on the way in which authority is to be wielded, as discussed in Chapter 2.

Principals sometimes have difficulty in consulting teachers and parents about substantive program issues. They complain, 'If I announce in advance that the decision is made and that the consultation is about implementation only, teachers say that all the big decisions have been made, the meetings are a waste of time, and they are being manipulated into giving tacit approval. If, on the other hand, I state in advance that the decision is not made but then fail to act on majority opinion, I am told that I was not upfront and that the consultation was an empty charade, a waste of time. What teachers mean by consultation is that I should listen to them and do what they say.'

It is usually neither truthful nor practically useful to announce in advance that one's mind is made up. However committed to an idea within his or her discretionary domain of authority a principal may be, there are factors that could cause change. For example, a senior administrator might order the principal not to proceed. (Such an order might result from strong parental complaints supported by the school board.) A group of key teachers including the vice-principals or indeed the entire teaching staff might threaten mass resignation, a vote of no confidence in the principal, or mass requests for transfer. Most principals would change their minds long before any of those events took place. Determination has its bounds. However, it is patently unethical to 'consult' with the implication that one has an open mind when the decision is all but foreordained.

Simple truthfulness is, as always, the best policy. Suppose there is a discretionary program the principal wants to develop and implement. Suppose there is reasonably strong research evidence to support it, certainly none to refute it — and no likely negative side effects. For example, the idea might be a four times a week, compulsory, twenty-minute period of fitness training for all students. The principal might well say to a staff meeting or to the appropriate staff committee, 'I am very committed to this change as our recent tests show most of our students are far from fit. I plan to ask all parents for comments in a parent newsletter and raise the matter with the PTA. Although I shall have to hear very strong reasons to be dissuaded, I would like to have comments and suggestions from all. I talked about the plan with the physical education teachers this morning as they will be very likely teaching much of the new program. Also, they will be losing some of their regular scheduled time to the new program. But some of the additional time will have to come from some other area, probably from social studies. Of one thing I can assure you, no teachers currently on staff will lose their jobs as a result of the change, but there will be some change in schedules. This is the consultation process I have in mind . . .'

One question that arises is whether or not it is ever legitimate for a principal to proceed with a plan that is opposed by a majority of staff. In principle the answer must be affirmative. There are some issues where teachers' self-interest conflicts with students' best interests; the responsible principal openly and evidently mediates such sensitive conflicts. However, teachers can also effectively disempower the principal by threatening a no confidence motion or mass resignation. Here than we may have a classic conflict between power and ethics. Obviously, the administrator must tread very carefully. If the issue is important enough, the principal may have to be prepared to resign, 'If a majority of you vote against the principle of increased regulation of students' homework, I shall offer my resignation.' Note that the principal pre-empts a 'non-confidence' motion by such a gesture. Principals are stronger when they offer to resign on a point of principle than if they wait to be, at least to the outside world, forced out. Note also that the motion is one of principle, not a detailed plan — so that teachers will have to vote directly on the issue at hand and will not be able to argue afterwards that their vote was not on the substance but on a badly thought out plan or poor implementation. But note also the danger: teachers may simply vote against the proposal as an easy way to get rid of an administrator who has proven demanding on different occasions on very different matters. When the lion is wounded, evey hyena circles to get its bite.

Clearly that situation would be a very unusual one and one that any sensible administrator would desperately try to avoid. But administrators should have some bottom line, some point beyond which they will not go to betray the interests of the students. There are often ways to avoid confrontation, by compromise or negotiation. Sometimes, higher authority is used. If principals recognize a problem, they may ask for a school district policy or for a new clause in the collective agreement. Sometimes, less ethically and more dangerously, many manipulate their change by means of carefully selected advisory committees in combination with threats or bribes to the disaffected. In short, there is no magic solution to the problem of confrontation on central, substantive matters. The good principal will try to lead teachers in a professional manner in positive directions in which at least the majority wishes to go. But there are times when the only ethical thing to do is leave.

Conclusion

It is ironical that most contemporary advice to principals from 'experts' in educational administration suggests they should be program leaders. Yet research into what principals do suggests that many have little involvement with program, particularly in the case of secondary principals. Our own experience with school principals suggests that elementary school benevolent despots are involved to some extent in school program; but secondary school bureaucrats, brokers, democrats as well as benevolent despots are usually not. Part of the difference stems from the greater complexity of the secondary schools and its subject differentiation. Just as important a cause is the bureaucratization of the secondary school, for which complexity is only one of several causes. In an informal organizational setting, power and authority can be wielded dexterously with little danger. Within a developed bureaucracy, only regular, already legitimate lines of authority may be used with impunity. Once again, then, we are returned to the theme of the first chapter — the need for a school to have a strong sense of commitment to a consensual set of purposes. Only then can a principal move with ease to change programs based on the initiative of teachers and administrators, and perhaps parents too. In the absence of such consensus, the principal is likely to be reduced to behaving bureaucratically, going through the motions of implementing programs of variable quality derived externally.

Many approaches to school change imply that once an innovation or new curriculum has been announced, the administrator's problem is to overcome all opposition. Implementation is simply getting over or around opposition, getting things done. The suggestion in this chapter is very different. Very likely, as currently produced, most new programs and innovations are not worth implementing — certainly if there is strong and professional opposition from teachers. The responsibility of the administrator is not to act as a bureaucratic cog in the wheel, not just to follow orders, but to bring about genuine improvement in the education of learners. This requires dealing with empirical evidence, continuing evaluation, teachers' professionalism, ethics, widespread consultation, consensual goal setting — least of all the manipulation of teachers' behavior. Ultimately, the principal remains an employee — of a government, of a school district or of a board of governors. It is unethical to force unprofessional change on teachers. But it is also unethical to undermine legitimate policies by quietly encouraging noncompliance. Bad policies should be challenged and confronted. The loyal administrator speaks honestly and openly to superordinates and subordinates alike, and leaves the job if there are fundamental, irreconcilable differences with either.

Further Reading

The US Department of Education booklet (1986) provides a useful summary of research on instruction, although inevitably it is somewhat superficial and occasionally contradictory. We know of no good analysis of the different ways administrators can organize classes for instruction. Barr and Dreeben (1983) is a good beginning. Streaming has been extensively but inconclusively researched. Everything seems to depend on the context. Jackson (1964) shows how streaming in the elementary school is to some extent a self-fulfilling prophecy. (Phenix 1964) gives a fine overview of curriculum from a philosophical perspective. Pratt (1980) is a good example of contemporary work on curriculum; generally sensible and mainstream, its premises are pragmatic. Thus, from our perspective, it lacks secure grounding in a justified educational philosophy although many of its conclusions and suggestions are unobjectionable. Barrow (1984) argues, as we do, for a degree of teacher autonomy, but his argument is based mainly on the inadequacy of the reaseach rather than on ethical and professional grounds. Fullan (1982), using a bureaucratic premise, gives a popular, mainstream approach to implementation. Huberman and Miles (1982) is one of a very few useful contributions to a relatively new research area, school improvement, a field that attempts to bridge the gap between school change and school effectiveness. Early work on school change, of which Sarason (1971, revised in 1982) is a classic, tended, in our view, to see change too much as an end in itself. School effectiveness, which we shall look at further in Chapter 9, has too often used very narrow criteria of outcomes. The school improvement literature attempts, not always successfully, to bridge the gap.

Chapter 7

Student and Program Evaluation

Why This Chapter?

Readers may be surprised to find this chapter in a book about school administration. Although teacher supervision is normally an important part of most books on and university programs in educational administration, student evaluation is usually not considered directly. Devoting a chapter, even a comparatively short one, reflects the position that it should be an important focus of a school administrator's attention. Increasingly, the effective schools research is showing that the student is indeed the centre of the educational process and that it is the student's rather than the teacher's behavior that requires most attention.

Suppose one is head of a large, traditional academic secondary school in Europe. The most important facet of student and school evaluation is likely to be success in external examinations. Even in the USA, some academic high schools are oriented to college entrance board tests and, through them, to access to the best universities. In those cases, it is understandable that the school administrator decides to give a low priority to internal student evaluation. Nevertheless, even in those cases it is unwise to ignore outcomes, or lack of outcomes, in domains other than the academic — moral behavior, aesthetic development, and expression in music, art and speech. Some elementary school administrators may also spend comparatively little time on academic evaluation; perhaps the school district requires regular standardized testing. In a few cases, teaching may be directed towards mastery, and that mastery may be adequately evaluated by a laid-on district program of sequenced tests by program-related criteria.

Even in the more usual situation where problems in student evaluation are serious and complex, some good principals will decide to choose different priorities. For example, the principal of an inner-city school plagued by violence, poor attendance, malaise and vandalism will reasonably address first the central issues of safety and order. But none of those situations explains why much more emphasis should be placed on teacher evaluation than on student evaluation — particularly in the light of the apparent lack of utility of most teacher evaluation policies.

This book has emphasized the importance of distinguishing goals and outcomes on the one hand from teaching methodology on the other. The school should reflect the public will about purposes and be accountable to the public for outcomes. The idea that professional teachers should take responsibility for their methodology is not of course an argument that can be empirically investigated, but it is one unlikely to be frontally refuted. However, critics of our position are likely to suggest that professionals should have major input into both purposes and methods of student and program evaluation because they are interested, knowledgeable and expert. In other words, disagreement is likely to be over degree rather than principle. Without taking an absurd, extreme position that teachers should not have responsibility for policy in evaluation at all, we do argue that, as in the case of goals and objectives, administrators should play a crucial part in evaluating outcomes, with a few exceptions. As part of their role, administrators should act on behalf of the public will to ensure that students are truly evaluated in terms of legitimate goals and objectives and not on a limited set of goals idiosyncratically selected by individual teachers.

This chapter is devoted principally to student evaluation; it is a major activity of the school. Once custody, safety and order have been established, the quickest way to attract negative parental attention is to fail to evaluate students or to evaluate them in some discriminatory or incomprehensible fashion. Once a school is in a position to evaluate systematically all the goals in all the domains with all students, most of the substance of desirable program evaluation is *ipso facto* accomplished. It is possible to evaluate program without evaluating the individual students, by using samples of students and by questioning teachers about students' behavior, but it is not possible to carry out effective evaluation of students without also at the same time making some kind of assessment of program.

Purposes of Student Evaluation

Purposes can be grouped under four major headings, two of which are most important in this context. The most obvious reason for evaluating students is to discover what is known, what is being learned — in short, to aid instruction. This process sometimes merely entails observing students' behavior (are they listening? do they understand?) and sometimes it involves pre-tests, post-tests and quizzes. *Formative* evaluation is that which takes place during rather than after instruction. As a general rule, it does not make sense to include results of formative quizzes in a *summative* grade (although the teacher may well comment on formative experiences, verbally to the student and parent and in writing on a report). One sensible way to teach is to measure what is known before instruction begins, and measure what is known after instruction and to provide evaluation only when one is satisfied that nearly everyone has learned what has been taught.

Student evaluation also forms a potent form of incentive to learn (as an extrinsic or maternal/purposive incentive in terms of the classifications used earlier in this book). As students become older, as they become more aware of the requirements of work or post-secondary study, they become increasingly motivated by grades. It might be more accurate to state the proposition somewhat differently: Adolescent students are frequently much less motivated than younger children by such other incentives as: automatic, traditional respect for teachers and adults; desire to please teachers and parents; fear; conformity to adult expectations; and intrinsic love of learning and discovering something entirely new. This last point is often misunderstood by educators, who find it puzzling when older children show less inclination to learn than younger children. It is often unfairly attributed to the inferiority of secondary teachers compared with elementary teachers. A much more likely explanation is that younger children make rapid progress as they learn new skills, such as reading, which they can apply immediately to their advantage. In contrast, adolescents are likely to be reinforcing or honing the skills they have either learned or are supposed to have learned but have failed to learn. Further, adolescents are distracted by their strong sense of sexual identity and by what seems at times to be distant adulthood.

If administrators should be professionally concerned with the instructional process in a generally informal, collegial manner, evaluation as diagnosis and incentive should be treated in the same manner.

This is not to recommend uninvolvement on the part of the administrator. In many schools, instructional assistance is an important part of the work of department heads and vice-principals, sometimes principals. Administrators should make sensible discretionary choices about where their work will have most impact. There may be a few policy issues in this area. For example, there may be a need for agreement on testing schedules, so that homework can be fairly and reasonably allocated.

Nevertheless, most administrators should be centrally interested from a policy perspective on the two remaining purposes of student evaluation — evaluation in terms of *norms* and *criteria*. Students must be compared with others — others in their school or country — because schools prepare the young for adulthood, a defining characteristic of adult society being the division of labor. And they must be assessed in terms of specific standards or levels of competence because most parents, as well as post-secondary institutions and employers, want to know what children have achieved as well as their ranking in relation to others. In practice, the two distinct notions merge. Teachers discriminate, for example, among pupils on the basis of the different things they know or the different standards or levels achieved.

The first two reasons for evaluating, powerful as they may be, are means to an educational or instructional end. Ultimately, administrators are interested in what their students have become (and in what they are becoming) — the use of diagnostic, formative quizzes and weekly tests is un-important in itself. On the other hand, norms and criteria are central to the school's purpose and function. They must be kept in perspective; they form part of a school's purpose, not the whole, and, ultimately, not the most important part. But, very likely, to a seventeen-year-old (and the parents), success in a program, grade average, graduation, certification, is the con-crete expression of the accomplishment of schooling.

Evaluation Policy in Elementary and Secondary Schools

The case was made earlier that, if there is some value in a common program for all pupils within a given school, the case is strongest in the early grades. That is to say, the differences among them are apparently less great when the children are five than when they are fifteen. It follows that criteria tend to have precedence over norms in student evaluation in the primary grades. Inevitably, children and their parents will make normative comparisons; such comparisons are not illegitimate, but they should not be stressed. In general, it matters much less in first grade that Maria is slightly ahead of Elizabeth in reading than that both have mastered the basic reading principles. So what should be stressed is that everyone masters the basic skills for beginning reading, beginning writing and the manipulation of number. All too must learn to behave. Thus home reports should stress the achieve-ment or non-achievement according to established criteria while normative comparisons should be limited to the exceptional, only the top and bottom five or ten percentiles in the first grade, perhaps the first and fifth quintiles by third or fourth grade.

In the middle grades, achievement of criteria and normative compari-sons become equally important. Parents and, of course, the students them-selves should know the level at which the student is working, for example, mid-seventh grade level, the objectives achieved (in terms of a must know, should know and nice to know classification), and the comparative progress in terms of the group with some other reasonable normative base for comparison.

In the middle grades, we suggested, sequential skill subjects, such as mathematics and language, should be taught within homogeneous groups or in sets, (i.e., synchronized classes divided by level of achievement). So students and their parents should know both the level of the group and the student's comparative placement within it. Where skills are most discrete, at least in the early years of instruction — social studies, fitness, art, beginning science — the classes should be formed heterogeneously. Once again, students will know their progress in this larger group as well as the level of the group. Thus a C in reading (fair achievement in an advanced group), may denote a better level of performance than a B in geography (good achievement in a heterogenous group). The reporting of such data in the middle grades is a complex matter sometimes puzzling and irritating to parents. But skilful evaluation should convey that complexity in as straightforward a way as possible. Parents' irritation is often justifiable; too often, schools provide only a part of the story, perhaps telling them that their child is making 'good progress' but neglecting to mention that the progress is being made two levels below grade. Once parents have established reasonable suspicions, anything complicated is suspect.

It is a straightforward matter to provide an approximate grade level equivalent, from a standardized test, in basic skill areas other than writing. A bar graph might show progress (in terms must, should and nice levels) in up to three or four areas within the subject (for example, computation, measurement, problem solving, algebra in mathematics) and a letter grade (A, B, C, D, E) or, less desirably, a 'percentage' grade (so-called percentages are in effect numbers on a line between, for example, forty and one hundred) could show progress in the group.

It becomes evident that the clear conceptual distinction between criterion evaluation and norm evaluation becomes confused in the complex reality of the middle grade. The evaluator in the middle grades must compromise between two incompatible but equally reasonable goals. One reasonably wants to avoid the continual comparison of the very weak student with the very strong (hence the emphasis on progress within a homogenous group); but one wants to keep learners and parents informed about the overall, normative progress — so that there is no misunderstanding in terms of future expectations. Pedagogy tells one to give every student a chance for success and praise and reward genuine improvement. On the other hand, the need for fairness, honesty and the importance of the distributive principle compels one to provide some overall rating. Thus in the middle grades most of all the choice is not between norms and criteria. One has to consider both which norms are to be applied (norms of the group or the norms of the age cohort) and which criteria (sequential criteria based on the student's current function and level, or age and grade based criteria). The middle school that encourages everyone by giving good grades is being very unfair to both weak and strong students. Weak students are misled into complacency; strong students are deprived of the challenge, reward and encouragement they should have.

At the high school level, when students are (i) in tracks or streams leading to a particular common goal or (ii) in levels of instruction tied both to their interests and abilities in their futures or (iii) in a sequential program with built-in steps and accompanying goals, criteria become somewhat less important — because the criterion is implicit in the program placement. Criteria would only be important if elementary-style heterogenous classes were continued into the high school, with each individual class containing a variety of students with a variety of levels of competence and a variety of future goals. Japan is an example of a country which approximately meets that last condition. That is to say, there is a minimum of segregation of students in the high school grades. Most students are promoted, most finish high school and a common program is the norm. Even here, however, normative comparisons become more important than achievement of criteria as students jostle competitively for limited places in post-secondary institutions of varying prestige. Instruction is comparable to what North Americans would call mastery approaches and nearly all students learn the must know components of the program and continue from grade to grade.

It is not that criteria become irrelevant in the high school grades. There are evident criteria for admission to college and university and for some forms of employment. The criteria however are built into programs. Thus it becomes axiomatic that the student who receives a B in a university preparatory program is believed by the teachers to be satisfactorily prepared for university entrance. In contrast, a B in fifth grade or eighth grade may mean almost anything or nothing depending on the circumstances in which the grade is given. Thus high school evaluation typically and reasonably dwells on norms, i.e., how well each student performs compared with others — in the class, in the school, in the school district, in the nation.

One sometimes hears it said that evaluation should take place in terms of oneself, but ultimately there is no such thing. Measurement is the description of quantity and quality — how big, how long, how many, of what type. Evaluation is the judgment applied to a description of quantity or quality. It is logically impossible to be judged, evaluated, in terms of oneself — there must always be some implicit external criteria, and in schools those criteria are developed, formally or informally, with reference to the behavior of others. No evaluation in school can completely exclude some kind of comparison with others. Even if one merely notes that Judy, in grade two, meets the criterion of adding two and two, there is an implicit statement that it is a reasonable skill to demand of people like her. One would not bother to observe that a six-month-old baby could not add two and two, or that an average ten-year-old could. Taken literally, no useful judgment can be made by ourselves in terms of ourselves — we are what we are and if all were known about us we would all be entirely explicable and 'right' — by definition. The French observe that he who excuses himself accuses himself. It would be accurate to state that truly comprehensive and knowledgeable, evaluative accusation explains all. Of course, advocates of this kind of evaluation usually mean in practice that the student should merely be evaluated in terms of change from a previous level of functioning. But of course any legitimate praise or regret is impossible without an external referent.

The practical policy for the principal becomes: Should students be evaluated more in terms of their age or grade cohort or in terms of 'people like them'. The first approach is traditional and well understood; it is universalistic and fair. On the other hand, it can run against pedagogical principles. The slower learner in grade four is constantly failed, or given marginal grades; the incentive for continued work is slight. But if slow learners are compared only with people like themselves, they and their parents may, if one is not very careful, become complacent.

One of the aspects of evaluation most criticized by parents is a teacher's or school's assumption that the progress being made is good 'for him'. The parents often assume, rightly or wrongly that the school has classified this little boy as a loser, a slow learner, or a learning disabled child — and thereby lowered the level of expectations. Obviously it is extremely difficult to know how much to expect of a child — but there is more danger in expecting a little than a lot. The basic principle of evaluation is one of comprehensive truthfulness — the parent and child should know both the level at which the child is working and the comparative achievement made.

There is a danger in trying to be kind and postponing the moment of truth and reality. Indeed, the motive for such 'kindness' is often questionable: 'kindly' deceit means that the teacher and principal do not have to confront a possibly angry parent with the fact that the child is performing well below level. It is mere sophistry to argue that academic achievement is not everything; of course it is not. Teachers should evaluate students in all the domains. The fact that evaluation should take place in all the domains in no way removes the responsiblity for being truthful in the academic domain. And the academic domain is important for future social distribution and is probably the domain in which the school has most general, widespread effect (Holmes, 1986a). The school should put less emphasis on the frequent student-by-student evaluation of areas over which it has little influence, except where those characteristics are known to influence progress in the areas where the school does have effect.

Overall, the organizational and evaluative principles outlined here are an attempt to reconcile two reasonable but sometimes incompatible principles. Basically, the answer is that the responsible administrator should ensure that both approaches are used — with normative comparisons being most evident in the senior grades when individual competition is necessary and inevitable, and with the level of mastery of skill development being most emphasized in the early grades. Nevertheless, both norms and criteria are necessary from primary grades to graduation.

Use of Must, Should and Nice

The categorization of elements of educational programs in three categories was suggested in Chapter 6. There should be a minimum level of competence required in every course. This minimum should be intensively taught and the assumption should be that every student should be able to reach this level. (We come later to the problem of failure and grade repetition, merely noting here there is not a necessary connection between failure to reach a level of competence and repeating a grade.) We have said that in first grade nearly all students should be kept together for instruction. But suppose it becomes evident that one child has no chance whatsoever of achieving the must know competence level — perhaps because of limited intelligence, perhaps because of learning disibility. The first recourse is help. Will extra time help? Can the parents help? Is assistance available from an aide or a volunteer? Is peer or cross-age drill available? But perhaps the problem is too great. Then, and only then, is separation the answer — and the child should then be prepared separately in the prerequisite skills for what the others are learning. Certainly there is no consensus in the research that wholesale segregation of children in special education classes is helpful. And other values — of social cohesion and community — speak against it.

This example illustrates several points. The competence level should not be arbitrarily moved up and down to accommodate unusual problems; but, equally, every child should have a genuine opportunity to succeed. The should and nice program categories will be small in the primary grades, but will increase in size as differences among students develop and as normative comparisons become more necessary. That is to say, as children grow older, the range in their 'mental age' increases as does their range of 'motivation' for work — attitude, organization, support from home, perseverance and other personal and cultural characteristics.

All three categories (must, should, nice) should be taught. All categories will not necessarily be taught to all students, but all students should have access to all objectives and learning material on request. All assignments, tests and examinations should reflect both the objectives and what has been taught. If the pass mark (level of competence) is, say, fifty (out of one hundred), then the weight accorded to must know items should be greater than half (sixty to sixty-five per cent perhaps); if honors or excellence is denoted by a mark greater than eighty, then nice to know items should not be weighted much more than fifteen. This division does not imply that a half or two-thirds of test and homework time must be allocated to must know items. In senior grades, it may well be that nice to know items, requiring analysis and synthesis, require much more time than must know items, requiring knowledge and understanding. Children who are learning individually or in a special segregated group should normally be evaluated separately — on what they have been taught. However, care must be taken to ensure that the parents and their children understand what is and what is not being achieved in terms of the criteria for the cohort. This does not imply that children who are far ahead or far behind their peers should be bombarded daily with news of their advancement or disadvantage. Daily evaluation will reflect the daily progress. But there must still be a written record of the normative information. It is also worth reminding parents and students that, once young people gain entry to a professional or training program, success in the program is a poor predictor of success in their career. Academics are only a foundation. In everyday life, other aspects of character are more important.

Evaluation in the Hard to Evaluate Domains

It is often said that school evaluation is not very important because only a limited set of objectives, usually academic objectives, can be measured. The really important things, it is claimed, such as self-concept and cooperating with others, are not easily measurable. Such comments reflect a lack of understanding of the school and its functions and a lack of understanding of measurement.

The stuff of schools is the academic program, even if academic success is not the first goal of the school, and it is in this domain that the school's effect is most evident. It is largely on the criterion of academic success that students are selected for post-secondary education, and it is post-secondary education that leads on average to the best jobs, the highest pay and the most favorable family circumstances. Thus it is simply absurd to suggest that the most important things, to parents and students, are things on which the school has much less influence and which have little relation to the students' accession to important symbols of success in modern society. This is not to assert that academic progress and future material success are or are believed by most parents to be the most important things in life. They are, however, the things over which the school has most control. A recurring theme in this book is that good character is the most important aspect of a young person's development. Some readers will disagree and argue that, perhaps, social attributes are more important. In any case, if many people believe that other things than academic and material advancement are the most important things in life, there may appear to be a contradiction. On the one hand, we suggest that academic progress is the appropriate emphasis for student evaluation; on the other, we assert that character is more important than academic knowledge and that academic learning not moral training is the stuff of schooling. The apparent contradiction can be resolved in several ways. Firstly, consider analogies with other areas of life. A store manager may spend several weeks training a new employee; the time is spent on technical aspects of sales, computerization, and so on. But that emphasis on technical aspects does not negate the fact that the entire training exercise is wasted if the trainee turns out to be a thief. Law schools spend most of their time (probably too much) teaching law, but the first quality many people look for, often in vain, in a lawyer is integrity. So, schools spend most of their time on academic tasks (if we include cultural and aesthetic as well as intellectual goals within that rather vague term). Secondly, the discussion here is of emphasis. Law schools should not exclude ethics and morality and neither should schools. Thirdly, character is probably most effectively taught by modelling and by direct teaching within context. Just as we best teach writing by ensuring that students understand the audience for whom they write and the purpose of the communication, so morality is best taught in a context (real or fictitious) where moral choices are made, i.e., through a study of literature, history and religion. So, an emphasis on academic stuff no more precludes character development than does discussion at home centring on politics, current events and family life.

As for the alleged problem of measurement, there is virtually nothing in the domains that cannot be adequately measured. Educators are often confused about what they are trying to teach — and one certainly cannot measure what one cannot understand or define. And there are some things we ought not to measure. In the moral and spiritual domain, educators should be very careful about invading individual privacy. Nevertheless, even in that domain, some evaluation, usually by exception, should take place. The student who shows conspicuous honesty or courage should be singled out for special praise. By the same token, dishonesty and cowardice should not pass without criticism. Groups should be formed and given opportunities to express and model good moral behavior. This perspective of school life is developed further in Chapter 8. Thus, while we agree that formal evaluation in the moral and spiritual domain should be much less prominent than in academic areas, we do see an important place for informal evaluation. Furthermore, as the next chapter will show, there are many ways to reward students for conscientious, persevering, caring, responsible behavior in important extra-curricular activities, activities that are often more important than the official program.

Expression in music, art and writing can be evaluated almost as reliably as can performance in mathematics and physics. Impression scoring of drawings is a quick, easily applied technique which provides excellent normative evaluation. As it provides no useful feedback, it is without instructional value, but it makes sense in a summative examination. Analytic scoring (according to a variety of weighted criteria), although often less reliable, can be used to provide both constructive criticism and a useful summative grade.

Evaluation of aesthetic appreciation in literature, music and art is sometimes difficult, not because measurement itself is difficult but because teachers are often undecided what it is they want. Some will argue they only want evidence of enjoyment. There is readily available evidence about that — many adolescents spend long periods of time listening to repetitive popular music and superficial television entertainment. For us, enjoyment is a comparatively insignificant goal for the school; it is discriminating enjoyment we should be seeking. It is even arguable that mere enjoyment should scarcely be classified as aesthetic appreciation. People may enjoy scenes of cruelty and humiliation but that experience cannot reasonably be classified within an aesthetic educational domain. Aesthetic development implies a knowledgeable appreciation of what is to valued — not just any low level positive attitude towards any sensory experience. So, in asserting that qualitive judgments about music, art and literature must and should be made, we join the aesthetic absolutists. We believe some art has more value than some other.

Judgments must and should be made in school; must, because the extreme, non-judgmental teacher still talks about one piece of work by a student as being an improvement over another, and should, because the inclusion of the arts as an important part of the school curriculum is based partly on the belief that levels of artistic expression and understanding can be improved, not just that the level of enjoyment can be enhanced. Discussion, question and tests can easily elicit information about students' tastes and discriminatory powers.

In this context, it is important to consider the use to which evaluation is put. Awards for achievement in language, mathematics and history go on written record, for future uses related to educational advancement and, ultimately, social distribution. The assumption when students are tested and examined is that students either did or ought to have done their best. But in areas like aesthetics, values and attitudes, students frequently know in advance what the 'right' answer is. Thus, if we were to give students a 'test' on morality and appropriate attitudes to work in order to elicit a score to be given to future employers, we would not be surprised if most students scored very high. But the utility of such a 'test' to the employer would be minimal. Most young people will give a truthful answer, if they trust the evaluator and if they understand than an honest, displeasing answer will not later be used against them. For example, students will usually be very willing to state which subjects they enjoy and which they dislike, which books and literature they enjoyed, which not and so on. But of course if a preference for the Hardy Boys to Susan Cooper is to result in a lower grade in reading, a powerful incentive to lie is provided.

Unfortunately, many attempts to extend evaluation to personal, moral, cultural, aesthetic and social issues lead to the encouragement of dishonesty. Even in literature, senior students sometimes pretend to like poetry and drama that the teacher likes in order to raise their mark for 'appreciation' or 'participation.' So the issue of what is done with the measurement and evaluation of these areas is crucial. Once again, we are returned to the central question of values and purposes. This book is written with the assumption, expressed in the goals developed in Chapter 1, that truth and compassion are good. Thus the expression of approval of lying and contempt for others should not be accepted — even though the consequence of rejection may sometimes be hypocrisy, i.e., some children will pretend to care about truth and compassion. In general, however, as truth is crucial to the educational purpose and process, it should be encouraged even when it elicits ideas and values other than those desired by the teacher or administrator. We are not here advocating a total right of free expression for children in all areas of school life. Such 'rights' often serve to promote trendy rebellion and rudeness. We do assert that evaluative exercises in, for example, moral and aesthetic domains, should be based on the mutual assumption of truth. Therefore every effort must be made to ensure the exercises do not unintentionally encourage dishonest replies.

The fact that only limited direct use can be made of the results of evaluation of certain facets of educational progress does not eliminate the worth of evaluating aesthetic appreciation, attitudes, and so on. Administrators ought to learn about the achievement of all stated goals if the goals are sincerely held. Some of the information may be of little interest to many students and parents — but it remains useful for program evaluation. Beyond that, there may be a report without comment of students' self-assessment of attitudes, (although even that cautious approach may sometimes raise the incidence of dishonesty unless the report can be essentially descriptive and unthreatening). For example, it is possible to report that the student dislikes reading and rarely reads but not that the student considers herself to be frequently dishonest in personal relationships. One approach is to keep students' responses to legitimate questions on file, for discussion in a non-threatening atmosphere with the student and, with the student's prior knowledge, the parent. It is always important that young people know exactly what is going to happen with any evaluation that takes place. In sensitive areas such as these it is absolutely vital. Thus, if information on even such a topic as a student's like or dislike of the different subjects is to be conveyed to parents, students should be told so in advance and should be advised not to answer the question if they do not want their parents to know. And questions invading personal privacy and internal family matters should not be asked.

The problems of evaluation in the so-called hard to measure areas have almost nothing to do with measurement, everything to do with evaluative purposes and integrity. Students understand at an early age regular school testing — what the tests are for and how they will be used. Measurements in other areas are not so clearly understood, not by students and not by parents and educators either. The purposes of measurement and evaluation must be thought through in advance. Care must be taken not to reward students for lying, or for saying the 'right' thing for the wrong reasons. All that notwithstanding, it is still useful for students, teachers, administrators and parents to know about attitudes and aesthetic judgments — and they can be measured if there is an atmosphere of mutual trust.

Some Policy Problems in the Administration of Evaluation

Apples and Oranges

One of the most common difficulties schools face in evaluation is in their attempt to combine a number of different variables in a single easily comprehended super-variable; the lumping together of apples and oranges.

There is no statistical law to prohibit the combining of variables — and variables are combined for simplicity's sake by the best of statisticians. The problem lies in the extent of dissimilarity among the combined variables.

Consider the following example. Ninth grade English teachers face a large number of goals and objectives. They are interested, among other things, in students attending class, participating in group discussions, completing homework, working hard, learning new skills, understanding, appreciating and interpreting literature and writing interesting, accurate and persuasive narrative and argument. To report individually on every facet of the program would be time consuming and pointless. Teachers might find themselves spending more time evaluating than teaching and parents would respond impatiently to the welter of data, 'Yes, but what grade did she get?' So, teachers and administrators sometimes decide to award twenty per cent for participation, ten per cent for effort, twenty per cent for assignments and homework, thirty per cent for tests, twenty per cent for projects.

Before turning to the crucial apples and oranges problem, consider some other less central objections to the combination of such different variables. We have argued that it makes sense to evaluate attitudes, behavior and conduct — providing they do not 'count.' Participation — and to a lesser extent, effort, homework and project completion — are examples of characteristics in which teachers are legitimately interested. The reason teachers want to evaluate participation is probably that they believe students themselves and other students will learn more when there is full participation and vigorous class discussion. Probably also they believe they can evaluate qualities in the students that do not emerge in written tests. However, as soon as students understand that participation 'counts', they are given the incentive to participate for all the wrong reasons — not because they have something important to say, but because they want to say something (or worse, even to show a willingness which they calculate in time will not be called upon). They play the game — and in so doing become cynical about evaluation, teachers and school. The game is to give teachers what they want in order to get high marks, not to learn something and demonstrate mastery of it. Students draw musical instruments from the school's store to show keenness — and then leave them in their lockers overnight. They sometimes stay after class to impress the teacher, not to learn. Direct assistance from parents and friends is sought for projects and homework — the purpose sometimes being to get a high mark for the assignment, not to understand anything that is presented. In contrast, the test remains the best and fairest way of determining exactly what is known and understood. It is true that tests can be perverted by meaningless memorization of facts soon forgotten. However, some memorization is important in most subjects and good testing ensures that empty rote learning is not rewarded. There is much to be said for the careful evaluation of student's behavior and conduct. But it should be an end in itself and it should be evaluated directly.

The matter becomes more complicated when programs require several discrete characteristics for success. Thus a teacher of commercial cooking may legitimately integrate, for certification purposes, skill, knowledge, cleanliness, temperament and punctuality. But even in that case the students should see and understand their evaluation for the different criteria. In academic subjects the situation is different. Of course, good behavior may be more important than knowledge of physics, but success in behavior should not be described as success in physics.

The central problem of apples and oranges lies in the linking of very dissimilar variables. A mark of seventy in English may reflect an enormous desire to please combined with minimal skills and knowledge, or, a high level of skills and knowledge with a minimal desire to please. That confusion is unhelpful to the student and parent as well as to future teachers, employers and post-secondary institutions. The sensible alternative is not to report separately on twenty different and confusing criteria but to report on the two, three or four most important criteria grouping similar factors together.

The achievement mark, which should reflect the level of achievement of the student within the group, should be just that — achievement, not effort, not personality, not participation and not even 'progress' or 'improvement.' There is of course an aspect of improvement within the achievement mark, particularly if the program is sensibly organized in a sequential manner. If students begin at roughly the same level in their homogeneous group or class, those who improve the most, and achieve the highest levels will also receive the highest grades. But that should not be confused with 'marks for improvement', where a student began a long way behind but who has made significant strides is given a higher achievement mark than a student who both began and ended ahead. Generally, the more advanced one is, the harder it is to demonstrate improvement. Thus, where 'improvement' counts, students often affect hopeless incompetence at the beginning of the course so that they can show improvement over the course by the end of the term. It is easier to improve if you are bad than if you are very good. Attendance, participation and attitude, and effort could well be reported separately, best with a three point grade system whereby the majority of students fall in a middle category and exceptions are shown above and below the norm.

Different Standards among Teachers

There are few things that upset conscientious students more than the unfairness of varying standards. It is galling to work very hard, enjoy one's classes, learn a lot and be given seventy, when a friend in another class does very little and receives a mark of eighty. Teachers sometimes seem surprised at the amount students know about what goes on in other classes. They should not be. Even in the junior grades, there is often considerable discussion, comparison and competition.

The obvious solution is shared testing — with common tests and examinations. However, administrators should be wary of interfering in teachers' discretionary areas and teachers' tests and examinations (as distinct from standardized tests) are closely linked to program content and the teacher's methodology. Persuasion and education are preferable in this instance to an announcement of across the board mandatory policy. Common items or examinations are often acceptable in mathematics in high school, but less so in third grade mathematics and not in high school English or history. Unfortunately, the problems are sometimes most serious where the solutions are least likely to be accepted.

The causes of the disparity among teachers are many: some teachers like to encourage students by giving high marks; others like to assure a high standard of work by setting a high standard of evaluation; some like to conceal their mediocrity behind high marks. So high marks may mean high or low standards, as may low marks. Where marks are used unprofessionally, individual administrative attention is called for, not school-wide policy. Otherwise, the principal should first encourage teachers themselves to solve the problems. Most often, the problem results more from different norms, traditions, habits and philosophies than from unprofessionalism or incompetence. One cannot simply assume that either high or low marks are good, the other bad.

In some circumstances, teachers may welcome the intervention of the administration, in which case a number of solutions can be worked through. Ultimately, administrators are responsible for ensuring some degree of fairness in the allocation of marks, particularly where the stakes are high: over failure or promotion in elementary school, access to program in middle and high schools; and in high schools generally where high school marks are important for students' futures.

Where external tests and examinations are few or unimportant, systematic difference in standards among subjects, as distinct from among teachers, becomes much more important. Typically, marks in English and history have a lower standard deviation than do marks in mathematics and physics. Thus both high marks and low marks are easier to get in mathematics than in English. The consequence is that bright students learn to take science and mathematics courses in order to boost their averages; those are the subjects where they wrongly appear to be best. In the same way, poor students congregate in English and the social sciences because those subjects are harder to fail. The not-so-hidden message is that mathematics and science are really important, but anyone can do English. This problem is less severe or non-existent where external examinations and tests evaluate all subjects by the same metric, i.e., grades in different subjects are allocated in the same proportions in totally different examinations providing the different courses enrol students of similar ability.

As the prevailing situation benefits teachers of maths and science, who increasingly get only the best students, it may be easier to change the habits of the teachers of English and history. This problem is particularly evident in schools using so called percentage marks. English teachers find it easier to give an essay a grade of A+ than to give it a grade of 100, the latter numeral denoting perfection in their eyes. So one solution is a change from numbers to letters where that is feasible.

The disadvantage of letter grades is that the broad bands that each denotes weaken competition. Although that may make letters more attractive in the middle grades, where competition is often less desired, it becomes problematic in the senior grades where competition for scholarships and programs with limited places becomes intense. Further, a grade change from one term to the next from A to B is upsetting, whereas a mark change from 81 to 79 is not so.

It is generally impractical and unwise to try to impose set formulae on teachers. Formulae remove most of the teachers' discretion. And formulae never fit all situations perfectly. Thus rules limiting the percentage of failures in high school courses are a confession of failure with respect to a workable evaluation policy. If the school has sound, well implemented policies in place concerning objectives and standards of evaluation, the failures in any particular course will thereby become justifiable. For example, it may be necessary to make a choice between reducing the demands of the must know component of the course and a high failure rate. It is unfair and unprofessional to demand both a high passing rate and a high must know component, unless there is evidence that the teachers involved are simply ineffective.

For example, suppose that, upon entering high school, students are permitted to choose their own level, track or stream. Some students will choose unwisely and will be unable to meet the demands of the course they select. For the teacher to change standards to the level of the students would be to change and misrepresent the course. Therefore, typically in such cases the failure rate is high. Some administrators try to apply a formula, for example, no failure rate higher than twenty per cent, on the grounds that it is pedagogically desirable to take students from where they are, as distinct from where they think they are or where they ought to be. There is no happy answer when two sound principles conflict. The conflict can be avoided, we have suggested, by structuring programs sequentially and placing every student in the correct spot in the sequence. In that case, every student has a genuine opportunity to learn and a good teacher will have a low failure rate. If that policy is not adopted, then the principal, not the teacher, must choose between a lower standard and a high failure rate, and must be prepared to justify the policy publicly.

Passing and Failing

Grade retention and promotion in elementary school are two of the most vexing evaluation problems and are often marked by an egregious lack of policy and inconsistent practice.

Our assumption is that grade retention, in which term is included spreading the work of three years over four, will continue. A review of psychological research on non-promotion proves inconclusive — some studies show slight benefit from non-promotion, others slight harm, others no difference. However, the main reason for maintaining the system has more to do with maintenance of a school's norms than with demonstrable individual benefit. If schools promote automatically, students are probably given less incentive to learn, and teachers to teach. It is true that some countries do not normally practise grade repetition, but they usually have other means of achieving the same ends. In Britain, for example, streaming is more widely practised in the middle grades, and in many junior schools, than is the case in the USA and Canada. Thus less able students are 'promoted' (as promotion is automatic there is neither incentive nor reward), but they are demoted to or remain within a lower group or stream. In some European countries students attend different schools according to their ability or level of competence. Japan is an exception here. It manages to combine virtually automatic promotion with whole class instruction and high levels of achievement. It is not clear to what extent this achievement can be attributed to the special character of Japanese society and the Japanese people and to what extent it is a result of the extremely direct instructional methodologies used. In any case, it will not be easy to transfer the Japanese approach to the more heterogeneous societies of USA and Canada.

One must be careful not to generalize too much about national systems. The fact that the Japanese approach cannot be easily transferred to the whole of North America does not mean it is inapplicable in every school. Many educators consider the policy of West Germany, Switzerland and Austria, whereby students are segregated according to their levels of academic competence, unfair and 'undemocratic.' But it must be remembered that in the English speaking world there is enormous *de facto* segregation; in the USA by residential neighborhood and by choice of private school; in Canada, by residence, private school and also by the now popular French immersion option, which recruits mainly middle class children; in England, by choice of increasingly numerous private schools as well as by parental selection among competing public schools.

Even though, within the North American context, we favor the principle of grade retention, its use should be sparing; there is little likelihood of it being notably beneficial to all the individuals concerned (but also little likelihood of its being harmful if it is carefully carried out). The practice we advocate is implicit in the instructional organization already described. Consider the first grade class with most students taking a common program in the basic skills. Two exceptional students are mainly working on their own, perhaps with special help from a teacher's aide. They are of superior intelligence (IQ over 120) and should probably be moved, with their parents' consent, to second grade during the year. The move might be preceded by some involvement in the second grade class for basic skill instruction. Two very slow students are also receiving special help. The same criteria should be used for grade retention as for grade acceleration: a combination of achievement and ability. But if every child is given a genuine opportunity to succeed, the number of grade repetitions should be very few. In practice, there should be a few cases of children spending an extra year to complete the first two grades, very few cases of grade repetition

Table 7: Sample Home Report (Grades 5 to 8)

Pinemarch Middle School
179 Philip Drive
Lancaster C4G 1D9
Tel. 693-4605

Principal: Katherine R. Wright, M.A.　　Homeroom Teacher: _____

Term: Beginning: _____ ;　Ending: _____

Student: _____ ;　Grade: _____6_____

Possible Days Attendance: _____ ;　Actual Days Attendance: _____

Academic Achievement and Effort

Subject	Teacher (if not known)	Grade Level Attained Sept.	Grade Level Attained June	Working Group (+ +, +, 0, -, - -)	Achievement in Group/Class (A, B, C, D, E)	Effort (A, B, C)
Reading — Comprehension	_____	_____	_____	_____	_____	_____
Language and Spelling	_____	_____	_____	_____	_____	_____
Written Expression	_____	_____	_____	_____	_____	_____
Mathematics	_____	_____	_____	_____	_____	_____
Geography	_____	_____	_____	_____	_____	_____
History	_____	_____	_____	_____	_____	_____
French	_____	_____	_____	_____	_____	_____
Science	_____	_____	_____	_____	_____	_____
Moral/Social Development/ Family Life/Health	_____	_____	_____	_____	_____	_____
Life Skills	_____	_____	_____	_____	_____	_____
Music — Expression	_____	_____	_____	_____	_____	_____
— Comprehension	_____	_____	_____	_____	_____	_____
Art — Expression	_____	_____	_____	_____	_____	_____
— Comprehension	_____	_____	_____	_____	_____	_____
Physical Education	_____	_____	_____	_____	_____	_____

Table 7:

Other Standing

Fitness (A,B,C,D,E)   _____

Psychomotor Development (A,B,C,D,E)   _____

Citizenship (A,B,C)   _____

Homework Completion (A,B,C)   _____

Participation in Class (A,B,C)   _____

Behavior in Class (A,B,C)   _____

Comments: _____

_____

_____

_____

_____

_____

_____

_____

_____

_____

_____

_____

Notes: Normal grade level in September in sixth grade is between 5.6 and 6.6, and in June between 6.4 and 7.4. A level two years ahead of grade in all areas indicates discussion of possible advancement if teachers' grades are also high. Achievement in the grade/class is in comparison with other students in groups/classes like this one. A is excellent, B very good, C good, D fair, E unsatisfactory. Similarly, in other standings A,B,C,D,E have the same meaning. Where the A,B,C scale is used most students receive B, with A reflecting exceptional performance and C severe problems. Students receiving E in three out of four basic skill subjects (reading, language and spelling, written English and mathematics) are usually required to repeat the year, those receiving E in two out of those four or receiving E in most subject areas are usually recommended to repeat the year. Students receiving E in any subject may be required to take the course in summer session in order to continue in the next grade in September.

in the next three grades, and then some retention as students move to different levels of school whose programs assume basic skills in number and language for success. Thus, in fifth grade, if there is homogeneous grouping either within classes or among classes in the basic skill subjects, it is not practically necessary to retain a student who fails to reach the must know level by the end of fifth grade. But of course it is incumbent on the administrators to ensure that parents know the precise circumstances of the movement to a sixth grade class. A well run, average elementary school should experience not more than two per cent grade retentions a year, and those should be concentrated in pivotal grades. As a result, no more than one-fifth of the age cohort should be over age on reaching ninth grade. A proportion somewhat smaller than that, perhaps ten per cent, should have experienced acceleration. The proportion should be smaller because it is usually easier to accommodate students doing additional work, who often require less supervision, than students who are working well below the level of the rest of the class.

The actual percentages will of course vary with the population served. Hard decisions have to be made in low achieving inner-city schools. Homogeneous grouping or streaming may be necessary earlier if all are not to be overcome by low expectations. Even here, very high failure rates are unlikely to be helpful.

Overall, there seems to be no good reason why all children should arrive in ninth grade at the same age. It seems sensible to provide less able students with additional time to reach a reasonable standard so that they will have a wider array of possible choices during high school. At the same time, it seems unlikely that many students will be prepared to spend two or three years more than their peers in completing a twelve year school program, so multiple grade repetition is not likely to be helpful. There may not be a single policy for all schools; but every school should have a clear policy.

Principles of Student Evaluation

1. *The purposes of evaluation should always be clear to students and teachers.* It is unlikely that a single test can provide diagnosis, an incentive for learning, measurement in terms of criteria and measurement in terms of norms.
2. *Most formal evaluation should focus on the academic stuff of the school*, which includes all the school's courses.
3. *Evaluation involves the exercise of judgment and can never be entirely objective.* One must decide what must be learned, and what need not be.
4. *Tests should reflect the must know, should know and nice to know breakdown of the course*, certainly when students' learning is differentiated.

5. *In the early grades, evaluation should stress mastery of sequential criteria in the skill subjects.* Little emphasis should be placed on normative competition among individuals.
6. *In the senior grades, evaluation should stress the comparative performance of students (in terms of other students and national norms) as well as the criteria of the programs.*
7. *Students should always know exactly what is expected of them.*
8. *Achievement in all domains should be evaluated, whether the criteria are good essay writing, physical fitness or articulate self-expression, effort or cooperative behavior.*
9. *It is possible to measure the level of achievement of most students according to most goals, but evaluation may make measurement difficult and may sometimes be unnecessary.* Goals in highly personal areas are often best evaluated in program terms (rather than every student), informally or by exception (only the exceptionally good or bad is commented upon).
10. *It is important to evaluate good behavior favorably and bad behavior unfavorably.* Evaluation of attitudes and, particularly, values, should be carried out with great care.
11. *Evaluation of very different and only slightly related characteristics, for example, achievement and effort, should be carried out separately and not combined in a single score.* Where a program, for example, professional cooking, requires success on several very different criteria, students should receive, in writing, reports on the parts as well as an overall grade or statement.
12. *School policies on evaluation are important but they should be sensitive to teachers' professional discretion in the area of teaching.*
13. *Evaluation is not a contract between the teacher and student.* Evaluation is important for parents, employers, post-secondary institutions and the community. All have a legitimate interest in the outcomes.

Program Evaluation

If there is a good, open, fair, universal, and consistent student evaluation policy and corresponding practice, it is unlikely that extensive program evaluation is generally required. Program evaluation is rarely carried out at the school level; if it is carried out at all, it is applied at the level of the school district, state or province. Serious, effective program evaluation at any level is relatively rare. There are doubtless numerous reasons for this, one being the enormous complexity of a totally valid evaluation, another being the reluctance of policy makers to pay large amounts of money for what may turn out to be bad news.

The following are situations where program evaluation, beyond good student evaluation, is sometimes helpful:

(i) Before, during and after the introduction of an entirely new program;

(ii) Where there are two or more very different approaches being used for the attainment of the same or similar objectives;

(iii) In areas where student evaluation is not systematically developed; and

(iv) Where there is some question or doubt about program goals and objectives.

New Programs

New programs are often introduced for the flimsiest of reasons; very often they are imposed from outside the school. The responsible school administrator will evaluate the school's achievement of the new program's stated goals and objectives before the program is implemented, during implementation and after implementation. This is important whether or not the goals and objectives are entirely new ones. Young people learn many things outside school and it should never be assumed that knowledge about a goal has been learned simply as a result of instruction directed towards the goal. The more educators seek to make their programs novel and complex, the more frequently it seems that the new goals are things that children might very well learn at home or in their daily lives, irrespective of school instruction. Very often competence in a particular task is related more to native intelligence than to any particular form of instruction. In such cases, it is very easy to attribute a level of attainment to instruction, after the event. New programs in elementary mathematics and science sometimes have objectives referring to the understanding of patterns. Intelligent eight-year-olds probably understand patterns anyway. It is fashionable to have goals concerning self-concept and tolerance for others; traits related to personality and character are likely to be learned more outside school than within given the small proportion of time that is actually spent in school. As neither term is conceptually clear (for example, the qualities of self-respect, modesty, self-assessment of ability and conceitedness are never distinguished from 'self-concept'), neither effective instruction nor effective measurement seems likely.

Different Approaches to Similar Objectives

Different approaches to teaching are not themselves problematic. Indeed, a situation where there are two very different teachers in the two second grade classes may be ideal; similarly, if half the tenth grade English teachers are devotees of the process approach and the other half supporters of the sequential, direct approach, free choice for students may be advantageous. We are not so naive to suggest that parents of students with linear, deductive learning styles will choose linear methods, and those with more inductive minds will choose more open, holistic approaches. Obviously, the motives for choice will be varied; equally obviously, children do not fall into two neat piles, the size of each exactly matching the available places in the classrooms. Nevertheless, an element of choice is often helpful where there is contention among teachers and among parents.

So, such situations do not in themselves call for comparative program evaluation, and, in any case, much of the most crucial information can be obtained from regular student evaluation by means of standardized tests and common examinations. Furthermore, a simple comparison of achievement among the two groups will not tell one which approach is better, even if the students in the groups are similar. Good teachers are, by definition, more effective than bad teachers; and a really good teacher could probably do better than a poor teacher whatever method is used. School program evaluation will not provide final or even good provisional answers to very complex questions.

Even so, program evaluation does become important where there is dispute. Perhaps a new department head is trying to impose a new program on reluctant tenth grade teachers of English. Perhaps, the primary consultant does not like the very formal second grade class, much preferring the other class based on active learning. Perhaps the principal believes that the reason seventh grade students are learning very little science is that they never study and learn something intensively.

In these and similar cases, program evaluation is an ideal first step in solving the apparent problem. By working with teachers to develop a comprehensive and fair program evaluation, the department head may come to a greater understanding of what the teachers are trying to do. By bringing the consultant and the primary teachers together, the principal can assure the traditional second grade teacher that teaching methodology is a professional choice and at the same time assure the consultant that there is genuine interest in program quality. And a review of the science program may lead to changes that will enhance achievement, whether or not they are the changes the principal originally had in mind. Nevertheless, it would be a mistake to swing into a program evaluation mode just because there is some untidiness, with teachers doing very different things. There is no intrinsic problem in teachers doing different things; more likely there is a problem if administrators believe everybody ought to be doing the same thing.

Values and Aesthetics

Evaluation of every student in some areas of morality, attitudes and aesthetics is not always appropriate, (but evaluation of moral conduct or behavior is appropriate). One reason is that evaluation may encourage students to give dishonest answers to oral or written questions. Another is that detailed, personal probing about deeply held values and ideas may well constitute an upsetting and unethical invasion of privacy. This is particularly the case if children hold beliefs they know to be unpopular with most other children and probably with teachers. Fundamentalist Christians, when they form a small minority, often feel excluded and derided. Children of such families are understandably reluctant to talk publicly about their family's beliefs and customs.

Nevertheless, if these constitute domains of significant goals, then program evaluation becomes doubly important. Precisely because every student evaluation is absent it is very easy to de-emphasize some very important areas. Some schools with quite good academic records are extremely poor in terms of expressing fundamental values. Indeed, it is possible to emphasize only those values conducive to academic excellence — with students becoming narrow minded and unpleasantly competitive. Similarly, many more schools give little thought to the development of aesthetic expression and understanding, with enjoyment and participation being the only criteria. Even schools which claim to give primacy to non-academic goals, preferring goals related to personal development, avoid central, difficult values that may sometimes cause confrontation — truth and courage, preferring to emphasize softer values without cutting edge — such as tolerance and self-concept. It is those domains that are often in most need of thorough program evaluation.

Problem Areas

Just as the single, best reason for evaluating (as distinct from informally advising) a teacher is a suspicion that the teacher is incompetent, so the single best reason for evaluating a school program is suspicion that it is ineffective. The statement seems so self-evidently valid that it is difficult to understand those who argue instead for enormous, bureaucratic programs to evaluate everything in turn, programs which usually fail by inertia. In any case, it is simply not practical to imagine that a school administration can usefully evaluate all school programs, unless there is a guarantee that neither the principal nor the programs will be changed for ten years.

Obviously, any program evaluation will set up legitimate fears, legitimate because one must assume that a professional principal will do something about problems that emerge from the review. So it should not be undertaken lightly, and once undertaken it should be carried out properly.

Carrying Out a Program Evaluation

Program evaluation contains six central components:

(i) Determination of the program's goals and objectives;

(ii) Consideration of the goals and objectives that might have been or may be appropriate but which are not actual goals and objectives;

(iii) Evaluation of the program's goals and objectives;

(iv) Collection of descriptive data on the way the program is carried out; (comment is also appropriate on what is not done, but care must be taken not to assume that the 'right' way is known in advance);

(v) Collection of attitudinal and performance data by means of (a) student tests; (b) student questionnaires; (c) teacher questionnaires; (d) parent questionnaires; (e) interviews; (f) observation; data should not be confined to the stated goals but should consider unintended side-effects;

(vi) Judgment of the program, its goals, implementation, practice and outcomes.

In the end, judgment must be made and judgment is very difficult without some basis for comparison. Achievement data should be compared with data from different but comparable schools, with students of similar age and ability. There should be comparisons among classes, before the new program and after. If the program is universal and discrete, then at least there should be comparison with similar students who have not taken the program, either before the program was introduced or in another school district.

On reflection, it is not surprising that student evaluation is an integral part of the daily life of virtually all schools, that teacher evaluation often figures prominently in district policies, if less prominently in school practice, but that program evaluation is rare, even at the district level. Program evaluation is not related, as is student evaluation, to a basic function of the school.

There are often good reasons for not carrying out a program evaluation. But, even so, a stronger case can be made for increased involvement in program evaluation than for the continued emphasis of teacher evaluation. Program evaluation is not a magic wand. The announcement of a problem is not the announcement of a cure. But at least program evaluation provides some guidance for improvement based on empirical knowledge of what children are not learning, rather than on administrators' idiosyncratic impressions about what and how teachers are teaching.

Program evaluation is the school's Cinderella — but for this Cinderella the chimes of midnight have not yet struck and the glass shoe is not yet in sight. The reasons are obvious enough: program evaluation is extremely difficult; there is no obvious material reward; it is sometimes confrontational; and it may sometimes be strongly resisted. But it is surely often necessary if one is not to continue throwing money after non-problems and ignoring the real problems of which there are many. The individual school principal cannot be expected to take major responsibility for program problems far removed from his or her personal responsibility. But in a small way, bad innovations can be resisted or removed and good and improved programs can be recognized and rewarded. Even the smallest school can ensure that its major goals are regularly evaluated, formally, informally or both.

A Check List for Program Evaluation

1. All major academic areas should be evaluated periodically by means of standardized tests reasonably reflecting the school's goals. Information about the student should go to students, parents and teachers; information by class should go to teachers and administrators; and test information by school should go to administrators and teachers. This last information should also generally be available to parents.
2. Comparisons by class or by school should be accompanied where possible by information about the social background of the students, their ability levels and their levels of achievement when beginning the program.
3. All students should be tested for writing composition regularly by means of some externally valid and reliable arrangement, for example, impression scoring by two or more scorers.
4. Records should be kept of school performance in physical fitness by grade.
5. Information on achievement in major areas should be made available in clear, graphic form, over time, in terms of school standing in comparison with other schools, to parents, teachers and students.
6. Public exhibition and competition in art, music and drama and sports should be sufficiently frequent to provide feedback on the quality of work in comparison with other schools.
7. Public records should be kept in clear graphic form of a variety of achievements and problems that provide indicators of the school's moral strengths and weaknesses: for example, incidence of physical violence on and off school property, drug involvement, alcohol involvement, bullying, graffiti, vandalism, false fire alarms, major and minor thefts, lying, incomplete homework, dropouts, suspension, expulsion; and incidence of successful class visits, out of school tutoring projects, successes in competitions, appearance of

school yard and buildings, community/school events, occasions of outstanding generosity, courage and kindness, success of graduates, community help programs.

8. Teachers and students who leave the school should be asked to evaluate their school experiences and make constructive suggestions for improvement — both when they leave and, for example, three years later.

9. Parents should be involved in major policy issues particularly with respect to goals and evaluation in sensitive areas. Parents who are not regularly involved in home/school projects should be reached by telephone or questionnaire. Public questionnaires about the school and its performance should be used fairly regularly, every year or two.

Further Reading

Most of the ideas in this chapter are developed more fully in Holmes (1982b). Although there are many texts on simple educational statistics as statistical approaches to evaluation, very little has been written in the areas most emphasized in this chapter, i.e., the administrative policy as distinct from the mechanical issues.

Chapter 8

Developing School Climate

(This chapter was written by Edward Wynne)

The phrase school climate is popular due to its metaphorical value. The metaphor suggests that school efficacy is affected by a pervasive but hard to clarify force. Unfortunately, there are other implications to the word 'climate' that are less appealing. It is very hard for human beings to influence our external climate — the weather tends to go its own way. It is true that one's capabilities for short-term weather prediction are relatively precise. However, long-term weather predictions are notoriously inaccurate — beyond simple truisms, such as winters being colder than summers. Even with the enormous power of modern computers, no one knows how to analyze the infinite number of variables determining long-range weather patterns.

In sum, one cannot either change or predict the weather — a poor augury for the worth of school climate as a stimulating metaphor.

There is a considerable body of research on school climate — which, unfortunately, is somewhat like the data on weather. Interesting, but inconclusive. Through the use of questionnaires administered to administrators, teachers and pupils, one is also able to identify patterns of attitudes and beliefs in schools. That combination constitutes the school climate. And different schools have notably different patterns. Sometimes, patterns have been associated with different forms of administrative style. Various agencies sell packets of climate assessment instruments to schools to help them evaluate their climate. Such instruments are designed to be completed by every adult in the school, and the results tabulated and analyzed. Sometimes such agencies provide further services, such as tabulating completed forms, producing printouts of the results, or providing interpretive reports.

The precise information generated by such processes varies. In general, the information is intended to assist schools in the analysis and change of existing policies. But one should not overrate the 'scientific' elements of the questionnaire process. The fact is that the relationship between measured school climate and pupil academic learning is usually non-existent, small or problematic. Relationships among adults, for example, usually tell us little about behavior and beliefs of students. Many instruments for measuring school climate are valid enough measures of the emotional life in schools; but even if those emotions have a 'warm' tone, it does not necessarily mean pupils are learning the right things. It is true that some research has identified statistically significant relationships among different sets of attitudes and administrative styles and students' academic learning outcomes. However, the statistical power of relationships has only been moderate. Furthermore, many of the school climate instruments now in use have not been tested against such criteria. There is no simple, widely recognized pattern of school climate which can be readily produced and which is known to lead to improved pupil learning outcomes.

All of this means that the school climate research — like research about the weather — is interesting, but leaves many matters subject to personal interpretation. For example, some schools may be more open to faculty input than others. Some researchers, who see parallels between political democracy and school management, claim such schools are 'better.' Unfortunately, the connection between such 'open' school management and better pupil academic, let alone moral, learning is hard to substantiate in the research. Indeed, there is a danger that aspects of climate, instead of being characteristics likely to favor the kind of student development we should like, become objects or ends in themselves.

Despite the inconclusive nature of much of such research, we take the position that school climate is changeable by human determination. We predict that continuing research will disclose additional ties between school climate and good pupil learning.

The following discussion largely relies on deduction and inference, sometimes making passing reference to the relevant research. The discussion will prepare readers to engage in more focused observations in schools and to make judicious choices among actions influencing school climate.

Elements of School Choice

Different elements combine to form a school's climate. For our purposes, we centre on four key elements: the *gratification* members of the community gain from being in the school; the *industriousness* they display while they are there; the *efficiency* with which they carry out their tasks; and the *predictability* of the school environment.

Gratification is important because it is hard to imagine an effective school where substantial proportions of the inhabitants (both educators and pupils) are distressed when they are in school. Without a significant level of gratification, many counterproductive tensions will inevitably arise.

Industriousness is relevant, since a goodly number of persons are capable of being gratified by non-demanding tasks. But a school is not some idyllic utopia — a lotusland. Thus, community members must spend much of their time engaged in demanding and productive activities. We have identified a set of educational goals; they will not be achieved without sustained effort.

Efficiency suggests the contrast between working hard and working competently. And hard-working community members, in order to be efficient, must simultaneously have their efforts directed towards rational ends — essentially, teaching and learning.

Predictability reminds us that schools are elaborate environments, composed of many persons who work together for long periods of time. There cannot be effective coherence among such persons and groups unless there are common expectations about what should be happening in the school next week, next year, and even six or eight years from now. This element refers back to the consensus we see as being important in the effective school.

The elements of climate are rarely in full harmony. It is easy to identify some potential areas of conflict. Gratification may conflict with efficiency (what is easy is not always productive). Less obviously, predictability may become boring; dull routine undermines industriousness. Furthermore, different groups in a school — the students, the teachers, the administrators — may attribute contrasting values to different elements. In sum, the management of school climate — if metaphors are applied — is probably more like the managing of a symphony orchestra than predicting next year's weather. And the fact is that there are undoubtedly better and worse directed symphony orchestras, although only musical experts can explain the difference.

The four elements imply that many aspects of school climate are largely influenced by the overall administrative efficiency of the school. For instance, one characteristic of an efficient school is that staff members come into work regularly, and on time. The proposition seems trite. Most readers recognize that regular and prompt attendance is particularly important in schools. Even in the best of schools, substitute teachers are but a lesser evil; there is always a loss of continuity in instruction, and often other distressing inadequacies. And, as for lateness, late teachers provide pupils with poor examples, waste instructional time, and (if they are late for staff meetings) diminish the efficiency of the group's efforts.

The exact mechanics applied to ensure regular attendance and promptness will necessarily vary. The measures used depend on the size of the school, the previous records of attendance and punctuality of the staff, and other factors. Still, if attendance and promptness are poor, administrators have an obligation — after briefly trying more temperate means — to take measures to hold the faculty to their professional obligations, i.e., requiring a carefully maintained sign-in sheet, monitoring teacher compliance, and generating different consequences for those who maintain good and bad records.

In the short run, measures to improve staff attendance and promptness may lower the on-the-job gratification of some faculty members — though the measures may subtly please others who do come in on time and are distressed by the free loaders.

Another example of conflicting priorities is the tension which may arise around decision making — which ties into predictability, efficiency and gratification. Efficient decision making requires some process of collecting information and counsel through a process which is not extremely time consuming. Predictability means there must be a regular structure of decision making; that structure should articulate both general principles, and concrete directions. In democratic countries, gratification is sometimes associated with provisions giving subordinate employees some say in the decision making process.

Combining these variables is a notable challenge. How much time should be spent on information collecting? How much weight should be given to consistency (an element of predictability)? How much say should subordinates have in the process? Should there be variations, depending on the experience and commitment of the school staff, the size of the school, and the particular issues involved? What variations are appropriate? We have discussed decision making in Chapters 4 and 6; our point here is that the elements of climate impinge on all aspects of administrative life.

School climate is a complex matter. Single-minded pursuit of one element, gratification, may undermine the wholesomeness of the environment. Conversely, single-minded pursuit of rational efficiency may be similarly dysfunctional. In the school, children and adolescents predominate. The school is not a factory and efficiency is unlikely to persist if efficient output is the only important characteristic of climate. We have advocated the use of mastery type, outcomes based instructional approaches in skill areas in the early years. Research suggests this will prove an efficient practice. However, we do not advocate that all goals at all grade levels should be approached by means of a single instructional approach applied by all teachers. The reason is not simply that research has yet to show that this kind of approach can be applied in all domains. More important, a healthy climate requires other elements as well as efficiency. Administrators should remember too that teachers as well as students will not like an environment in which efficiency appears to be the only thing that counts.

Many of the elements affecting school climate are referred to in other chapters in this book. The way those elements work is determined by the basic administrative structure of the school. That structure should encourage the development of industriousness, predictability and efficiency — among both adults and pupils, and to some degree among pupils' families.

The remainder of this chapter will focus on the fourth element of school climate: gratification. As we have said, gratification of its inhabitants is not paramount; but, like the string section of an orchestra, it is important.

School Spirit and Gratification

'Good school spirit' is a term educators popularly use to suggest that people in the school like being there — they are proud of their school. The term has a certain juvenile tone; and it is often applied among children. Perhaps that usage trivializes the term. If so, that is unfortunate. One important aspect of the term is its direct recognition by children and adolescents. Its appeal stimulates common interests among adults and pupils in schools. Such commonality across generations has much to do with gratification. In particular, it means that pupils are not prisoners, and the adults not jailers. Instead, it means they are people of different ages, knowledge levels, and amounts of authority — but engaged in a common mission. And that mission is carried out under the auspices of the school.

A healthy school spirit may be treated as an equivalent of gratification. In other words, for adults and pupils (and families) to find a school a gratifying place, there must be high levels of school spirit.

Much of the succeeding discussion will focus on the development of school spirit among pupils. But a prior condition for the development of such student attitudes is the concurrent development of equivalent attitudes among faculty. And, furthermore, if we see students (and parents) developing high levels of school spirit, we should recognize that such patterns are, also, a powerful indicator of high levels of staff spirit. In other words, all of the policies and activities which effectively stimulate school spirit among pupils must have their counterparts in the adult community.

The term school spirit is popularly associated with matters such as successful athletic teams, or other publicity-generating activities connected with a school. And, undoubtedly, such matters do have a bearing on school spirit. The problem with an athletic emphasis, however, is that many schools, for various reasons, will have not had conspicuously successful teams. And younger children typically do not even engage in such competitive activities. Thus, a solely 'athletic' approach largely removes school spirit from the control of many administrators. It becomes external weather over which they have little control. Good times come and go depending on the quality of the coaches and the teams.

Fortunately, there are many measures — other than emphasizing athletics — which educators can take to improve school spirit. A first step to attaining such control is to perceive the relationship between school spirit and the more formal term community. School spirit is simply the popular substitute for that more esoteric term. When we recognize that parallel, we also become conscious that there is a substantial body of thought about the characteristics of vital communities. Such perceptions can be used to derive

237

general principles. Those principles can then be applied in the cultivation of school spirit. Furthermore, the perceptions can be placed alongside existing research findings on school practices. It will then become evident that many schools deliberately do practise a variety of community-building measures, which simultaneously enhance their school spirit.

First, we present an abstract definition of the principles underlying in-school community. Those principles will then be refined and illustrated with examples of actual school practices — both good and bad — that demonstrate the basic points. Furthermore, as we proceed, readers will recognize that the applications of some of the principles are controversial. Different educators have different opinions about how far a school should go to build community. The opinions of the authors about such conflicts will be evident to readers. However, it is not essential that readers agree with all of our preferences. Such unanimity is certainly impossible and probably undesirable. The more important point is for readers to be presented with a set of ideas and arguments for certain priorities. Administrators and teachers will choose their own directions. Once again, we emphasize the importance of professional discretion.

A Definition

A community is a bounded environment, which persists through time. Its inhabitants share important common goals, and such commonality is reinforced by aesthetic and intellectual appeal. If the community comprises substantial numbers of people, it must also include vital subcommunities, which replicate the central characteristics of the larger community. The subcommunities and the community maintain mutually supportive relationships among and between one another.

Obviously, these analytic statements require amplification and, eventually, enrichment by the presentation of examples. The idea of boundary means that people know when they join or leave a community, and that other community (or non-community) members within the boundaries can easily be identified. Furthermore, boundaries can be more or less permeable. Impermeable boundaries keep out intruders, and make it hard for people to enlist in the community without undergoing substantial initiating procedures. Conversely, when boundaries are permeable, people can enter and leave readily. Moreover, newcomers may intrude, visit or join.

Different social systems apply a variety of boundaries to maintain community. They can be visible and tangible — such as walls, fences, hedges, or even locked doors. Or they can be visible and symbolic, such as codified uniform dress for members, or other indicators — badges, behavioral patterns, cut of hair, or mode of dress. Community membership may also be demarcated by other less visible attributes — a certain language or dialect; the possession of a credential indicating membership of a profession;

membership of a formal group for which beliefs, commitments and initiation rites may be required; or membership of a religious sect.

Various combinations of bounding principles may also be applied in practice. Peshkin (1986) studied a Christian evangelical elementary school in Illinois. All of the school's students were members of one church. Substantial portions of school time were dedicated to Bible study. The pupils all dressed in a neat, trim fashion. All school faculty were members of the sponsoring church. A main conclusion of his study was that high levels of cohesion and good feelings prevailed among pupils and faculty. Pupil academic learning — as measured by test scores — was also at a good level. Peshkin, however, was troubled by the 'parochialism' prevailing in the environment. As we have mentioned, shared values are involved in building and maintaining in-school community. Other researchers have studied contemporary public school environments, and concluded they were often incoherent — without a sense of collective purpose (Coleman and Hoffer, 1987).

Vital communities must persist over time if inhabitants are to perceive the relationships that occur in them as significant. Thus, at the moment of birth of a community, community spirit may be low because members do not know if their relationships will persist. But, after they have been together for several years, and expect leadership to persist for still more years, their feelings about each other will become richer.

This is likely to be the case in a new school in a new community, where administrators, teachers, pupils and parents are strangers with few immediately obvious ties. Good stewardship may well bring about a strong community in a few years. In contrast, a school set up as a consciously alternative school may initially appear to have strong grounds for community; as a minority the newly formed community is conscious of its difference. If the differentiating values are strongly held, the community may build strongly and quickly. But if the single differentiating factor masks a host of competing motives, survival may be more difficult.

The idea of common goals means that no member can have important attainments or losses without other community members being similarly affected. To recite an aphorism, 'All for one, one for all.' Such commonality inspires members to become deeply engaged in observing and caring for each other. Commonality must be reinforced by aesthetic and intellectual appeals. The point is that, on many occasions, community members are tempted to ignore their collective obligations, and pursue more individualistic (selfish?) goals. To moderate inevitable tendencies, effective communities must persistently remind members of their collective purposes. Such reminders occur via a variety of means. Many of such means are artistic. Community members sing songs together, recite poems, see, read and reflect on artistic materials, or learn to respond to symbols emphasizing such commonalities.

Furthermore, at other levels of perception, rational arguments are recited about the virtues of commonality. In religious schools, students are frequently reminded of how easily they will lose their religious identity in an outside, hostile or uncaring world. The quality and efficiency of both the aesthetic and intellectual appeals partly reflect the imagination, skills and energy of the persons designing and presenting such materials.

The idea of vital subgroups means that once a community extends beyond a certain size — more than five to ten people — regular, close relationships among all members will be impossible due to the limits of time. Members will thus be prone to develop subgroup relationships. This is normal, and typically healthy. Persisting larger communities will encourage the formation of such subgroups, and simultaneously invite those subgroups to mesh their own immediate principles and goals within those of the larger community. To put it simply, probably one reason all political states support the institution of marriage is because, 'It is not good for man to live alone.' By encouraging marriage, political states simultaneously encourage families and married couples to have supportive attitudes towards their country. Conversely, a large community where members are not rooted in small, proximate groups will find its members afflicted with persisting emotional instability.

The preceding analysis suggests that there are both immutable and mutable elements to a community. Some environments have certain characteristics which make it difficult or impossible for them to have community spirit — like airport terminals, where many travellers and visitors, for their own private purposes, briefly pass through on their way elsewhere. There may be community spirit among the terminal employees, but that is made difficult by the numerous visitors. Conversely, some other human environments have strong potentialities for developing community: a family, including parents and their young children; the crew and passengers of a ship on a long and difficult voyage; or a military unit surrounded by a ruthless enemy. But, beyond such external and defining characteristics, there are important matters of choice and decision: conditions of entry or exit may be established; general goals may be identified and publicized to encourage members to work together; and elaborate and imaginative systems of community-building by means of structure, symbols and art may be created and given prominence in everyday life.

Community in Schools

Certain aspects of school life naturally tend to generate communal feelings. Many adults are likely to have been there for long periods of time; It is not uncommon for teachers to have served in the same school for over ten years. And, depending on the organization of the school involved, the scheduled length of pupil enrolment can run from two to eight years. Schools also invariably have different forms of boundaries.

They have walls which separate them from the outside world. Depending on neighborhood factors and school policies, their walls, doors and fences have varying degrees of permeability. Schools also are frequently in locations which isolate them from disturbance or intrusion. All of these factors heighten the level of self-consciousness among members of the environment; they know each other, they are often in contact for prolonged periods of time, and there are few strangers or intruders.

But many of the preceding factors are subject to variation. We know that differences in the length of pupils' planned enrolment — between two to eight years — can be considerable. These variations are partly the outcome of adults' decisions about appropriate forms of school organization, for example, two year or three year junior high or middle schools, compared with kindergarten through eighth grade. And, as for avoidance of intrusion, some schools establish policies — or fail to establish them — which make them more open to disturbing intrusion. Some schools are more prone to welcome visits or unwelcome invasion. Student and teacher mobility varies — for internal and external reasons.

Beyond the matter of natural forces for community enhancing or undermining such forces — there can be deliberate policies to stimulate in-school community (school spirit).

A first step is to take measures, if necessary, to diminish the permeability of school boundaries. Such boundaries are typically described in two ways: the boundaries of the school's enrolment area (sometimes called the attendance or catchment area), and the boundaries of the school and its grounds. One traditional form of enrolment area is the neighborhood school. In this situation, all of the children in one defined area attend one designated school. Sometimes, such attendance areas are also relatively small in size, and all pupils live within walking distance of the school. In such a situation, pupils, and their families, are often in touch with each other on numerous occasions, for example, playing, shopping, in neighborhood and church activities. It is also possible that school employees live in that same neighborhood. This proximity encourages in-school community.

Such cosy situations have become less frequent due to a variety of political and technological changes. Some of these changes require brief mention here. A preference for larger schools has encouraged boundary enlargement. And social and political policies have often encouraged more out-of-area busing of students to specific schools. Thus, we have witnessed the deployment of powerful forces for the promotion of diversity. Furthermore, throughout much of North America, the values concensus which once surrounded public education (and much of public life) has become less coherent. This breakdown of consensus has inevitably had its effects on the levels of in-school consensus.

Despite such handicaps to developing in-school community, there are many measures schools can take to foster in-school cohesion; in particular, measures to heighten the vitality of school boundaries. They can establish symbol systems which increase membership demarcation — school uniforms (covering 100 per cent of the pupils), or they can encourage the use of school jackets or bookbags and other materials bearing school symbols.

Another boundary forming system is the magnet school established in some communities. These are public schools where the pupils (and their parents) deliberately choose whether to enrol, compared to reflexively attending their neighborhood school. In these schools of choice, the administration may not automatically enrol each applicant; sometimes unusual conditions are established consonant with the school's special emphases, for example, a talent for mathematics, or dedication to the arts. Such criteria can be used to favor pupils and families whose values are congruent with the unique goals of the school. This congruence may overcome the disadvantage of a geographically dispersed enrolment area. But it does require the school (and its administration) to develop a clear image of the values it hopes to foster. Then, it can articulate strong and plausible enrolment criteria. Coleman and Hoffer (1987) describe such schools as values communities. Parents share common values, but not common lives, as they do in functional communities.

Obviously, certain forms of criteria would be clearly unwarranted, for example, a criterion based on race. However, depending on the political and social environment, other criteria might be considered defensible, for example, willingness to do considerable homework, accept an honors code, or attend a single sex school (we should recall that single sex schools have been the dominant educational norm through Western history, and are common in many other modern societies).

Theoretically, pupils who are rejected by magnet schools have not been denied access to public school. They have merely been refused entry to programs for which they were unqualified. After all, if someone is very poor in math, he or she cannot be expected to pass courses in electronics or physics, which an engineering high school might require for its students. But, like other issues relating to in-school community, the matter may be more complicated. One can easily imagine a situation where magnet schools cream off the interesting pupils — those who are academically able, or come from motivated and coherent families. The traditional neighborhood schools will be left with pools of less adept pupils and will be less able to build strong community boundaries than before.

Conversely, when there are no magnet schools, more motivated families and pupils are expected to be committed to schools which apparently do not meet their children's capabilities. Furthermore, only so much compulsion is possible in a democracy. There is evidence that some families move out of neighborhoods, or refuse to move in, because they are unsatisfied with the public school options put before them. In this light, it may be better to keep such families invested in the public school system, compared with trying to compel them to use schools whose community they cannot accept. In any event, as we have emphasized, the policies for building school spirit are affected by profound value issues. It may be gratifying to imagine that an extremely heterogeneous group of pupils and families may be welded into a coherent, supportive, multicultural school community. However, the fact is that such achievements are extraordinarily difficult, or even impossible. Indeed, effective multicultural schools seem to outsiders to reflect an extraordinary degree of assimilation. There are enormous problems in imagining, still less building, a strong community school that is genuinely committed to contradictory, incompatible multi-ethnic goals.

Common Goals

Thus the matter of common goals is also important, and relatively complex. In a reflexive sense, most people in schools have common goals. Many teachers perform essentially similar tasks, and all pupils, one hopes, want to excel in learning. But such common aspirations are inadequate examples of common goals. They are similar goals, each held by separate community members. A truly binding common goal is one which can only be attained by all members of a group at the same time; if one group member fails to attain it, then none of them succeeds. But in most classes, one pupil may receive 100 per cent on a biology exam, while others may fail. The common wish to succeed in biology is not particularly binding — and may be divisive if some students lose interest.

When goals are truly common, as on athletic teams, every group member, regardless of likes and dislikes about other team members, has strong motives for wishing all of the team's members to do well. Such commonality is a powerful incentive for building group ties.

Structurally speaking, many schools have low levels of common goals. It is up to skilful educators to overcome this serious deficiency. The main problem is the essential nature of the regular work of students and teachers. As already pointed out in Chapter 7, pupil grading systems have an essential normative, individually competitive aspect. Secondary schools have to divide students — in the sense that not all can be prepared equally for the same future. Some will win university scholarships. Some will go directly to work at comparatively low pay. Most grading systems generate strong incentives for pupils to want others to do poorly. After all, if one pupil is a mediocre performer, and everyone else is even worse, a teacher is under some pressure to give the mediocre student an A. That pupil is still the best in the class. Furthermore, if pupils take time away from studying to aid other pupils, that generosity may lead to penalization: they give less time to their own learning, and also help inadept pupils to improve their performance and become potential competitors for recognition and high grades.

It is true that few pupils carefully think through this whole, highly individually competitive process. Still, it is widely recognized that, by high school, more able pupils are often regarded by other pupils in a critical light, for example, as nerds. But few pupils criticize the school athletes who put in long hours of drill to win praise for the school and honor for themselves. The potentially successful athletes also add to the prestige of the whole school. But pupils with mediocre grades rarely feel better because other pupils in their classes earn As. In most European countries, sports are less highly valued in secondary school. Sometimes, special academic schools have a more strongly intellectual character where academic success is respected. But even there, individual competition is strong and the sharing of common but individualized goals is not particularly helpful for building school spirit.

The individualization of teachers' work is not quite as focused as that of students. Most teachers receive some benefit if other teachers do a good job teaching, and they also suffer problems if other teachers do a poor job (and they have to work with ill-prepared pupils). Still few or no teachers receive extra pay or conspicuous honors as a result of the joint contributions of the teaching staff. Like the typical recognition process affecting students, teachers, too often, fail or succeed very much on their own. Such patterns make it hard to encourage teamwork among teachers. Teachers, too, are concerned to build their own classroom subcommunities, which are not always drawn in to the school community.

The educator's task is to moderately transform the recognition structure of the typical school or classroom. The transformation should generate more forms of collective achievement and recognition for pupils and teachers. Such proposals are not original to our era. For instance, the Lancastrian tutorial schools of the nineteenth century applied many forms of group competition, and contests among rows of pupils in classrooms are a long-practised tradition. Many contemporary schools have already taken some such equivalent steps. Team athletics, in particular, and extra-curricular activities in general, are fertile fields for such measures; as are any activity where groups of students excel — or fail — as a group: the dramatic society's performance, the art show, the musical evening, the basketball team, the school's success in fund raising for the community chest. Sometimes, such groups can have a class or intra-class base. Thus, there can be academic contests between classes and between groups within particular classes.

Another strategy is the encouragement of various forms of team learning. This enlists pupils in learning activities where their individual success is partly dependent on the learning efficiency of a team — or group. This process requires the assignment of learning responsibilities to groups — or teams — of students. Such responsibilities can be allocated to groups taking into account the age of the pupils, the experience of the teacher, the subject matter, the pupil's previous learning experiences with teamwork, and the length of the learning activity involved. The design and evaluation of group learning activities can be a complex and developmental process. As might be expected, a number of researchers have been working on such matters. They have developed a variety of types of learning activities.

Some general principles follow:

1. Groups should not go beyond four or five members, unless they will be working together for long periods of time (two or three members are often appropriate).
2. The product to be produced by the group, especially if a grade is to be given, should be relatively clearly defined in advance.
3. Some of the group's work and planning should occur during free time, away from adult supervision.
4. The teacher should be able to casually observe some of the groups' planning meetings, and make low key recommendations.
5. If teams are asked to produce long-range products (taking one to ten weeks), they should first have brief 'practice' sessions, for small fractions of their total grade.
6. The longer the group is asked to work as a team, the more important it is that a system be designed to weigh the value of each member's comparative contribution (simply providing the same grade for all members is only warranted for brief projects).
7. On some occasions, each group member should produce his or her individual project; but a total group grade will also be calculated, and the group will thus be encouraged to stimulate each member to excel.

The encouragement of such team-learning will never extinguish the need for all traditional grading and assignments. Still, much more can be done in teaching to foster group loyalties than is usually the case. Although traditional, individual grading is still required, team-learning and grading serve to promote learning by individuals — as well as providing other benefits.

Some general principles should also be articulated about all school-related group activities. All elaborate forms of such activities need to be accompanied by significant incentives. As pupils get older, the forms of such recognition should become increasingly elaborate. Warm 'thank yous' may do for groups of first graders; groups of junior high pupils may need personal notes sent to their parents; and groups of high school seniors may appreciate mention in the school paper, being recognized on the public address system, and so on. After all, in adult life, a variety of rewards is used in our working lives and employees are rightly resentful when something appears to have been done to no purpose. Similar recognition should be provided for activities with shared goals. Sometimes, such recognition systems already exist. In athletics, many schools already support systems of athletic letters, announcements of coming games and victories throughout the school, pep rallies, audiences watching teams perform, mention in the school paper, and so on. And such recognition systems often succeed in generating considerable enthusiasm among students. But sometimes the recognition systems for group activities — especially non-athletic ones — are thin or non-existent. The effect is to situate school spirit within a subset of activities and to give unintended stardom to athletic prowess, particularly among boys.

To improve such deficient systems, one simply needs to apply the ideal athletic recognition model: give groups notable identities, either in individual classrooms, or schoolwide; devise a system of comparative scoring; design competitive systems so there is a good likelihood of many competitors winning; keep track of scores, and give the results appropriate publicity; and, over time, manipulate the formation of teams, so almost all pupils have a chance to belong to one or more winning teams.

All of the foregoing activities take administrative time and energy. But recall the example of competitive sports. Many pupils already dedicate enormous energy to pursuing success in athletics — far more energy than most pupils dedicate to academic learning. That energy is partly invested due to the recognition systems now maintained by adults. Similarly, if adults create equivalent recognition systems for other group activities, we should see similar learning benefits dispersed through the whole school. In times past, a few (usually boys') sports teams often provided a large part of school spirit. That cannot work in many places today — even if one wants it to. Alternative more broadly-based programs should be developed.

The matter of inter-group competition moves us ahead to the vital topic of subcommunities, as parts of the whole school community. The formation of teams, and subgroups, which has just been recommended, obviously is congruent with the policy of encouraging subcommunities. Such competing groups provide pupils with sub-bases in their schools — bases which are generally subordinate to wholesome adult supervision. After all, adults oversee the contests the pupils are striving to win.

Another tool for the formation of such groups is the homeroom (or division), typical of departmentalized schools. In departmentalized schools, such bases are important sites for the encouragement of community. However, if such communities are to flourish, then other elements of community must exist: groups persisting for several years, under the supervision of one persisting advisor, with frequent, regular meeting time set aside, and assigned collective responsibilities and recreational activities. Homerooms and divisions currently vary widely in their adherence to such principles.

A most successful tradition of English private boarding schools is the house system. The house is a subcommunity cutting across age/grade lines. In boarding schools, houses often live and eat together. Houses are the focus of intra-school competition in debating, chess and sports. The house system has not worked as well in day schools, where the divisions often seem unreal and arbitrary. Nevertheless, some day schools have managed to make such divisions work. Like the homerooms, the house works best when it has some functional reality; for example, just as the homeroom teacher should teach the homeroom class something, ideally students should take some classes together in their house. The trick is to give each house enough identity to create loyalty and belonging, but not so much as to create divisiveness, as one would if one set up black, white and Hispanic houses in a multiracial school. It must be remembered that subgroup climate must reflect and recapitulate the community climate.

Aesthetic and Intellectual Appeals

Community members can be encouraged to recognize their common goals, and give great significance to such goals, by means of aesthetic and intellectual appeals. An old story makes the point about the importance of appearances in such matters.

William the Conqueror was at the prow of the first Norman ship to reach England in 1066. As a true leader, he jumped from the ship to the beach, before the eyes of all his men. He landed on the sand, slipped, and fell on his face. The soldiers looked aghast at this bad omen. William, a brilliant leader, grabbed a handful of sand in his fist, scrambled boldly to his feet, and shouted, 'First man to seize English soil.' And his men leaped from their boats, and marched to battle.

William's imaginative conduct served a variety of purposes. It transformed an embarrassing episode into a bold achievement. Also, many of his followers probably tacitly realized the imagination and daring underlying his act of transformation. They felt heartened being led into battle following such a leader. And so — perhaps unfortunately — daring and imagination are especially important in developing and articulating aesthetic and intellectual appeals: unfortunately, because these characteristics are in limited supply.

Various formal aesthetic and intellectual devices and techniques are effectively applied in schools to foster commonality. They can be summarily catalogued, and then selectively discussed in greater depth: assemblies, class opening ceremonies; memorial occasions; the celebration of holidays as part of a school's program (not simply through taking the day off); appropriate announcements via the public address system or in periodic publications for the staff, parents and families; giving prominence to symbols of the school, the community or the nation; various statements of purpose or philosophy, including school pledges frequently recited by pupils and faculty; processions; parades; festive occasions; homecomings; and dramatic and musical performances.

These activities, when they work, attain their effects by stimulating appropriate emotions among members of the school community. The emotions generated can include: mutual affection and respect; collective pride and determination; a recognition of shared values; good humored fun; and shared mourning and disappointment.

Like other community-building activities, such efforts require forethought, and the commitment of resources. One principal tells how his school regularly conducted an elaborate Halloween festival: many pupils and teachers came into school dressed in outlandish costumes, some class time during the day was absorbed in a best costume contest, and an orderly, all-school neighborhood parade was conducted. The principal notes, 'I realize that such activities take a lot of learning time from the day. But I believe such activities, overall, are worth such a loss.' Obviously, the decision is a matter of judgment.

The commonalities emphasized by such techniques can heighten a variety of emotional ties. The ties may be simply among members of the subcommunities in a school; or between the subcommunities and the whole school; or between the school and the external community, even the nation; or between the school and the communities of the past (our ancestors) and the future (our descendants). All such acts of intercommunity engagement may heighten the community in the school, since members of the school community find their own sense of community enhanced via their recognition of shared values. For example, when the school observes some national (patriotic) holiday, community members not only feel closer to the nation, but also to each other, knowing they share important values.

There are other practical and conceptual issues connected with the use of aesthetic appeals. Sometimes, such assemblies and other occasions make demands on the pupils: will they maintain order if brought together in a body and asked to stay respectfully silent for a period of time? Of course, the reply is, 'It depends.' It depends on the models presented by adults, the values pupils are taught to attribute to the occasion, and the level of discipline prevailing in the school. Another issue concerns the commitments which adults believe it is proper to transmit to pupils.

For instance, in some American public schools, certain adults do not believe it is proper to encourage pupils to recognize certain relationships based on formal religion: such recognition might be inconsistent with the legally defined purposes of those schools. Thus, American public schools are often reluctant to encourage the expression of commitment inherent in many pupils' religious beliefs (for example, through celebrating the religious significance of Christmas). Again, those who believe it is important for pupils to have international affiliations — in contrast with national ones — may disparage the celebration of national holidays in schools, or strive to supplement them with more international concerns. And so on.

The sum of the matter is that community is based on bodies of shared feelings and values. If school citizens hold many discrepant values, then it will be harder to organize activities for the symbolic expression of collective values; such ceremonies may even foster tension, not unity. And so one long-term goal of school administrators is to gradually form a school staff and pool of students (and families) with generally congruent values. Such a process can provide a variety of benefits to the school; in particular, it can generate a base for the symbolic and intellectual expression of collective values.

Since much of the preceding discussion has focused on affecting students, some direct mention should be made about attaining equivalent effects on the teaching faculty. Community among faculty simply involves teachers participating in school-related activities which are roughly the counterparts of those prescribed for pupils. Faculty must be encouraged, and required to work together in small groups, as well as individually. The faculty must be provided with collective, contructive goals — as well as individual ones. Potential new teachers must be carefully assessed to ensure their values are generally congruent with those prevailing in the school. Faculty stability is generally a desirable characteristic of a school. Ceremonies, rites, clear and elevating statements of purpose, and good humored fun must all be significant elements of teacher relationships. And teachers, in appropriate ways, must feel at ease sharing some of their concerns with students.

Conclusion

To re-emphasize some major themes, good school climate is fostered by:

1. Encouraging persons sympathetic to the school's overall goals to enlist in the school environment, and keeping unsympathetic persons from enlisting, or persisting.
2. Encouraging members of the school community to form into small, persisting groups, whose goals are congruent with the overall values of the school.
3. Maintaining a vital administrative structure for the overall school.
4. Recognizing that effective school operations require a continuous concern with the balancing of four elements: gratification, industriousness, efficiency and predictability.
5. Using appropriate combinations of aesthetic, ceremonial and intellectual appeals to heighten the collective identity of community members.
6. Fostering activities — including systems of academic learning — that encourage the pursuit of collective goals by students and faculty members.
7. Recognizing that some of the means of pursuing good school climate are controversial. Effective pursuit requires judicious compromises, plus a willingness to engage, where necessary, in tactful confrontation.

Further Reading

Wynne's (1980) book *Looking at Schools: Good, Bad and Indifferent* provides an extended discussion of school climate based on observations and reports from his students. The emphasis is on patterns of discipline and control. Holmes (1985d) and Anderson (1982) provide overviews of the literature on climate. McDill and Rigsby (1973) provide some of the original research establishing clearly the importance of school climate to student achievement. Coleman and Hoffer (1987) illustrate the close identity between school community and educational outcomes. More practical assistance is provided by: Howard, Howell and Brainard (1987); McGrail, Wilson and Rossman (1987); Slavin (1986) and Wilson and McGrail (1987).

Chapter 9

The Administrator and the Effective School: Bringing about Improvement

The Effective School

It may seem strange that the notion of the effective school is only directly addressed as we near the end of the book. But we chose not to base the book on 'effective schools' research. This book is intended to help those interested in school administration reflect on good practice. It is not simply a recipe for the application and implementation of the findings of effective schools research.

We began instead with the centrality of purpose — and that theme has emerged over and over through the chapters. Effective schools research, like all empirical research, is contained by the questions the researchers address. They are for example necessarily limited by the available criteria of success. The criteria established in the first chapter go well beyond what is typically researched (Holmes, 1986a). In any case, empirical research cannot attempt to determine what is right or wrong, what is ethical and moral, or how vigorously particular principles should be applied. The discussion of many important aspects of school life, such as grouping, scheduling and student evaluation depends almost entirely on rational argument related to underlying values and philosophies, hardly at all on empirical research. Thus we have throughout the book deliberately avoided constraining discussion to those few issues which can be profitably addressed through empirical research. Even in those areas where empirical research has been active, extravagant and dubious claims are frequently made.

We do not disparage empirical research, but it cannot be used as a single or dominant source of advice on most important school questions. Rather it provides a few, rather limited answers to a very specific and small set of questions.

There are numerous useful summaries of the effective schools research (Purkey and Smith, 1983; Northwest Regional Educational Laboratory, 1984; Rosenholtz, 1985). The purpose of this chapter is to put the research in perspective and to draw some rather general conclusions for the school administrator.

Effective Schools Research — the First Phase

Before the advent of the computer and large scale social research, two themes central to the study of the effective school had already been developed. The first concerned the effect of home background on school achievement. It was with evident distaste that Hollingshead (1949) and Havighurst (1962) chronicled the extent to which children of affluent parents gained educational advantage over the poor within comprehensive supposedly 'democratic' school systems. Liberal reformers had hoped, both in the USA and in Europe, that as equal opportunity in terms of access to educational programs became generally available, the result would be greatly increased social equality; at least, it was felt that access to post-secondary education would be unrelated or only slightly related to social and ethnic origin and sex.

But Hollingshead's early research was a preliminary warning, with implications understood neither by him nor by others at the time, that, as schools become more and more alike, and as nearly everyone attends, intelligence and home culture are the most important factors to explain which young people move up the economic ladder and which do not. Hollingshead saw the inheritance of parental success as being at least partly the school's fault. But today it is becoming increasingly apparent that if fault there is, it is that of the parents.

The first theme then in the first phase was social inequality; but the second concerned the anti-intellectual, or at least the non-intellectual, character of the democratic, comprehensive American school. Coleman (1961) wrote a classic study of the American high school showing that the powerful male peer group was less interested in academic success than in cars, sports and the opposite sex, the female peer group in appearance, dress and the opposite sex. It is ironic that his later more famous study (1966) totally ignored the potential contribution of school climate to school effectiveness. Thus it is probably fair to say, with the benefit of hindsight, that two of the most central difficulties with school effectiveness research are evident in research completed before the movement really began, around twenty years ago. In developed countries, where classrooms, books and materials are readily available and where teachers are educated up to or beyond their level of competence (extra training for the most part does not seem to improve teaching), it is intellectual curiosity, desire to learn, positive attitudes to school and teachers, moral support, language and culture, all of which children bring with them from home, that are most crucial to their relative development. Insofar as differences among schools are important, we should by now recognize that schools do not always systematically operate as if academic achievement were an important goal — at least not in Britain or North America. In short, as schooling is equalized, home differences (which are far from being equalized) become more crucial. Schools do not compensate, partly because they are similar and not strongly intellectual, and partly because the more academic schools and tracks are populated by children of ambitious parents (Holmes, 1988b).

The Second Phase

The first phase ended with the publication of Coleman's epic American research (1966) and with the first round of international studies (see, for example, Purves and Levine, 1975). With the advent of computers, high spending governments and the belief among educators that technical improvements would revolutionize the school, large scale research into the school factors most relevant to school effectiveness was undertaken. We shall not review here (see Holmes, 1978b) the significant weaknesses of Coleman's landmark research (1966). However, several of his important findings have not been refuted either by subsequent research or by re-analysis of his data. They are:

(i) The character of the student body explains more of the difference between schools than do any qualitative or quantitative differences in the schools themselves.

(ii) Although individual teachers may differ greatly in quality, differences in instructional quality by school are difficult to establish, presumably because (a) most schools have average numbers of good, bad and moderate teachers; and (b) differences in quality are not either attributable to or even strongly related to differences in teachers' quantity of experience or training.

(iii) Material conditions in schools (buildings, materials, expenditure) do not explain much of the difference in achievement among schools.

Coleman's research was by no means the end of school effectiveness but it was the beginning of the end. To some extent, it weakened both the critics who thought schools were part of a capitalist plot and the Polyannas who thought that 'democratic' schooling was the answer to an inequitable social system. Coleman's somewhat disappointing findings were not challenged by the first round of international studies which, like Coleman, found few school differences with a fraction of the potency of differences in home culture.

The Third Phase

Researchers after Coleman gradually picked up the pieces and began to research the non-material factors he had ignored. His earlier study of the American high school gave impetus to researchers to examine the effects of school climate — typically operationalized as the expectations teachers have of students and students have of one another (McDill and Rigsby, 1973; Holmes, 1971).

253

A series of studies in different countries, using different methodologies, in both elementary and secondary schools, had led to a set of characteristics associated with so called effective schools: academic climate of high expectations among teachers and students; the use of universalistic discipline; a safe and orderly atmosphere; frequent and immediate rewards for good performance; regular monitoring of student achievement; community involvement; and strong leadership. Probably the single most influential study in the literature has been the Rutter study of secondary schools in southwest London (Rutter *et al.*, 1979).

What the bulk of the effective schools research shows is that, generally in the English speaking world, slightly better academic performance (typically in the basic skills) is to be found in schools possessing the effective school correlates in good measure. Rutter went further to claim that his most effective school obtained better achievement with the lowest social band of students than did the least effective with the highest band. That statement is more credible when it is recalled that Rutter's schools were quite homogeneous in terms of socioeconomic background; that is to say that the highest band did not in fact differ greatly in socioeconomic terms from the lowest band.

The Fourth Phase

Since the early eighties, the emphasis has changed from effectiveness studies to improvement studies. It is one thing to know what school characteristics co-exist with high achievement levels; it is another thing to (i) introduce those characteristics and (ii) improve academic achievement as a result.

At this point in history, two very different strands of research have come together. In Chapter 6, we referred to the implementation literature. As well as being based on case studies, the mainstream literature excluded important factors such as the worth of the change being introduced and the ethical problems inherent in changing teachers, or in giving them a sense of spurious ownership. To that not inconsiderable set of problems, the effective schools research brings its own as the two traditions merge. It assumes that academic achievement is the principal school goal (indeed it seems to assume that it is both the major school function and the major school goal). Effective school advocates have also assumed that less successful schools have only to act out the effective school behaviors to bring about improvement. To further compound a difficult situation, experimental improvement efforts rather obviously require the direct involvement of the schools and school district to be improved. In contrast, effective schools research involved the observation of inert, operating schools, and improvement research involved mainly the objective observation of improvement efforts in progress (Huberman and Miles, 1984). Needless to say, school people do not always want to change in the ways suggested by the outside observer.

It is too early to comment fairly on the success of this last phase, which is still in progress. It is clear enough however that the task of improving schools along effective school lines is a daunting one and will be characterized by some failure. It would be naive indeed to believe that every school in every improvement plan will improve. Indeed, it may well be that a genuine success rate of twenty-five per cent may be considered admirable. Holmes's experience with a New Jersey school improvement project (1988a) suggests that even coordinated state efforts to help volunteer schools to improve may run into major difficulties.

In sum, the effective schools research is an important part of history in educational reasearch. We do know some correlates of more and less academically effective schools. But we do not know how improved effectiveness, even in academic areas, can be brought about. Both the implementation and the improvement strands of research, both limited in scope and generalizability, have significant shortcomings when applied to applying effective schools findings.

The Problem for Administrators

The Criterion

The first and most important problem facing some people wanting to bring about school improvement is reaching agreement on what constitutes improvement. Is it test scores? Examination results? Parent satisfaction? Pupil satisfaction? Teacher fulfilment? We are not suggesting that different goals are simply irreconcilable, although some are. But clearly the effective schools program is most relevant if one is interested in the goals measured by effective schools research.

Here once again, and most crucially, school administrators are forced to confront the issues of educational purpose addressed in Chapter 1. Perhaps there was a time when educators, like physicians, could assert that their purposes were patently obvious. Everyone 'knew' why children went to school. That innocence, if indeed that is what it was, has passed. This book is full of problems grounded in policy; the school principal cannot just get on with good management. Management science tells us little about universalism and particularism, or which program to evaluate, or whether to teach about abortion, or how to deal with anti-semitism in *The Merchant of Venice*; and the lowering of important moral, ethical, philosophical and political issues to the level of managerial difficulty makes the principal at best a bureaucrat or broker, certainly not an educator. We decided earlier that school administrators claimed to be and ought to be professional educators.

The goal orientations educators support may be encapsulated under six headings. The first is liberal, cultural education: children should acquire more knowledge of our world, our humanity and our culture, together with the traditional academic skills including skills of investigation, data collection, hypothesis testing and evaluative judgment used in the physical and social sciences. A second is education as preparation for the future. Improvement in education here means the production of more students with the capacity and skills required by colleges and employers. A third orientation defines education as a voyage of self-discovery; personal fulfilment and self-knowledge are its ultimate goals. A fourth orientation is to social equity and equality. The task of the school is to prevent parents from passing economic advantage and disadvantage to succeeding generations. This can be attempted by educating all equally and by providing post-secondary opportunities based on fair distribution among different groups rather than on competitive testing. A fifth orientation is to individual development. We live in a competitive world, so improved education would better help young people learn to compete and achieve — the goal being not self-discovery but success. A last orientation is to character — to the development of good, healthy, citizens who can help those around them make the world a better place through family and community.

We can label those six orientations: liberal, technocratic, progressive, egalitarian, neo-conservative and traditional. All six orientations have legitimacy in our society and most readers will have some sympathy with most or all. But clearly, priorities will vary and improvement schemes will not be identical irrespective of the developers' prime motivation. At the same time as one considers lofty ideals, one has also to consider the school's functional realities (the custody, social distribution and basic skills discussed in Chapter 1). Although we see worth in most of those orientations, readers will not be surprised to hear that the last orientation is of particular importance to us. We do not expect a majority of readers to share our perspective, but we do hope it will be considered — along with the others. We also, it will be evident, have sympathy with the thrust of the effective schools research, which is consistent with the technocratic, liberal and neo-conservative orientations, but not at all with the progressive.

Now, how is all this relevant to effective schools research and to the implementation of its findings within the school? Educators will be attracted to one or more of the six sets of orientations on which improvements could be based. The school effectiveness research assumes that primacy is to be given to academic work, or perhaps in a few cases to academic work and character development. But if teachers do not share that assumption, and it is surely very evident that many do not, it is very difficult to see how the necessary changes can be adequately implemented. In particular, many teachers, perhaps the majority, particularly at the elementary level, place their faith in personal development. The principal who tries to bring about a massive change based on a rather contrary philosophy is unlikely to be successful.

Indeed, one possible explanation of the effective schools research is that effective schools are those where the principal and teachers subscribe to the value of the criteria attested to by effective schools research. They have high expectations of students and make strong demands of them because they want children to learn; they monitor achievement because they care about the children and their achievement. They apply strict discipline because they work to a standard. And the principal is a good leader partly because the principal looks good in the school that achieves the goals it wants to achieve and partly because the principal is leading in a direction where the people want to go. That explanation is too pat, too neat; the complexity of life is not so simply explained. But we think it is likely to be a part of the truth. Indeed, our interest in character is not at all inconsistent with the effective schools research. The two orientations, to character and to academics, are complementary. Crucial aspects of character — respect for truth, diligence — are necessary for continued academic success.

One thing is true by definition. If the principal is to bring about improvement, then leadership must be exercised. This is of course not the same thing as saying that improvement can only take place if the principal exercises leadership. But if the principal is to bring about improvement, it is first highly desirable if not absolutely necessary to bring about some consensual agreement on school purpose. And that is where we began this book. The consensual purpose need not and should not be identical for all schools; but a continuing good school needs some transcendent value — probably and preferably (from our perspective) beyond intellectual development, material advancement, personal success and social equality. The point is not to convince teachers, parents and students that academic achievement is the only worthwhile criterion of education, although it is one. Rather is it to focus clearly on a framework of goals.

Many of the goals listed in Chapter 1 are straightforward, obvious. Many are easily achieved. It is certainly an error to concentrate only on the clear, achievable objectives — improved physical fitness, better test scores in the basic skills, better manners, a clean and pleasant environment. But it is a far greater error to concentrate mainly on 'higher level' objectives: to improve decision making skills, to learn how to learn, to understand issues of world peace and world hunger, to achieve self-fulfilment. There is nothing absolutely wrong with that latter set. Any educator can think of some worthwhile learning that could be captured within any of those objectives. The problem with many so-called 'high level' objectives is that they are inadequately conceptualized. The fact that anyone can think of something to do for such complex objectives is not comforting; it suggests that what will be done will be varied, vague and ill-defined. And so long as people disagree about what is is they are trying to do, no one can really know if it is or is not done. Some abstruse, 'high level' objectives are often conceptually confused.

Consider the case of decision making. Everyone would like young people (and old people) to make better decisions. But consider the form and purpose of instruction to that end. We would argue that decisions must first be good, i.e., they must be congruent with a virtuous life reflecting fundamental values. A pragmatist might argue that decision making is improved by practice; children from the earliest age should be faced with choices, with increasingly important consequences as they go through the grades. A cognitive rationalist would argue that children should be taught a decision making structure whereby they match options with an array of criteria, each criterion weighted for its significance — all in terms of estimated consequences; and so on. The debate is not really about instructional methodology, but about ends, about what decision making is and what purpose it serves.

Teachers at all levels (from primary to graduate level) often observe how little learners seem to learn from what is taught, 'After two weeks of reviewing European geography some of my 12-year-olds can only identify two countries on a map.' There is a case for simplifying what is taught — at least to the point where the teacher knows exactly what it is.

What is true about teaching in general is even more true about school improvement. It should be very clear exactly what it is that is to be improved. There is disagreement (within the effective schools movement) between those who believe one should begin with instructional change within a few classrooms and those who believe one should begin with school climate. There is no conclusive research yet to guide us on such choices. Moreover, the problems of experimental research in education are so great that any major claims based on a few studies will be suspect. However, knowing what we do about instruction (i.e., very little), it would be unwise to be overly optimistic about effects of incremental changes in instructional methodology in a few classrooms of a large school. But that generalization would not hold in the situation where there is general recognition of an instructional problem (for example, poor reading and writing skills in a small inner-city school) and a determined school-wide effort to do something about it.

The effective schools research emphasizes school level factors; not surprisingly because it was those factors that the research investigated. Even so, it makes sense that administrators should attempt to change school level characteristics, generally accepted as being within the sphere of legitimate authority, rather than intra-classroom characteristics, where administrative interference is likely to be resisted on ethical as well as other practical grounds.

The criteria for improvement chosen by school administrators, in conjunction with others (teachers, parents, students and senior administrators) should vary with the situation in the school and the beliefs of those involved. For example, the school plagued by discipline problems, incomplete home assignments, poor attendance and vandalism will surely begin by improving its handling of discipline and by involving the school community in efforts to create a positive, caring climate.

The following general principles with respect to choosing effectiveness criteria are based only partly on the effective schools research; more fundamentally they are based on the educational philosophy embraced in Chapter 1. We return again to this integrating theme in the final chapter. Suffice it here to remind the reader that good character is assumed to be a fundamental educational goal and that academic achievement is considered the legitimate stuff of the school.

Principles for Selecting Effectiveness Criteria

1. *The effectiveness goals should be clear enough for success to be possible and evident at all.* School climate is an obvious candidate. No one can miss clean and tidy halls and washrooms. Group rewards for classes demonstrating school spirit (not self-satisfaction) and helpfulness to others, perhaps to senior citizens or hospitals, become a visible focus for the effectiveness movement. One of the authors visited several schools in a massive British school improvement project. He was told by those running the project that the introduction of computers to the schools was only the tip of the iceberg and that they were really planning fundamental change as a prototype for the twenty-first century. But the students were quite mystified when asked if the project had anything to do with other changes beyond the introduction of computers. Some approved, some disapproved — depending on whether they enjoyed using computers. The point is not just that the changes were not evident to the naked eye, but the students were not even aware they were supposed to have taken place.

2. *The effectiveness goals should be faithful to the thrust of the improvement rationale.* If improvement is to concentrate on the academic and moral/spiritual domains, then care must be taken not to become so involved with a host of activities that they actually distract teachers and students from the major purposes.

3. *Effectiveness goals should be inclusive.* This principle may appear to conflict with the previous one. It may appear difficult for goals to be consistently faithful and inclusive. Surely everyone cannot be academically and morally superior; and many legitimate school activities have little relationship to either form of superiority. Neither objection is crucial. Academic improvement should not focus only on the excellence of the few but on the improvement of the many. There is nothing to prevent a school from focusing simultaneously on improvement in specific directions in all domains — but that will require a powerful consensus and will, without which an unfocused, general attempt to improve will surely founder. The main point here is that it is very unlikely that a school community will be made more effective by attempts to help a small group

improve. That does not exclude special efforts to help a small group of non-readers as part of an overall reading thrust.

4. *The effectiveness goals should be guided by effectiveness research.* This does not mean that all schools should simply adopt the summary conclusions listed earlier. Their assumed objectives, as we have said, are limited. Nevertheless, it is hard to believe that any improvement can take place in unpleasant, unsafe and undisciplined environments. It is difficult to believe that a climate inhospitable to one's purposes will be conducive to their attainment. The main thrust of the research is that one has to work intensely and intensively on what one considers really important.

5. *The effectiveness goals should be contained within a transcendent vision of the school and its mission.* This principle may appear to conflict with the simple clarity required to satisfy the first principle. The argument here is that the improvement changes should be more than short-term, instrumental, *ad hoc* changes that will, for a time, buy peace and attract favorable attention. The word transcendent, for which we know of no reasonable substitute, may be off-putting to some readers; it may sound pretentious, grandiose, silly, or simply overly ambitious — certainly not clear. One effective school one of us visited is situated in an inner-city area of poverty and destruction in a large American urban centre. Its transcendent image is a peaceful and purposeful haven where young people have a chance to build lives for themselves better than those promised by their environment. The improvement objectives themselves in this particular school are exceptionally mundane — but the vision is not. Obviously not every student in the school will have a comprehensive sense of that vision, but one may be surprised by how many do. Another effective school visited is a small, traditional school which is extraordinary only in the fact that it does the ordinary things extremely well — but only by chance. It has no ambition to radicalize education — or the community. Its vision is to be a healthy, superior organ within one very commonplace small town. A girls' private school within Toronto, which is probably effective, avoids the girls' school stereotype (with aggressive, overly self-confident women victorious in field hockey); it has developed a quiet community of thoughtful and caring girls who are encouraged to develop the life of the mind. The transcendent vision need not be (should not be) esoteric, mystical and incomprehensible; but it should lie above and beyond any improvement plan and short-term objectives.

Bringing about Improvement

The most important factor in the implementation of school improvement is commitment — the sense of identification with the improvement goals. The starting point must be philosophical. Suppose that a middle school is generally lax, and is achieving mediocre academic results, considering its reasonably strong and supportive pattern of home culture. Suppose further that the administrators and the parents are strongly committed to improvement of (i) academic performance (i.e., in the basic skills, in writing, in science, in history and geography); (ii) behavior (i.e., reduction in: squabbling, rudeness and jostling in the halls; smoking in the school neighborhood and in the school's washrooms; vandalism in the neighborhood — some on the way to and from school; and the incidence of pornography, sexual experimentation, drinking and drugs); and (iii) musical expression (i.e., development of a school band and choir).

A few staff are also enthusiastic. Many others are indifferent or cynical, 'We have heard all this before. Everything's always our fault of course.' More than a few are openly hostile to any suggestion of a new thrust, 'The problems have always been with us and always will be. Most of them come from the parents themselves anyway. If they spent less time grubbing for money and more time with their kids, our lives would be much easier. What we should be doing is providing education to help these poor kids understand the poverty of their lives, to give them choices, to let them fulfil themselves. What we don't need are higher test scores and a disciplined élite school band to beat the hell out of Southview in the city band festival.'

Obviously, an effective school thrust in that school could easily be doomed before it begins. The principal has several options. The most unreasonable option is to go ahead ignoring the open and covert opposition. At best, there may be some short term gloss, only to be forgotten altogether or added to the cynics' history of failed innovations. Another option is to seek a transfer to a more congenial school.

That last point is not meant facetiously. One of the features of bureaucratization of school districts is the extent to which the allocation of administrators and staff is carried out arbitrarily, centrally and randomly, in such a way that the matching of administrators', teachers' and community purposes is impossible. In Japan, the bureaucratization, in terms of assignment, is far more rigid; but in Japanese schools there is a clear, uniform, national sense of purpose lacking in western, English-speaking countries. In Japan, the regular transfer of teachers and principals serves to reinforce the central purpose by deliberately preventing local alliances, allegiances, deviations and rebellions. Too many school districts in the western world have bureaucratic form without any central commitment or purpose — the worst of both worlds.

One other option for the principal is to divert parental criticism into community oriented activities whose involvement in the school is tangential and superficial. But that is weak, cowardly, because, in this particular case, the principal recognizes the problems and shares many of the community's views and ideas about what ought to be done. The principal may build herself a good reputation — but she will have avoided doing what she knows she ought to do.

However, to expect that fundamental opposition among staff can be converted into enthusiastic commitment is unrealistic. Some accommodation from senior administration must be sought. Let us suppose the district staff is supportive. The senior administrators are well aware of the community disaffection and have received numerous complaints about the school. The principal should seek committed support for a difficult undertaking, and, particularly, a willingness to transfer some staff members to other schools under agreed conditions. This powerful incentive must be used with enormous care. It is likely to antagonize teachers, their union and some parents. It should be evident at this point that the option of a possible transfer for the principal herself was not raised frivolously.

If reasonable district support, beyond verbal encouragement, is not forthcoming, the principal should reconsider the improvement plan. Perhaps there is some kind of limited compromise that will work around those deeply opposed; however, the opposition of teachers with considerable informal authority should not be underestimated. A half-hearted plan is sometimes more easily defeated than a full-fledged idea. The principal must spell out her plan, likely consequences and ideas to deal with various contingencies — and make sure she knows exactly how much support she can expect. It may be helpful to have the idea approved, formally or informally, by the district school board.

If support from the senior administration is forthcoming, the principal should use the newly acquired power with the greatest care. First, the temptation to use the transfer weapon to get rid of weak teachers must be absolutely resisted. Community support for the effort must be strongly in place before the actual processes begin. The principal should acknowledge frankly that some teachers may not like it. Otherwise, parents will find it difficult to see why some strong teachers leave, and that may well happen. In most bureaucratized school districts, where teachers have tenure, there is tacit acceptance that most schools have their share of mediocre and average teachers. Other principals, as well as district staff, will understandably object if the improvement plan consists of exchanging weak teachers for strong ones. Transfer, even voluntary, should be a last resort, and should not be used to get rid of the incompetent or mediocre (see Chapter 4).

The principal's responsibility is, once the outline of the improvement plan is developed, with input from teachers, parents, administrators and students, to identify the teachers who are fundamentally and philosophically opposed to the new emphasis on standards, quality, excellence and accountability. With luck, they will turn out to be few in number. Many others with weak philosophical convictions of any kind will have gone along with the minority for a variety of motives including unwillingness to make extra effort and respect for their more powerful colleagues' informal authority.

Many administrators will argue that obvious opponents of a plan should be ignored and excluded until support has been gathered informally from a significant group. That kind of approach will sometimes have success, at least in the short term. However, it can be seen as being manipulative and in the long term may well generate even more hostility and opposition. Those who are apparently strongly opposed should be approached directly with the problem, early in the process. The school is going to go, the principal hopes, in a direction of which they appear to disapprove. The principal would like those who feel professionally uncomfortable to consider whether or not they would prefer to transfer to some other school. Such transfers must appear to be, as they are in fact, professionally responsible; these particular teachers do not like the school's planned direction so they are moving somewhere more congenial. It may be best to deal with all those affected at one time initially, to ensure that all receive the same message. There are dangers in identifying potential opponents in this way and in a sense labelling a particular group and obviously this tactic should not be used if such a group does not in fact exist. But if there is strong, concerted opposition, it should be confronted — not in an antagonistic, personal way but as frank, open admission of the problem.

The outcome of this open approach is not predictable. There may be obdurate refusal to discuss the matter, 'We shall take this up with the union.' Teachers may say they will stay and fight. At least, however, the problem has been identified and both sides understand the position of the other. If there is deliberate sabotage of the plan, the principal has good grounds for mandatory transfer later on. At best, one or two of the most valiant opponents may take up the option, provided they are able to transfer to another school they would like to go to and providing that the transfer is not seen as demeaning. Another possibility is that the teachers may appear to accommodate the new plan by moderating their opposition, 'I am all in favor of excellence, quality and all that stuff. I just don't want the administration breathing down my neck giving reading tests to my seventh grade class every week.'

It is evident that this straightforward approach may consolidate the opposition of the group of hard-liners. By bringing them together, the principal may give them a sense of collegiality and togetherness they previously lacked. If the plan fails, one can be sure that failure to bring key, informal leaders 'on side' will be blamed; and to some extent that blame will certainly be reasonable. But, blithely ignoring fundamental opposition as one proceeds with a caricature of a plan to which few are committed and many opposed is dishonest and unproductive. Even if voluntary or involuntary transfers do not take place (and most teachers do not like to transfer unless the idea clearly originates with themselves) this approach focuses the staff on the plan. Criticism and objections from the small group philosophically opposed will be seen, by parents and teachers, as being generally unconstructive. Papering over the problems and pretending that everything is rosy and that there is just a little initial reluctance on the part of people who are afraid of change only permits those opposed to sabotage the plan covertly and overtly with little fear of direct opposition or action. The principal must remember that the goal is not to appear to implement a new plan or to get superficial acceptance. The goal is to get commitment to substantive change.

At the same time as the opposition is dealt with, by removal, identification or neutralization, the remaining staff must be given a combination of incentives to become involved. The incentives, as outlined in Chapter 2, should be solidary, material and purposive (or intrinsic, extrinsic and unilateral). Over the long term, purposive incentives are the most important; it must be possible for improvement in the students' manners, behavior and achievement to be readily visible to teachers. In the short run, material incentives are important. Parents must be persuaded to support, praise and reward teachers for their efforts. (They might send in notes of praise to teachers when something good happens to their child, rather than letters of complaint when something bad happens, they might put on a dinner for the teachers, with students waiting at table.) Teachers should be given time and money to go to conferences and in-service programs to learn about the improvement ideas — and to become more supportive. Solidary incentives must be used more carefully; typically, teachers rely on these incentives least (Cameron, 1984; Lortie, 1975). Committees and teams can easily become burdens of extra work rather than rewarding collegial experiences. It should also be remembered that committees usually wane and die. Committees should be given a clear task, a leader, authority and a clear life span. It is always possible to expand a committee's activities; but it leaves a bad taste if a committee gradually falls into inactivity without completing its central work. Structures for permanent improvement should be built into the fabric of the organization.

Solidary incentives are probably more important for parents. Community agreement on how to handle adolescents may strengthen parental willpower. The school can help guide and develop such agreements, for example, no friends in the home without supervision; no acceptance or condoning of smoking, drugs, sexual relationships or unsupervised use of alcohol; no visiting after 8.00 p.m. on school nights. Many parents like to become involved with other parents in helping their children's school if they can see a direct link with their own family. Parhaps the new band will need new instruments and new music, or money to visit other parts of the country or buy uniforms. Parents may run fairs, fashions shows, dances, whist drives, bridge clubs, book and cake sales — whose benefit lies far more in community feeling and involvement than in the money raised. Parents may also be involved in the substance of change in the school. They may help coordinate staff, parent and student consultation on appropriate dress, behavior and punishment. They may help with the administration and scoring of tests.

The involvement of teachers in out of school affairs is delicate. Clear expectations or, worse, demands will only undermine the improvement project; however, fewer things will strengthen the staff/community bonds more than the voluntary involvement of teachers and parents in a common, community endeavor in situations where the underlying parent/teacher conflict does not arise. A few teachers becoming genuinely enthusiastic is better than most teachers drearily doing their duty. Realistically, a compromise may result: most teachers will voluntarily understand the importance of the joint endeavor and will accept with reasonably good grace some normative involvement. Once again, the isolation of the opposition helps here too. It is very easy for the opposition to curry disfavor concerning administrative requests or demands, but very difficult to attack voluntary and enthusiastic involvement in activities enjoyed by their colleagues. A little supportive funding from the district can be helpful perhaps for a dinner to thank those who helped organize the main activities, or a party after the academic awards night.

The commitment of students is probably almost as important as the commitment of parents and staff. There are three ways in which students provide potential for improvement and greater effectiveness in the schools. Most obviously, students bring individual personal and cultural characteristics to the school — the school may make use of these characteristics but will have comparatively little effect on them. Collectively, students help create the school's climate which in part reflects their different and common characteristics. The school's organization of students may influence the development of this context. For example, schools that are tightly streamed (by achievement or ability) may create two cultures within the school — one essentially pro-education and pro-school, the other essentially antagonistic. The school's task is to bring out and develop the best characteristics and to ensure that rewards are open to all segments of the population, but only as a response to good work. Thirdly, there is growing evidence that the ecology of the community served by the school is also an important influence (Coleman and Hoffer, 1987). Thus the school population not only brings individual characteristics to the school and common and shared values but also may be actively influenced by continuing values and behavior of parents in particular and the adult members of the community more generally. We do not claim that the school has an enormous opportunity to direct the ecological characteristics of the community, but it does potentially have the chance to augment, develop, identify and channel those characteristics that are supportive of its consensual purposes. If students are to become committed to certain aspects of school life then those aspects must be emphasized by the school, there must be rewards associated with excellence, with improvement and with continuing industriousness. Material incentives, in the form of good grades, prizes, awards and praise, should be supplied. Solidary incentives, generally neglected in most schools outside the areas of sport and music, can be provided in the form of team and class cooperation and competition, as described in Chapter 8. And purposive incentives — in the form of advanced placement, special reading groups, science and geography displays, special visits — are also helpful.

Through all this activity, the transcendent purpose of the school should be visible. If the special assemblies, the prizes, the awards, the trips become mechanical gimmicks they will quickly lose effect, and will probably not survive. Indeed, it is important not to plan large numbers of activities requiring enormous amounts of individual effort on a continuing basis. It may be necessary to curb enthusiasm. Exciting school assemblies may work for a year — but inspiration will fail and they will soon appear to be contrived, mechanical. Better to have an annual series — perhaps six special assemblies in late winter. Better to have an arts festival once a year over a week than to try to put on a new public dramatic performance every month (although there might be a class or house or grade presentation each month). Somehow, the spirit of the school must be allowed to grow; for example, this is a school whose academic work is respected and whose artistic performance is notable.

The principal and other significant leaders, formal or informal, must model the school vision; if the principal's interests outside school life are limited to television, beer and baseball, then the chances of the school being seen as being intellectually and artistically alive are greatly reduced. The best the principal of that kind can provide is benign but ignorant encouragement — and any praise or prizes from that source will be suspect by the knowledgeable; and it is the knowledgeable who must develop the school culture. Of course, every principal cannot be a Renaissance model — interested and expert in all fields of endeavor. But the principal should show genuine commitment to some form of endeavor and should delegate leadership and commitment to other formal or informal leaders in the areas where interests and expertise are lacking.

Throughout this discussion, we have talked, for simplicity's sake, as if the principal were alone as an administrator, as she is in a small elementary school. In large schools, vice-principals, administrative assistants and department heads all carry portions of the administrative responsibility. Opposition from within the administration is even more dangerous than from individual teachers. It should go without saying that the administrative team must work collaboratively with clearly delegated responsibilities. There may on occasion be legitimate dissent. For example, a vice-principal may like the idea of an arts festival, but disapprove of any competitive aspects. That dissent should be compartmentalized, segregated, cauterized; the simplest way is to keep that vice-principal, openly and deliberately, away from the administration of the arts festival.

The following principles are useful guides in the implementation of school effectiveness ideas:

1. *The school's improvement goals should be central to the entire undertaking.*

2. *The familiar factors generally associated with academically effective schools should be kept in mind, but should not become a simple-minded formula to be followed slavishly.*

3. *It is highly likely that many of the effective school correlates are manifestations of commitment — they are rational ways for professionals who believe in effective school goals to behave.* If this hypothesis is correct, there is little to be gained in persuading people to behave spuriously in ways that are inconsistent with their underlying *beliefs.* Deviant beliefs must be changed, removed, neutralized or limited within an understood, specific context.

4. *Those who are philosophically opposed to school improvement based on effective school ideas should be encouraged to move to other schools not involved with the same idea.*

5. *The principal should be personally committed to the effective school program.* The principal who is a manager — leading first this way then that, depending on current trends and local politics — is unlikely to be an effective educational leader, as teachers and parents will correctly infer the lack of genuine commitment. It is possible for others to provide leadership around a passive or neutral principal, but it is not easy. But that does not mean that all effective principals must be the dynamic centres of all activity that one thinks of as characterizing the 'super-principal.'

6. *Incentive systems should be carefully deployed for parents, teachers and students so that all may benefit from the improvement process.* They should be carefully and openly planned in a nonmanipulative way and consideration should be given to both shortterm and long-term needs for awareness and maintenance.

7. *Substantive change should be built carefully into the fabric and organization of the school so that it becomes difficult for positive change to be gradually abandoned.* For example, an annual festival of the arts should involve parents and artists in the community. The involvement of students helping (for example, the sick or the elderly) in the community should be established in the schedule. In return, senior citizens may become an active and helping part of school life both as volunteers and perhaps as audience and participants. Comparative test results should be published openly and regularly, September to June gain scores tabulated and parents encouraged to watch their own children's progress. Parents' interest should be directed to other areas as well as progress on standardized tests — progress in writing, in musical expression, in debating and

in team participation (in roles demanding leadership and participation). The activities should be regularized and predictable — expected.

8. *Administrative change should be efficient.* It should not require frequent and lengthy meetings or numerous committees for survival. Increasing absenteeism and increasingly infrequent meetings will soon kill a program dependent on continuous cooperation. Where in-service, texts, new courses and materials, prizes are required, there should be an automatic and simple way of supplying them. There should be key individuals responsible for planning and coordinating all activities; the leaders may be formal leaders (administrators) or informal leaders. Responsibilities should never be left vaguely to some committee or group, particularly if the chair is reluctantly or self-importantly doing a duty.

9. *The school's transcendent image should be reflected in all major sets of activities.* Enthusiasm will sometimes lead to the suggestion of inappropriate activities — all in a good cause. For example, if money is required, a parent or teacher may decide that kitsch in form of Christmas ornaments should make money, or vulgar works of art or popular records of low musical quality. The administrator must ensure that all school activities are reflective of high quality in all areas of the school purposes — academic, moral, social, aesthetic and physical.

Further Reading

The issue of policy development for making schools more effective is the topic of a forthcoming book edited by Holmes, Leithwood and Musella (forthcoming). Chapters by Holmes, Wynne, Davis, Musella, Leithwood and Louis are relevant here. Huberman and Miles (1984) take a useful look at problems in school improvement. Kirst and Meister (1985) provide a valuable cautionary note, pointing out how much easier it is to introduce regulatory changes as distinct from changes related to teachers' everyday instructional practice. For those unfamiliar with the school effectiveness research, the following are particularly recommended: Coleman and Hoffer (1987), Hallinger and Murphy (1986), McDill and Rigsby (1973), Purkey and Smith (1983), and Rutter *et al.* (1979).

Chapter 10

The Professional Administrator as Educational Leader

This book has been organized around a number of themes that impinge on school administration: functions of schools; educational goals; the use and limits of power and authority; the deployment of the school's wealth — instructional time; buildings and materials, teachers and students; formal and contractual relationships, informal quasi-contractual relationships and the idea of social exchange; the importance of symbolism and tradition; professional ethics; program and change and evaluation; accountability; and effective schools ideas. Overlying all these themes is the idea that educational administrators are professionals with considerable choice about how they use their time and how they behave.

In addressing these themes, we have tried to accomplish several purposes. Most writing about school administration can be divided into two major categories, the first being more popular today than the second. The more fashionable approach is one that appears to be scientific. It often describes or is explicitly based on research 'findings.' We accept the contribution of many kinds of educational research — survey, statistical, functional, phenomenological. However, a book about school administration, about being a principal, should be founded (explicitly or implicitly) in principles. To these, research makes only a secondary contribution. Research cannot tell the principal what he or she ought to do in any but the most obvious circumstances. It cannot distinguish good from bad ethics. Much research is essentially descriptive. Statistical research in education leads only to low level conclusions. So writers of this kind are either reduced to peripheral issues relatively free of values or they jump unconvincingly into pseudo-science, going far beyond their data. A secondary category of writing, most often found in non-refereed journals, consists of advisory, hortatory prose, often based on 'practical experience' and 'war stories.' That kind of writing can also be valuable, always provided again that the goals of the writer are very clear and provided the reader is given an opportunity to see how much similarity there is between the circumstances in which the recommended practice 'worked' and his or her own. There is also some writing that falls into neither of those two major categories. Increasingly popular are case studies, 'thick' descriptions of schools or principals in action; a fine example is Peshkin's *God's Choice* (1987). Good case studies make fascinating reading for the scholar, but there is a danger, just as there is a danger in the war stories, of practitioners assuming that ideas that worked or did not work in the case study will or will not work similarly for them. That is to say, even if the writer avoids (and it is hard to resist the temptation) generalizing, readers are apt to generalize for themselves, particularly if the successful practices match their own predisposition.

There is nothing conceptually new in the organizing principles of this book. Obviously it draws from and therefore has most of the weaknesses of both the major categories. We do place some faith in empirical research; and our conceptualization of practical problems necessarily stems from our own knowledge and experience — and what we see as important reflects our own educational and personal values. We have also adopted the position that research findings and established practice are insufficient. In our title, belief comes first. Before one can act purposefully, one should believe. Clever books and articles claiming, accurately or not, to tell educational administrators how they can be effective, irrespective of their purposes, are at best misleading, at worst miseducative. We believe educators should use their discretionary power and authority to further the interests of their students. And we have clearly set out, in Chapter 1, what we believe those interests to be. Those who reject our educational purposes should clarify their own, and ensure they have genuine community support before they enlist others (professionals, the public, students) in their cause.

Throughout, we have had two persisting purposes — to educate and to train. Our first and most general interest is to help teachers and principals reflect on professional practice — to consider the implications of how they choose to spend their administrative and managerial time, to think about the moral worth of their choices and of the consequences. But we also hope that some sections of this book will encourage and enable administrators to choose more effective and more efficient ways of spending their time — to put more effort into student evaluation; less into teacher evaluation; to put more time into developing comprehensive award systems for students, less into counselling individuals who reject discipline for a variety of personal problems often not related to the school; to put more time into involving more students in comprehensive curricular and community service programs, less into complex implementation processes related to a new curriculum replacing a perfectly serviceable old one; to think more about the experiences of students in school and less about public relations and grand planning; and to encourage teachers more in their day-to-day work with students, instead of developing elaborate in-service programs for new curricula whose effect is unknown or known to be negative.

The two purposes — education and training — overlap. Efficiency and effectiveness are of no value if the goals they address are themselves meretricious. And that returns us to a central theme. Good schools have some consensual purpose — and this book offers little practical advice to administrators in schools where there is and can be none. Further, it is not immaterial what that purpose is. Formal education should develop the kind of person we want in our society. In pluralistic societies, such as those of the USA, Canada and Britain, that ideal citizen is more varied than his or her counterpart in the USSR or Denmark (the USSR has a centralized state ideal and Denmark has a homogeneous population). For that reason, we have more varied schools to reflect the special wishes of strongly dissenting minorities. Even the schools serving the vast middle majority must recognize the varied interests and wishes of parents. But there must remain a solid core of common values — truth, justice, courage, care for the other person, together with those traits necessary for harmonious life in a school setting — respect for family, adherence to reasonable rules, courtesy, dilligence, personal responsibility, punctuality and dependability. The school must reflect, reward and honor work in all the domains — the moral and academic particularly for without a moral purpose of right and wrong the school should not exist, and without academics it would have little substance.

Critics of the approach taken in this book may well argue that our failure to separate fact from value is a crucial weakness. Yet it is precisely that intermixture that reflects the book's contribution. Educational administration is not centrally about theory and practice. There is little genuine theory in education. Education is an applied field, while genuine theory is more a property of basic disciplines. Educational administration is twice removed from the disciplines and it should not be surprising that the field has not produced much genuine theory. In our view, the study of educational administration is about the discretionary use of the authority in educational systems. The educational administrator uses discretion to make decisions to maintain, direct, change and improve schools. The principal's role can be described and divided up in countless ways, but there are two inescapable components: a hierarchical, bureaucratic component; and a discretionary role as educational leader. The notion of education necessarily contains moral components; that is to say it is at least minimally concerned with good and bad. In our view, education in schools ought to be centrally concerned with good and bad, and it sometimes is. Even today, there are many schools where it is considered more important to turn out good people who are probably good at mathematics than good mathematicians who may not be good people.

In that context, it makes little sense to see the principal as a middle manager, interchangeable with someone of similar rank in a soup factory or insurance company. A private business is concerned centrally and necessarily with profit — not to the exclusion of everything else, but centrally. This is not to say that ethics (including honesty) in business are unimportant, merely that business has a guiding goal different from that of the school. A school is about the development of children. It simply does not make sense to suggest that the principal of a small, ultra-progressive suburban school is or ought to be interchangeable with the principal of an inner city public high school (let alone with the manager of an abattoir or an advertising agency). It is awkward if a senior administrator in a free market organization privately favors state-run, socialized control of industrial production. But it is unthinkable, not awkward, for an atheist to administer a Christian fundamentalist school. We are saying then not only that this *is* so, that schools *are* about good and bad, but that they ought to be, indeed that they ought to be more involved than they now are. It is unacceptable then that schools (and their administrators) should attempt to be neutral about values except for those minimally necessary for the maintenance of organizational continuity. Even though total agreement about which values in which order of priority schools should sustain is often absent, nearly everyone seems to approve some value based program — whether it be peace education, sex education, global education or religious education. The real question then is not whether we should have values, but which they should be. The school principal should not be neutral about central educational values, although he or she may well be positive, negative or neutral about a particular specific program in, for example, peace education.

If one thinks of the principal in the local, public school, it is not useful or sensible to separate fact from value. Yes, she has a managerial responsibility to deliver program, discipline children and manage teachers. But we shall be more upset if we hear she has lied to her pupils than if we hear she has mismanaged program implementation; the one is a breach of trust, a truly unprofessional act, the other may be an error, or, at worst, a sign of possible incompetence in one endeavor.

This moral role as model — a model of values, of aesthetics, of culture — is an undercurrent of the principal's life. Of course, we do ask too much of the principal — certainly in modern times. Principals are still to some extent secular priests, with whom those outside education frequently feel uncomfortable, as though they feel they ought to act intellectually or morally in their presence. Despite the legal difficulties in defining and requiring a moral role, most people still care about the principal who lives with a 19-year-old boyfriend or girlfriend — more than they do about the same behavior in a sales clerk, service station operator or journalist. The reason is that, even in modern times, most people believe principals should set a good example.

A television program recently featured a teacher in a public school who had written several allegedly anti-semitic books. The position of the producers, supported by the Premier of the province concerned, was that the teacher should be dismissed, although it was agreed that the teacher was excellent and never introduced his political views in the classroom. We cannot judge that particular case without knowing more about the impact of his views on the school community. We do not know whether the writings really are anti-semitic and we do not know whether the students believe their teacher to be racist. But our moral position is clear. We do not believe that a teacher or school administrator should continue in the job if he or she is known to deliberately and consistently flout the basic moral values for which the school stands. Applying this to particular cases is very difficult, but the basic principle is widely (not universally) accepted.

So the principal is more than a professional who must exercise discretionary choice. The principal must also act in a moral way. The educational administrator must be distinguished in two respects from the business manager.

First, the educational administrator generally has much broader discretionary authority in areas directly affecting the personal lives of clients (pupils and their parents); or the products (if students are seen as analogous with the widgets produced in a factory). Second, although many employers may prefer to employ people who have moral personal lives, the personal life of the teacher and principal are particularly relevant to their employment.

School districts usually avoid codifying these issues for good reason. Specifying a clear set of traditional expectations would exclude large numbers of current incumbents and future applicants (as well as conflict with codes of individual human rights). But to exclude such expectations expressly and contractually would strike at the core of many parents' sense of what an education is. It is uncomfortable for the principal to live in such ambiguity. But all problems cannot be solved by written contracts. The family is a better analogue for the school than is the industrial shop floor.

It does matter which educational goals the principal, with others, selects and emphasizes. Suppose strong traditional Presbyterian parents discover that their children's principal is living publicly in a homosexual relation with a 19-year-old youth. They will likely want to remove either the principal or their children. At the same time, it is obviously not possible in most communities for the principal to reflect accurately all the beliefs and values of nearly all members of the community. There must be some compromise. There must be some match between the principal's overall educational vision and that of the community; but there may be areas of difference and the principal may have to stay silent about some aspects not absolutely central to his or her philosophy.

We must make a troubling distinction between moral conduct and beliefs. The problem is not so serious if a principal is occasionally unfaithful to his or her spouse, or drinks too much, or drives too fast. We all err and no one knows how sincerely we regret our actions. But consistent moral conduct that goes against the values espoused by the school is especially serious because it seems to undermine the school in a deliberate way. So much the worse if it is flagrantly public. This distinction is troubling because it appears to encourage hypocrisy; immoral beliefs are acceptable in private, even immoral conduct if it is discrete and irregular. There are no tidy lines; the fact that a wider range of moral conduct is acceptable today than was once the case makes the problem less serious in practice — but the principles require reflection.

The Future Principal

The suggestion that a principal might be chosen partly on the basis of beliefs or, more likley, moral conduct instead of skills and competence will be unsettling to many teachers. But those upset should consider a few obvious cases. A candidate who has had no involvement with blacks is turned down as principal of a school with a large black minority for that specific reason. A principal who is openly opposed to open immigration from Latin America and Asia is transferred from a school with large Hispanic and Asian minorities. A liberal Baptist is rejected as principal of a fundamentalist Christian school. A Deweyan progressive applicant is rejected as principal of a strongly traditional school. A strongly traditionalist principal is rejected as principal of a progressive school. Not every reader will concur with all those hypothetical decisions; but most will surely see contexts where they are at least defensible.

The argument here should not be exaggerated or taken out of context. Because some strong fundamental differences in values and lifestyle are legitimate reasons for rejecting or choosing administrators, it does not follow that any value difference is sufficient.

This problem may be becoming more serious. As long as society represented a clear consensus, dissenters, rightly or wrongly, were allowed little say in the running of public schools. Educators represented the middle, consensual majority. As minorities of various kinds are increasingly seen as legitimate in pluralistic, western societies, their treatment in schools becomes more problematic. If a fundamentalist principal tries to 'impose' (i.e., express) her beliefs in a public school, her behavior will be seen as unacceptable. But suppose a secular humanist expresses his beliefs, by word and behavior, to a fundamentalist minority of pupils.

The practical answer to this dilemma today is usually for the school to withdraw as far as possible from contentious value issues. Yet such a retreat from values is evidently contrary to the ideas developed in this book. The good school, as we have presented it, has clear purposes and puts character development as a central focus. We have gone further, to suggest, with Coleman and Hoffer (1987), that ideally a school should be a functioning community reflecting shared values by administrators, teachers, students and parents.

Logically, this may lead to the breakdown of the public school system into parts serving different interest groups. That issue is discussed more fully elsewhere (Holmes, 1988b). We are neither for nor against schools separated by values; we believe that the values represented in Chapter 1 in fact reflect a broad spectrum of modern society. However, forced to make a choice, we obviously stand for schools with clear, consensual value systems led by administrators representing those values. If that means some specialization of schools by values, and it undoubtedly does in some areas, so be it.

The school is coming to a critical crossroads — perhaps it is already there. Either it must re-establish some public consensus for a transcendent vision of the educated person and the educated society, or it must accept division. Perhaps both choices will be made, in different places. Rural, traditional, homogeneous communities may retain the consensual common school, while divided and socially differentiated, urban communities will choose division. That is what appears to be happening now.

Over the last few decades, aspiring principals have come to suppress their philosophies and beliefs, to become value-free managers who can supposedly run any kind of school with equal efficiency. But the research is showing that what schools most need is a sense of purpose, a sense of direction — and the new managers cannot or dare not provide it.

Thus in grounding the role of the principal in some public consensus we are not unaware of the dangers. The consensus may simply be torn apart. It is simply not possible to forecast to what extent social division will replace consensus. However, we are suggesting that attempts to act without consensus, to ignore value issues and differences, to replace administrative choice by managerial efficiency, will lead to school collapse (indeed, that has already happened in some urban communities).

Now it will be argued that the common school should be maintained at *any price*, even if it means that school management must rely on a lowest common denominator of rules to ensure safety. The purpose of this book has not been to defeat that argument; rather the book is grounded in the assumption that the argument is fallacious. Briefly, that course of action, of retreat to a value-neutral position on all the issues except those that affect the continuity of the school and the safety of its occupants, is opposed for three reasons:

1. In the long term it is infeasible; if the school administration stands for nothing the school will inevitably be overtaken by those with sufficient power who do stand for something — the principal will be turned into a simple bureaucrat or a power broker — but the school will not remain value-neutral;
2. It is already becoming evident that retreat to value neutrality will not assure the common school's future; the retreat from values in urban, public schools leads to increased enrolments in special schools (both private and public) with a clear sense of direction;
3. Schools without a clear, focused, coherent educational mission are miseducative and ought not to exist.

The Role of the Principal

This book is far from encyclopedic; there are numerous parts of the principal's life about which little or nothing has been said. For example, district staff have been referred to only in passing. There are numerous important policy issues affecting the principal, only a selection of which have been discussed. The scope of the principal's activities is large. Consider such a list of activities. It includes:

- completing forms and questionnaires
- developing curriculum in all subject areas
- teaching students
- scheduling classes
- evaluating curriculum
- conducting assemblies
- hiring and firing teachers
- allocating duties
- suspending teachers
- testing students
- conducting meetings
- leading teachers
- assessing test results
- running extracurricular activities
- working with teachers as colleagues
- admitting students
- evaluating teachers

- suspending and expelling students
- directing shows and programs
- writing policies
- punishing students
- making speeches
- talking to parents
- managing support staff
- managing buildings and supplies
- running fund-raising activities
- managing a budget
- purchasing
- running a cafeteria
- running a sports program
- attending school events
- organizing transportation
- public relations activities
- scheduling in-service courses

There are few jobs that are quite so varied. It should not be thought that most principals do most of those things. In fact, the typical principal is probably involved in only a fraction of those activities on any one day. Many secondary principals never teach and have almost no involvement in program development and evaluation. Many elementary principals have little involvement with pupils except for purposes of control and spend no time on extracurricular activities. Work which fills most of the time of one principal is scarcely attended to by another. Part of the explanation is delegation, but much is simply choice of priorities.

This book takes a position quite opposed to that taken by most writing about school administration. Most writers are at pains to avoid or appear to avoid any statement that appears to be value laden or philosophical. They usually fail because any writing about schools makes countless value assumptions. But the values are usually implicit, hidden. In this book, values, judgment, discretion, fairness, ethics and professional behavior are prominent. Education begins and ends in values. However, we have avoided suggesting that all principals should adopt a particular personal style or define their role in the same way.

Principals are enormously varied in their personality and skill. Schools are enormously varied in their composition and context. And the potential set of activities for the principal is enormous. Certainly there are many activities that are of lesser priority; they are ones we have argued are furthest removed from educational impact on students. But there remains an enormous variety of choices.

Some readers may wish to label the philosophical underpinning of this book. We see it as stemming from the Judaeo-Christian, classical tradition. While one does not have to share the philosophy to accept much of the commentary, a totally different philosophy (based on Marx or Bertrand Russell or Dewey for example) would lead to many different conclusions.

We have tried to engage educators in thought about what schools are really doing and what they ought to be doing. One must recognize and accept much of the reality of the environment in which one lives. Schools cannot be hostile bodies seeking to undermine or overthrow the legitimate authority outside the school. But educators have a responsibility above and beyond that necessary to be compatible with the external world. They should look beyond, to what it means to be a good citizen, a good person at this time in our history. They must accept the present as well as the immediate future — but never with smug satisfaction that what exists is somehow the best possible. They must accept that many children lead lives constricted, blighted even, by television — but they should not lower the gaze to suit what is fashionable and popular. Quite the reverse, the educator's task is to turn the heads of the young away from the glitzy, superficial baubles of our civilization, to seek again the fundamentals, to drive for a life and eventually a world of justice. The job of the educator is like that of the good missionary; not the caricature who looked at the surface of people considered primitive, seeking to change that surface by means of bras and Bibles; but the authentic missionary who tried to identify and celebrate the good that lies within all of us. The principal should be the leader of the flock. It is good to know some effective and efficient ways of getting things done; but it is better to know the way.

References

ADLER, M. (1982) *The Paideia Proposal*, New York, Macmillan.

ANDERSON, C.S. (1982) 'The search for school climate: A review of the research', *Review of Education Research* 52, 3, pp. 368–420.

BARR, R. and DREEBEN, R. (1983) *How Schools Work*, Chicago, University of Chicago Press.

BARROW, R. (1984) *Giving Teaching Back to Teachers*, Sussex, Wheatsheaf Books.

BEREITER, C. (1981) 'A constructive look at follow through results', *Curriculum Inquiry*, 12, 1, pp. 1–22.

BLAU, P.M. (1964) *Exchange and Power in Social Life*, New York, John Wiley.

BLAU, P.M. and SCOTT, W.R. (1962) *Formal Organizations*, San Francisco, Chandler.

BLOOM, A. (1987) *The Closing of the American Mind*, New York, Simon and Schuster.

BLOOM, B.S. (1976) *Human Characteristics and School Learning*, New York, McGraw-Hill.

BOWLES, S. and GINTIS, H. (1976) *Schooling in Capitalist America*, New York, Basic Books.

BRIDGE, R.G., JUDD, C.N. and MOOCK, P.R. (1979) *The Determinants of Education Outcomes*, Cambridge, Massachusetts, Dallinger.

BROOKOVER, W.B. and LEZOTTE, L. W. (1979) 'Changes in School Characteristics Co-incident with Changes in Student Learning', East Lansing, Michigan State University.

CAMERON, K.F. (1984) 'The Effects of Social, Demographic and Attitudinal Characteristics on the Preferences Expressed by Teachers for Strategies Intended to Reduce Redundancy and Layoffs', Unpublished EdD Dissertation, Toronto, OISE.

CHALL, J.S. (1983) *Learning to Read: The Great Debate*, New York, McGraw-Hill.

CLARKE., P.B. and WILSON, J.Q. (1961) 'Incentive systems: A theory of organizations', *Administrative Science Quarterly* VI, pp. 129–166.

COLEMAN, J.S. (1961) *The Adolescent Society*, New York, Free Press.

COLEMAN, J.S. *et al.* (1966) *Equality of Educational Opportunity*, Washington, DC. Department of Health, Education and Welfare.

COLEMAN, J.S. and HOFFER, T. (1987) *Public and Private High Schools*, New York, Basic Books.

COLEMAN, J.S., HOFFER, T. and KILGORE, S. (1982) *High School Achievement*, New York, Basic Books.

COOLEY, W. and LEINHARDT, G. (1980) 'Instructional dimensions study', *Educational Evaluation and Policy Analysis* 2, 1, pp. 7–25.

DELAMONT, S. (1980) *Sex Roles in the School*, London, Methuen.

DREEBEN, R. (1968) *On What is Learned in School*, Reading, Massachusetts, Addison-Wesley.

DURKHEIM, E. (1956) *Education and Sociology*, Glencoe, Illinios, Free Press.
DURKHEIM, E. (1961) *Moral Education*, New York, Free Press.
Ethics in Education (1987) OISE Press Vol. 7, No. 2, 2–16.
FELDWEBEL, A.N. (1964) 'Organizational climate, social class and educational output' *Administrators', Notebook* XII, 8.
FULLAN, M. (1982) *The Meaning of Educational Change*, Toronto, OISE Press.
GATHERAL, M. (1979) 'Super research: What to do if they use it against you', *Learning* August-September, pp. 71–8.
GERTH, H.H. and MILLS, C.W. (1958) *From Max Weber: Essays in Sociology*, New York, Oxford University Press.
GREENFIELD, T.B. (1986) 'The decline and fall of science in educational administration', *Interchange* 17, 2, pp. 57–80.
GROSS, N. and HERRIOTT, R.E. (1965) *Staff Leadership in Public Schools*, New York, John Wiley.
HALLINGER, P. and MURPHY, J.F. (1986) 'The social context of effective schools', *American Journal of Education* 94, 3, pp. 328–55.
HALPIN, A.C. (1966) *Theory and Research in Administration*, New York, Macmillan.
HARGREAVES, D.H. (1967) *Social Relations in a Secondary School*, London, Routledge and Kegan Paul.
HAVIGHURST, R.J. *et al.* (1962) *Growing Up in River City*, New York, John Wiley.
HILLOCKS, G.S. (1984) 'What works in teaching composition: A meta analysis of experimental treatment studies', *American Journal of Education* 93, 1, pp. 133–170.
HODGKINSON, C. (1978) *Towards a Philosophy of Administration*, Oxford, Blackwell.
HOLLINGSHEAD, A. (1949) *Elmtown's Youth*, New York, John Wiley.
HOLMES, M. (1971) 'A critique of neo-progressive trends in Canadian education,' *Interchange* 2, 3, pp. 63–80.
HOLMES, M. (1978a) 'Multiculturalism and the school', *Black Presence in Multi-Ethnic Canada*, editor V. D'Oyley. Faculty of Education, UBC, Vancouver pp. 239–58.
HOLMES, M. (1978b) 'Formal education and its effect on academic achievement', *Canadian Journal of Education* 3, 3, pp. 55–70.
HOLMES, M. (1979) 'Instructional Time and Academic Achievement', Toronto, Ministry of Education.
HOLMES, M. (1980) 'Forward to the basics: A radical conservative reconstruction', *Curriculum Inquiry* 10, 4, pp. 384–418.
HOLMES, M. (1982a) 'Significance of authority in contemporary education', *Teacher Education* 21, October, pp. 18–27.
HOLMES, M. (1982b) *What Every Teacher and Parent Should Know About Student Evaluation*, Toronto, OISE Press.
HOLMES, M. (1985a) 'The secondary school in contemporary western society: Constraints, imperatives and prospects', *Curriculum Inquiry* 15, 1, pp. 7–36.
HOLMES, M. (1985b) 'Requirements for education: A review of S.B. Sarason's *Schooling in America*', *Interchange* 16, 3, pp. 74–81.
HOLMES, M. (1985c) 'A response to Sarason', *Interchange* 16, 3, pp. 87–9.
HOLMES, M. (1985d) 'Organizational climate in schools, *International Encyclopedia of Education: Research and Studies*, HUSÉN, T. and POSTLETHWAITE, N. (Eds) Oxford, Pergamon Press, pp. 3707–3710.
HOLMES, M. (1986a) 'Models of the Relationship Between Students', Achievement in School and Later Success, Toronto, Ministry of Education.
HOLMES, M. (1986b) 'Comment', *Interchange* 17, 2, pp. 80–90.
HOLMES, M. (1986c) 'Traditionalism and educational administration', *Journal of Educational Administration and Foundations* 1, 2, pp. 40–52.
HOLMES, M. (1988a) 'The principal's leadership and school effectiveness' Paper presented to the American Educational Research Association, New Orleans.

HOLMES, M. (1988b) 'The fortress monastery: The future of the common core', *Cultural Literacy and the Idea of General Education*, WESTBURY, I. and PURVES, A.C. (Eds) NSSE Yearbook, 87, 2. Chicago, University of Chicago Press, pp. 231–258.

HOLMES, M., LEITHWOOD, K.A. and MUSELLA, D.F. (Forthcoming) *Policy for Effective Schools*, Toronto, OISE Press.

HOWARD, E., HOWELL, B. and BRAINARD, E. (1987) *Handbook for Conducting School Improvement Projects*, Bloomington, Indiana, Phi Delta Kappa Education Foundation.

HOY, W.K. and MISKEL, C.G. (1982) *Educational Administration: Theory, Research and Practice*, New York, Random House.

HUBERMAN, A.M. and MILES, M.B. (1982) *Innovation Up Close: How School Improvement Works*, New York, Plenum Press.

ILLICH, I. (1970) *Deschooling Society*, New York, Harper and Row.

JACKSON, B. (1964) *Streaming: An Education System in Miniature*, London, Routlege and Kegan Paul.

JACKSON, P.W. (1968) *Life in Classrooms*, New York, Holt, Rinehart, Winston.

JENCKS, C. (1979) *What Gets Ahead? The Determinants of Economic Success in America*, New York, Basic Books.

KARWEIT, N. (1978) *The Organization of Time in Schools: Time Scales and Learning*, Centre for School Organization of Schools, Baltimore, The Johns Hopkins University.

KELSEY, J.G.T. (1983) 'The Assessment of Administrative Performance in Schools' Paper presented at the Annual Conference of the Canadian Association for the Study of Educational Administration, Vancouver, British Columbia.

KIRST, M.W. and MEISTER, G.R. (1985) 'Turbulence in American secondary schools', *Curriculum Inquiry* 15, 2, pp. 169–186.

LACEY, C. (1970) *Hightown Grammar*, Manchester, Manchester University Press.

LEITHWOOD, K.A. and MONTGOMERY, D.J. (1986) *Improving Principal Effectiveness: The Principal Profile*, Toronto, OISE Press.

LIGHTFOOT, S.L. (1983) *The Good High School*, New York, Basic Books.

LORTIE, D.C. (1975) *Schoolteacher*, Chicago, University of Chicago Press.

McDILL, E.L. and RIGSBY, L.C. (1973) *Structure and Process in Secondary Schools: The Academic Impact of Educational Climates*, Baltimore, The Johns Hopkins University Press.

McGRAIL, J., WILSON, B.L. and ROSSMAN, G.B. (1987) *Looking at Schools: Instruments and Processes for School Analysis*, Philadelphia, Research for Better Schools.

McGREGOR, D. (1960) *The Human Side of Enterprise*, New York, McGraw-Hill.

MACINTYRE, A. (1981) *After Virtue*, Notre Dame, Indiana, University of Notre Dame Press.

McPHERSON, R.B., CROWSON, R.L. and PITNER, N.J. (1986) *Managing Uncertainty: Administrative Theory and Practice in Education*, Columbus, Ohio, Charles E. Merrill Publishing Company.

MARITAIN, J. (1943) *Education at the Crossroads*, New Haven, Connecticut, Yale University Press.

MAUSS, M. (1954) *The Gift*, Glencoe, Illinios, Free Press.

METZ, H.M. (1978) *Classrooms and Corridors*, Berkeley, California, University of California Press.

MINTZBERG, H. (1973) *The Nature of Managerial Work*, New York, Harper and Row.

MURNANE, R.J. (1975) *The Impact of School Resources on Learning of Inner City Children*, Cambridge, Massachusetts, Ballinger.

NORTHWEST REGIONAL EDUCATIONAL LABORATORY, (1984) *Effective School Practice: A Research Synthesis*, Portland, Oregon.

PESHKIN, A. (1986) *God's Choice*, Chicago, University of Chicago Press.

PHENIX, P.H. (1964) *Realms of Meaning: A Philosophy of the Curriculum of General Education*, New York, McGraw-Hill.

PORTER, J., PORTER, M. and BLISHEN, B. (1982) *Stations and Callings*, Toronto, Methuen.

PRATT, D. (1980) *Curriculum Design and Development*, New York, Harcourt, Brace, Jovanovich.

PUNCH, M. (1977) *Progressive Retreat*, Cambridge, Cambridge University Press.

PURKEY, S.C. and SMITH, M. (1983) 'Effective schools: A review', *Elementary School Journal* 83, 4, pp. 427–452.

PURKEY, W.W. (1970) *Self Concept and School Achievement*, Englewood Cliffs, New Jersey, Prentice-Hall.

PURVES, A.C. and LEVINE, D.U. (1975) *Educational Policy and International Assessment*, Berkeley, California, McCutchan.

RAPHAEL, D. and WAHLSTROM, M.W. (1986) 'The semestered secondary school and student achievement: Results from the Second Ontario Intermediate Science Study', *Canadian Journal of Education* 11, 2, pp. 180–3.

RAPHAEL, D. and WAHLSTROM, M.W. and McLEAN, L.D. (1986) 'Debunking the semestering myth', *Canadian Journal of Education* 11, 1, pp. 36–52.

ROSENHOLTZ, S.J. (1985) 'Effective schools: Interpreting the evidence', *American Journal of Education* 93, 3, pp. 352–88.

RUTTER, M., MAUGHAN, B., MORTIMORE, P. and OUSTON, J. (1979) *Fifteen Thousand Hours*, London, Open Books.

RYAN, D.W. and HICKCOX, E.S. (1980) *Redefining Teacher Evaluation*, Toronto, OISE Press.

SARASON, S.B. (1971) (second edition 1982) *The Culture of the School and the Problem of Change*, Boston, Allyn and Bacon.

SARASON, S.B. (1983) *Schooling in America*, New York, Free Press.

SARASON, S.B. (1985) 'A reply to Professor Holmes', *Interchange* 16, 3, pp. 82–6.

SEWELL, W.H. and HAUSER, R.M. (1975) *Education, Occupation and Earnings*, New York, Academic Press.

SHAKESHAFT, C. (1987) 'The equitable distribution of education: Are we reproducing our own oppression?' *Ethics in Education* 7, 2, pp. 2–5.

SHILS, E.A. (1981) *Tradition*, Chicago, University of Chicago Press.

SIZER, T.R. (1983) *Horace's Compromise*, New York, Houghton-Mifflin.

SLAVIN, R. (1986) *Using Student Team Learning*, Centre for Research on Elementary and Middle Schools, Baltimore, Johns Hopkins University.

STINCHCOMBE, A.L. (1964) *Rebellion in a High School*, Chicago, Quadrangle Books.

SUMMERS, A.A. and WOLFE, B.L. (1975) 'Which school resources help learning?', *Business Review*, February, Federal Reserve Bank of Philadelphia.

TRAUB, R., WEISS, J. and FISHER, C. (1976) *Openness in Schools: An Evaluation Study*, Toronto, The Ontario Institute for Studies in Education.

TYLER, R.W. (1950) *Basic Principles of Curriculum and Instruction*, Chicago, University of Chicago.

US DEPARTMENT OF EDUCATION, (1986) *What Works: Research Teaching and Learning*, Washington, DC.

WALBERG, H.J. (Ed) (1982) *Improving Educational Standards and Productivity*, Berkeley, California, McCutchan.

WALLER, W. (1965) *The Sociology of Teaching*, New York, John Wiley (Science Editions).

WEINBERG, I. (1967) *The English Public Schools*, New York, Atherton.

WILEY, D.E. (1976) 'Another hour, another day: Quantity of schooling, a potent path for policy', SEWELL, W.H., HAUSER, R.M. and FEATHERMAN, D.L. (eds) *Schooling and Achievement in American Society*, New York, Academic Press, pp. 225–65.

WILKINSON, R. (1964) *The Prefects: British Leadership and the Public School Tradition*, Oxford, Oxford University Press.

WILLIS, P. (1977) *Learning to Labour*, Farnborough, England, Gower Publishing.

WILSON, B.L. and MCGRAIL, J. (1987) *Measuring School Climate: Questions and Consideratins*, Philadelphia, Research for Better Schools.

WOLFE, R.M. (1977) *Achievement in America*, New York, Teachers College Press.

WYNNE, E.A. (1980) *Looking at Schools: Good, Bad, and Indifferent*, Lexington, Massachusetts, Lexington Books.

WYNNE, E.A. (1988) 'Another kind of sex education', *Ethics in Education* 7, 3, pp. 11–12.

Index